THE X RESOURCE

ISSUE THIRTEEN

PROCEEDINGS

9TH ANNUAL X TECHNICAL CONFERENCE

SPONSORED BY THE X CONSORTIUM

BOSTON, MASSACHUSETTS
JANUARY 30-February 31, 1995

O'Reilly & Associates, Inc.

A PRACTICAL JOURNAL OF THE X WINDOW SYSTEM

THE X RESOURCE

TABLE OF CONTENTS

ISSUE THIRTEEN

THE X RESOURCE

TABLE OF CONTENTS, CONTINUED

ISSUE THIRTEEN

THE X RESOURCE: A PRACTICAL JOURNAL OF THE X WINDOW SYSTEM

O'Reilly & Associates, Inc.

The Official Publisher of the
X Consortium's X Technical Conference Proceedings
and approved publisher of X Consortium public review specifications.

PUBLISHER

Tim O'Reilly

EDITOR

Paula M. Ferguson
(O'Reilly & Associates, Inc.)

EDITORIAL ADVISORY BOARD

Jeff Barr (Visix Software, Inc.)
Todd Brunhoff (North Valley Research)
Kevin Calhoun (Informix Software)
Ellis Cohen (Open Software Foundation)
Wayne Dyksen (Dept. of Computer Science, Purdue University)
Jim Fulton (Network Computing Devices, Inc.)
Ronald Hughes (CrossWind Technologies, Inc.)
Bob Joyce (Aspect, Inc.)
Phil Karlton (Silicon Graphics, Inc.)
John Buford (University of Lowell)
Mark Linton (Silicon Graphics, Inc.)
Stuart Marks (Sun Microsystems)
Chris Peterson (Investment Management Services, Inc.)
Ralph Swick (Digital Equipment Corporation)
Bob Scheifler with the staff (X Consortium) (acting as a single board member)

CUSTOMER SERVICE AND ADMINISTRATION

Marianne Cooke

COPY EDITING

Nancy Crumpton

COVER AND INTERIOR FORMAT DESIGN

Edie Freedman

PRODUCTION

Mike Sierra

ILLUSTRATIONS

Chris Reilley

From the Editor

Welcome to the 9th Annual X Technical Conference. This issue of *The X Resource* contains the conference proceedings. Many thanks to the program committee and the X Consortium staff for their help in preparing this issue.

How This Issue is Prepared

This proceedings issue is prepared much differently from regular issues of *The X Resource*. The conference program committee (listed on the next page) selected the papers. The deadline for submission was December 19, 1994, just one month before the conference. Given that it takes three weeks to print a publication of this type, there is no time for editing or production. Therefore authors were required to supply camera-ready copy. All of the submissions that were not in FrameMaker were converted to FrameMaker to make the final formatting easier. Thanks also go to the authors who helped in the conversion process.

This tight schedule was chosen to make sure that the X Conference papers reflect the state of the art now - not six months ago. So if you see some inevitable slight problems in the papers, please consider that a small price to pay for the most current information.

Write for The X Resource

We're always interested in good articles, papers, and documentation for *The X Resource*. Contact the editor to discuss any ideas you have or to get our current list of desired topics. Also consider these topics which we'd like to cover more than we have been:

- recommendations for X-specific, large-scale engineering methodologies
- detailed design tutorials for important user interfaces or graphics techniques
- case studies of real, shipping X-based products
- reviews of important non-standard (possibly non-free) tools

Enjoy the conference!

Paula M. Ferguson
Editor

9th Annual X Technical Conference
Program Committee

Stuart R. Anderson, AT&T GIS

Steven C. Bilow, Tektronix

Doug Blewett, AT&T Bell Laboratories

Craig Groeschel, Metro Link

Mark Hatch, UnixWare Technology Group, Chief of Technology

Selwyn L. Henriques, Tech-Source Inc.

Kaleb Keithley, X Consortium

David Lister, Adobe Systems

Stuart Marks, SunSoft

Prof. Patrick Powell, San Diego State University

Glenn Pinkerton, Colorado Softworks

Ralph Swick, X Consortium

Testing X-Clients Using Synlib And FocusMaps

Sankar L. Chakrabarti[*]

Abstract

Automated testing of X-clients is commonly implemented by some form of "record-and-playback" technology. This paper describes a method of testing in which the recording step is eliminated. Testing automatons, called agents, are created using a C-language library called Synlib. The Synlib agents manipulate the graphical user interface of X-clients in just the same way a human user would do and verify expectations coded in them. These agents use a construct called "FocusMap" to identify the objects of interest during execution. The FocusMap construct is a key board mediated navigational model of the windows under test. The paper describes the construct and its use by Synlib agents. Synlib agents using FocusMaps are robust and highly portable. They do not require the target application to be modified in any way; nor do they require that the application to be relinked to any customized library.

Naming GUI objects of interest

Testing an application with a Graphical User Interface (GUI) often involves the user interacting with GUI objects of interest and then verifying the results of such interaction. Whenever an automaton is used to test a GUI application - the test designer faces the following issues:

- How to name the GUI objects of interest in the test program or the test script? and

- How should the automaton map a named object to the desired structure on the display?

Naming GUI objects of interest and identifying them during execution is an important issue in the design and implementation of automated GUI testing systems.

---

[*]Sankar L. Chakrabarti is an R&D Engineer at User Interface Technology Division, Hewlett-Packard Company, 1000 NE Circle Blvd. , Corvallis , OR 97330 (sankar@hp-pcd.cv.hp.com).

Most of the tools used in testing X-clients are based on some form of "record-and-playback" technology. These tools solved the naming problem in one of the two ways: Either they used the (x,y) location of the object on the display as a proxy for its name; Or they use the internal path name of the widget implementing the GUI object of interest as the name of the object itself. The early implementations of record-and-playback technology such as tmon, xtm, Synergy[*] and XRunner 1.0[†] belong to the first group. More recent tools such XRunner 2.0, VistaREPLAY[‡], Xsimul.test[§], QA Partner[**] and QATS [1] follow the second strategy.

Whereas naming objects by location results in fragile tests, the second approach requires that the target application, i.e. the application to be tested, be invaded with some customized code. This invasion could take the form of modifying the application or may be disguised as relinking the application to special library supplied by the vendor. These modifications enable the testing automaton gain access to names of the widgets in the target application. The necessity of having to modify the application for testing have made this approach unacceptable in many situations. This paper describes a third approach to naming GUI objects in test programs. In this approach, the logical organization of the GUI objects within a window is specified by a construct called "FocusMap". The testing automatons, the agents, are implemented using a C-language library called "Synlib". During testing, a Synlib program uses FocusMaps to navigate to the desired GUI objects within a window. It will be shown that this naming strategy is effective, and results in robust and highly portable test programs without having invade the application in any way.

Using Synlib To Create Test Agents

If Synlib is used to test GUI applications, the "recording" phase of the "record-and-playback" procedure can be completely eliminated. Rather than manually recording a script to capture the interactions of an user with an already functional GUI application, in our method a test engineer decides what the properties and behavior of the target application should be. Using functions provided in Synlib, the test engineer creates a C-language program to describe those properties. These test programs are called Synlib agents. The target application need not be functional at the time the agent programs are created. Once the target application is functional the agents are executed against them. Agents manipulate the target applications in the same way a human user

---

[*] *tmon, xtm, and Synergy are successive generations of record-and-playback tools developed at Hewlett-Packard Company and used to test X-windows based products within the company. A version of the xtm tool has been available in the public domain under the name "Client Exerciser Tool". Interested readers may send e-mail to the author for more information and documentation on these tools. The name Synlib is derived from "Synergy Library" since this work originated from the author's effort to provide a library interface to Synergy - a record-and-playback tool widely used in Hewlett-Packard Company.*

[†] *XRunner is a product from Mercury Interactive Co. 3333 Octavius Drive, Santa Clara, CA 95054.*

[‡] *VistaREPLAY is a product from VERITAS Sofware Corporation.*

[§]*Xsimu.test is a product from Qualtrack Corporation.*

[**]*QA Partner is a product from Seague Software Inc. 1320 Center Street, Newton Center, MA 02159.*

would and verify the expectations coded in their programs. The programmers interface for Synlib is somewhat large and therefore, in this paper, we will not get into that subject in any significant detail except to mention that Synlib provides following types of capabilities:

- Functions to name objects of interest. Such objects include windows, regions, locations, keystrokes, focusmaps, focus paths etc.

- Functions to deliver pointer and keyboard events to named objects.

- Functions to synchronize delivery of input to the state of the target applications.

- Functions to retrieve text from selected objects in window.

- Functions to verify if a desired window has assumed a desired state.

Readers are referred to Synlib User's Guide[2] for an overview and functions available in Synlib. Users may augment the test program with any other functions to access and verify file or system resources to create more effective and penetrating tests. This paper will describe how Synlib agent solve the naming problem using FocusMaps and FocusPaths. Later in the paper an example shows a test program constructed using Synlib functions.

Using Keyboard access to name objects

One way of naming the object of interest would be to ask how the object could be accessed by a sequence of keystrokes. If an object in a window is accessible by a unique sequence of keystrokes relative to that window then the sequence of keystrokes could be used as the name of the object of interest. For example take the window showed in Figure 1.

Figure 1: Mouse Dialog Window

This window is displayed by the "dtstyleManager" application on the "CDE" desktop[*]. The purpose of this dialog is to let the users customize the behavior of the "mouse" on their systems. The widgets constituting the window are so constructed that : when the window is mapped the keyboard focus is on the pushbutton "OK". Whenever the focus is on the "OK" button, a <TAB> keystroke will shift the keyboard focus to the "Default" button whereas a "Down-Arrow" keystroke will shift the input focus to the "Cancel" button. Based on this behavior one could imagine a naming scheme as shown in Table 1.

Object Name	Window Name	Key Sequence
OK	Style_Manager_Mouse	NULL
Cancel	Style_Manager_Mouse	<DOWN_ARROW
Help	Style_Manager_Mouse	<DOWN_ARROW> <DOWN_ARROW>
Default	Style_Manager_Mouse	<TAB>

Table 1: Key Strokes as proxy for object names

The symbol "Cancel" could be used to name the object where the input focus will be if after mapping, the "Style_Manager_Mouse" window receives a <DOWN_ARROW> keystroke. Similarly "Help" could be the name of the object where the input focus will be after the window has been mapped and has processed two consecutive <DOWN_ARROW> keystrokes. A GUI object on the display could thus be uniquely named by tuple: < <window_name> <key-stroke-sequence>>. Following this strategy the "Cancel" button on the Style_Manager_Mouse would be named: < Style_Manager_Mouse <DOWN_ARROW>> and the name of the "Help" button would be : < Style_Manager_Mouse < <DOWN_ARROW> <DOWN_ARROW>>>.

By including the name of the window within the name of the object, it is possible to identify the "Cancel" button even if more than one window on the display would contain similar "Cancel" buttons. This naming scheme could also be implemented using by simple macro expansion. The problem is that the simple naming scheme would not work - since the exact sequence of keystrokes needed to reach a desired object is not a static value, rather it depends on and varies with the current location of input focus in the target window. For example, assume that input focus has somehow been placed on the "Cancel" button. In this state the "Help" button is reached by only one <DOWN_ARROW> keystroke. So the name of the "Help" button would have to be change to: < Style_Manager_Mouse <DOWN_ARROW>>. The name of the "OK" button would become < Style_Manager_Mouse <UP_ARROW>>. In short a naming scheme of static binding of object names to specified keystrokes will not work.

We need a scheme in which the keystrokes needed to traverse from one GUI object to another is dynamically computable depending on the current location of input focus. What we need is a map

---

[*]*CDE or Common Desktop Environment is product jointly developed by the Hewlett-Packard, International Business Machines, SUN Microsystems, and Unix System Laboratories. For more information the reader should contact the participating companies.*

describing the relative location of various GUI objects in a window, and a specified set of rules which in association with the map enable us to navigate from one object to another during execution of the program. Synlib's response to these needs is a construct called "FocusMap". A focus map as will be seen later is a map of keyboard traversable objects in a window. The distance between two objects in this map is measured in terms keystrokes - the details of which are hidden by the concept of "FocusPath". A specific set of access rules dictate which keystrokes are to be employed to move the input focus to and from a focus element to its neighbor. The rest of the paper describes the current implementation of these three concepts.

The X-applications built with OSF/Motif widgets are a particularly suitable domain for testing the use of this naming strategy. OSF/Motif style guide[3] has proposed a detailed model for navigating among widgets in a window. The style guide recommends that applications must be designed for dual accessibility; i.e. an user should be able to control the application by using either pointer or keyboard devices. A Synlib program which is actually a proxy of the user, should therefore be able to access and select any object of interest within a window by delivering suitable sequence of keystrokes. Current implementation of FocusMap and Synlib functions manipulating focusmaps draws heavily on this navigation model. Default rules built in first implementation of Synlib assume the input model of the target application to be compliant with OSF/Motif proposal. As we continued to develop, we found that the FocusMap concept can be extended and customized to non-compliant applications as well. In this paper however we will limit our discussion to the use of FocusMap and Synlib to the testing of OSF/Motif compliant applications only.

FocusMap and FocusPath

Synlib views an X-window as an assortment of focus elements. A focus element is a named region which can receive keyboard input. The focus elements in a window can be organized into groups. A FocusMap itself is a list of such groups. Traversal within members of a group is accomplished by "arrow" keys; while traversal among groups is achieved by <TAB>, <F10> or other keys depending on the type of group being traversed to or from. A FocusMap is a logical layout of focus elements within a window. A FocusMap describes two things: it states the kind of foci elements present in a window; and the grouping of such elements if any. Following the declaration of types and the ordering of elements declared in a FocusMap, Synlib applies it own rules to decide how to access the objects indicated in a focusmap. This process will be informally described using some examples. The Synlib User's Guide should be consulted for a detailed explanation of these ideas.

A FocusMap has the following syntax:

```
FOCUSMAP :: (FocusMap <item_name> [< <MENU_GROUP> <<FOCUS_GROUP>n> | <MENU>])
MENU_GROUP :: (MenuGroup <item_name> <MENU_GROUP_MEMBER>n)
MENU_GROUP_MEMBER :: ( <item_name> ([<name_list> | <SUB_MENU>],)
MENU :: (Menu <item_name> ([<name_list> | <SUB_MENU>] n))
SUB_MENU :: <item_name> ( SubMenu <item_name> ( [ <item_name> | SUB_MENU]n))
FOCUS_GROUP :: ( FocusGroup <item_name> (  <name_list> n))
item_name :: a string indicating name of an item or the name of a group
             of items.
name_list :: a list of names
```

A FocusMap may contain zero or more FocusGroups and zero or one MenuGroup; or a FocusMap may be describing a menu. A FocusGroup is a collection of focus elements. A Menu is a collection of focus items one or more of which can lead to individual SubMenu. A MenuGroup is a collection of Menus. The symbols: FocusMap, Menu, MenuGroup, FocusGroup and SubMenu are reserved names. They should not be used as user chosen names in describing a FocusMap.

Default Access Rules

Synlib assumes the following in processing FocusMap and in accessing GUI objects during execution.

- Order of declaration of FocusGroups within a FocusMap and the order of declaration of focus elements within a FocusGroup or a Menu are important.

- When a window is mapped the input focus is automatically set to the first focus element in the first FocusGroup declared in the FocusMap to be attached to the window. If the focusgroup has no children then input focus is assumed to be set to the FocusGroup itself. If the FocusMap is describing a menu, then on mapping the input focus is assumed to be set to the first item in the menu.

- A <TAB> key stroke will shift the input focus from the current FocusGroup to the next FocusGroup declared in the FocusMap. A <Shift-Tab> key sequence will transfer focus to the previous FocusGroup.

- Whenever input focus enters/re-enters a FocusGroup, the first child of the FocusGroup, if it has any, receives input focus.

- MenuGroup is accessed by a <F10> key. The first declared element within the MenuGroup receives input focus when the window receives <F10> key. Traversal within elements of MenuGroup is achieved via <LEFT_ARROW> or <RIGHT_ARROW> keys. A <Return> keystroke displays the pull down menu associated with the members of a MenuGroup. <Escape> key removes the focus from the MenuGroup and returns the focus to the previous location.

- Elements within a Menu, SubMenu or a FocusGroup are traversed via <UP_ARROW> and <DOWN_ARROW> keys.

- A SubMenu is accessed by a <RIGHT_ARROW> key from its parent.

These assumptions comply with the Input and Navigation Model proposed in the OSF/Motif Style Guide.

Example FocusMaps

Here are two examples of focus maps:

```
! FocusMap for the Mouse dialog  window obtained by selecting the
! Mouse icon of StyleManager
!
(FocusMap SetMouseAttributes
     (FocusGroup BottomButtons ( OK Cancel SeekHelp))
```

```
        (FocusGroup Default) (FocusGroup MouseIcon)
        (FocusGroup Right) (FocusGroup Left)
        (FocusGroup Transfer) (FocusGroup Adjust)
        (FocusGroup Double_click)
        (FocusGroup Acceleration)
        (FocusGroup Threshold))

   ! FocusMap for the main StyleManager window. It contains one MenuGroup
   ! and 8 FocusGroups. The SubMenu declaration is only an example to
   ! display the syntax.
   !
   (FocusMap StyleManager
     (MenuGroup MenuBar (
          File (Exit)
          Help (Overview Tasks  Reference On_Time
   ! You can access a submenu from the item UsingHelp.
                 UsingHelp (SubMenu ThisIsFake
                           (item1 item2 item3))
                 About_Resources)))
   ! End of MenuGroup description
   ! Describe the order of icons
     (FocusGroup Icons (ColorIcon FontIcon Backdrops
                        Keyboard Mouse Beep
                        Screen Window StartUpRules)))
```

The FocusMap SetMouseAttributes correspond to the window shown in Figure 1. The FocusMap StyleManager describes the organization of focus elements of the window in Figure 2.

Figure 2: StyleManager Window

FocusMap SetMouseAttributes is a linear sequence of ten FocusGroups. The first declared group BottomButtons have three children - named OK, Cancel and SeekHelp respectively. The order of declaration of the FocusGroups and the elements within a FocusGroup are important. The actual name of the focus elements need not match with the corresponding labels on the display. In the example, the labels associated with the objects on the display are mostly used to name the corresponding focus items in the FocusMap - merely to improve understandability. Note that the focus item named "SeekHelp" actually corresponds to the "Help" button on the window.

The FocusMap StyleManager has one FocusGroup named "Icons" and one MenuGroup named "MenuBar". The FocusGroup "Icons" has eight focus elements. The MenuGroup "MenuBar" has two members: File and Help. Since the components of a MenuGroup are themselves menus - the declaration indicates that if the item pointed to by "File" or "Help" are selected, they will each display a menu. The components of the menu are indicated by the names in parentheses following them. The pull down menu from "File" will have only one item which we have chosen to name "Exit". The pull down menu from Help will have six items - whose names have been chosen as: Overview, Tasks, Reference, On_Time, UsingHelp and About_Resources. The declaration also indicates that a SubMenu will be available from the item "UsingHelp". The SubMenu itself is being named "ThisIsFake" where as the given names for its items are item1, item2 and item3.

Building a FocusMap

Building a FocusMap is like building a program

A FocusMap for a window can be built without having a functional implementation of the window. A FocusMap is a description of the input model of the window in a defined syntax. Thus building a FocusMap is very much like building a program. The user imagines what GUI objects should there be in a desired window and how they should be grouped. The individual objects are named and their desired groupings are described in a FocusMap expression using the syntax shown above. The FocusMap description can be stored in a file and the file is supplied to a Synlib agent during execution.

Interactive building of a Focusmap

Of course the FocusMap for a window can also be constructed after the window has already been implemented. The correspondence between the keyboard traversal and the FocusMap description is so close, that the FocusMap for a window can be easily created by following the movement of the location cursor as the window processes keystrokes. Following steps will be helpful in building FocusMaps for windows which have already been implemented:

1. Set the window manager resource "keyboardFocusPolicy" to "explicit".

2. Map the desired window on the display. Let "MyFocusMap" be the name of the intended focusmap.

3. Determine the FocusGroups within the window: When the window is mapped the location cursor will be on some object on the window. That object represents the first FoucsGroup of the FocusMap. Choose a name, any name, for the object. Let us call it Group1. At this point the FocusMap "MyFocusMap" will look like this:

```
(FocusMap  MyFocusMap
   (FocusGroup  Group1)
```

Then deliver a "<TAB>" keystroke to the window. If the location cursor moves to a different object then a new FocusGroup has been uncovered; a new name need to chosen and the name need to be assigned the type "FocusGroup". Continue doing the same till the location cursor returns to the object where it was when the window had mapped. At this point all FocusGroups in the window have been revealed. If the window had contained 3 FocusGroups then the FocusMap would be:

```
(FocusMap  MyFocusMap
   (FocusGroup  Group1) (FocusGroup Group2)  (FocusGroup  Group3))
```

4. Determine focus items within each group: Shift the location cursor to the group of interest and press the "<DOWN_ARROW>" . If location cursor moves to a different object, then

a focus item within the current focus group is being revealed. Continue doing so till the location cursor returns to the original position within the FocusGroup. Choose distinct names for each of the focus items within a group and declare them following the prescribed syntax. Assuming that Group1, Group2 and Groupt3 has zero, one and four items respectively - the focusmap would become:

```
(FocusMap  MyFocusMap
    (FocusGroup  Group1)
    (FocusGroup  Group2 (item1 item2))
    (FocusGroup  Group3 (item1  item2  item3 item4)))
```

5. Determine MenuGroup and its components: In most applications the MenuGroup is visible as a bar across the top part of the window. Deliver the <F10> keystroke to the window to reveal a MenuGroup. If it exists, the first item within the MenuGroup will receive the keyboard focus. Choose a name for the this item. Now press <RIGHT_ARROW> key to move focus to reveal the next item in the MenuGroup. Continue doing so till the first item in the MenuGroup receives focus. At each stage choose a name for the new item receiving focus. Declare these names in the focusmap in the order they received focus. Assuming that the menubar had three items and that their user given names are "PullMenu1" etc. the FocusMap at this stage would be as follows:

```
(FocusMap  MyFocusMap
    (MenuGroup  MyMenuBar (PullMenu1 PullMenu2  PullMenu3))
    (FocusGroup  Group1)
    (FocusGroup  Group2  (item1 item2))
    (FocusGroup  Group3  (item1  item2  item3 item4)))
```

6. Determine the menu items within each pull down menu on the menubar: To do this set focus on each item on each member of the MenuGroup, press the <RETURN> key to pull down the menu associated with this menubar item. For each item in the menu choose a name for the item and declare them as a list in the order of their traversal with <DOWN_ARROW> key. Associate this list with the name from which the menu was pulled down. The focusmap declaration at this stage might be as follows:

```
(FocusMap  MyFocusMap
    (MenuGroup  MyMenuBar
        (PullMenu1 (Exit)
            PullMenu2  (BackTrack HomeTopic History)
            PullMenu3  (OverView Tasks Contents)))
    (FocusGroup  Group1)
    (FocusGroup  Group2  (item1 item2))
    (FocusGroup  Group3  (item1  item2  item3 item4)))
```

7. If a menu item has a submenu, then first put keyboard focus on the menu item and then press the <RIGHT_ARROW> key to reveal the submenu. The items within the SubMenu is represented by a list of names in the order of their traversal using <DOWN_ARROW> key, and later the list is to be associated with the item from which the SubMenu was accessed. Assuming that a SubMenu was spawned from the item "Tasks" above and that the SubMenu had three items in it, the finished FocusMap could be:

```
(FocusMap   MyFocusMap
    (MenuGroup   MyMenuBar
        (PullMenu1 (Exit)
            PullMenu2 (BackTrack HomeTopic History)
            PullMenu3 (OverView
                        Tasks (SubMenu TaskNames ( Move Copy Delete))
                            Contents)))
    (FocusGroup   Group1)
    (FocusGroup   Group2   (item1 item2))
    (FocusGroup   Group3   (item1   item2   item3 item4)))
```

NOTE: that all names declared in a FocusMap are chosen by the user. There is no dependence on the internal names of the widgets or the widget hierarchy which may have been used to implement the object underlying the focus item.

Using FocusMaps and FocusPaths to access objects of Interest

The main purpose of a FocusMap is to express the user view of the access properties of various input enabled objects within a window. An input enabled object is an object within a window which can accept input focus. Assisted by a FocusMap, the user or a Synlib agent can navigate to a desired object, select the same and control the application owning the object. Individual items in a FocusMap are identified by their FocusPaths. This section describes how Synlib uses FocusPaths and FocusMaps to identify objects of interest on the display.

FocusPath

A FocusPath is a string to name an individual element in a FocusMap. A FocusPath is a dot ("."") separated string of names encountered in traversing from the top, the name of the FocusMap, to the referenced item itself. For example: the focus item "Mouse" in the focusmap "StyleManager" is named by the FocusPath "StyleManager.Icons.Mouse". Similarly the "item2" in the submenu "ThisIsFake" is named by the FocusPath "StyleManager.MenuBar.UsingHelp.ThisIsFake.item2".

Synlib uses FocusMaps and FocusPaths to dynamically compute the sequence of keystrokes needed to set focus to a a desired location. Assume that an window named "style" which corresponds to the focusmap "StyleManager" is mapped on the display. Synlib would bind the name "StyleManager.Icons.ColorIcon" to the object having the input focus in the "style" window. This is because its access rules dictate that the after mapping a window, the first element in the first FocusGroup will receive input focus. Once a FocusMap has been anchored to the ground, i.e. a certain component within the FocusMap is bound to a known object on a specified window, Synlib can dynamically compute how to access any other object named by a FocusPath simply by consulting the FocusMap. The example below explains how.

A Synlib Test: How FocusMap is used in navigating a window

Assume that a test needs to be developed for the following properties of the Style Manager application: That on electing the Mouse icon on the window will present a dialog for the user to set attributes of the pointer device for that display.   The dialog presented is expected to have the following property: (a) its title will be "Style Manager - Mouse"; (b) it will unmap if the "Cancel" item in the dialog is selected. Also that selecting the "Exit" item in the File menu will terminate the Style Manager application by unmapping its main window. A sample agent to verify these assertions is shown below.   Although the main purpose here is to explain how Synlib programs use FocusMaps to control the target application, a brief description of the other Synlib functions will be provided as they are encountered in the program. The Synlib User's Guide should be consulted for a complete discussion of functions provided by Synlib.

```
#define DIALOG_TITLE "Style Manager - Mouse"
#define WINDOW_TITLE "Style Manager"
/** Following FocusPaths are declared in a object file named: test.objects
FocusPath  MouseIcon "StyleManager.Icons.Mouse"
FocusPath  Cancel    "SetMouseAttributes.BottomButtons.Cancel"
FocusPath  Exit      "StyleManager.MenuBar.File.exit"
******/
main ()
{   Display *display;
    Window  *window_list;
    int match_count,  result;
    int      time_out = 30;
    char    *wtitle;
    display = SynOpenDisplay (NULL);
    result  = SynParseObjectFile ( "test.objects");
    /* the contents of the file test.focusmaps is shown above */
    result  = SynBuildFocusMap ( "test.focusmaps" );
    result = SynNamewindowByTitle ( display, "style", WINDOW_TITLE,
                                    PARTIAL_MATCH, window_list, match_count);
    result = SynSelectItem ( display, "style",  MouseIcon);
    if (result == SYN_SUCCESS)
      { result = SynWaitWindowMap ( display, "MouseDialog",  time_out);
         result = SynGetWindowTitle ( display, "MouseDialog", &wtitle);
         if ( strcmp ( wtitle, DIALOG_TITLE) == 0)
            printf ("ASSERT_1:  PASS;  Mouse dialog found.\n");
         else {
            printf ("ASSERT_1: FAIL; Title Expected: %s, Title Found: %s\n",
                    DIALOG_TITLE, wtitle);
            exit (1);
            }
         result = SynSelectItem ( display,  "MouseDialog",  "Cancel");
         result  = SynWaitWindowUnmap ( display, "MouseDialog", time_out);
         if (result == SYN_SUCCESS)
            printf ( "ASSERT_2: PASS; Selecting Cancel Button Unmaps Mouse
Dialog.\n");
         else
             printf ("ASSERT_2: FAIL; Cancel  button does not function.\n");
       }
    /** Select the FontIcon of the StyleManager  - just for fun. */
    result = SynSelectItem ( display,  "style" ,  FontIcon );
    /* Terminate the Style Manager window **/
    result = SynSelectItem ( display,  "style" ,  "Exit" );
    result =  SynWaitWindowUnmap ( display,  "style" , time_out);
    if ( result == SYN_SUCCESS)
      printf ("ASSERT_3: PASS Selecting Exit Menu Unmaps Style Manager.\n");
    else
      printf ("ASSERT_4: FAIL Style Manager Exit Menu does not function.\n");
    SynCloseDisplay ( display);
}
```

SynOpenDisplay: All program using Synlib functions must initialize themselves calling SynOpenDisplay(). This function internally calls XOpenDisplay() to connect to the desired display and also sets up data structures required to support Synlib functions.

SynParseObjectFile: Synlib recognizes a variety of objects and it is customary to declare them in file called a "objects" file. This function will parse an objects file and store the object definitions for later use by the Synlib program. FocusPath is a type of object recognized by Synlib. The contents of the file "test.objects" referred to in this program are shown in the commented lines at the top of the program. In this example the only purpose of using the objects file is to provide an alias for the FocusPaths used by the program.

SynBuildFocusMap: This function parses a file containing description of FocusMaps and creates their internal representations. The program described above could be executed with the focus map file shown earlier.

SynNameWindowByTitle: This function searches the display opened by SynOpenDisplay for a window whose title matches the string "Style Manager"; if found the function registers the window in a database maintained by Synlib under the program chosen name "style". Once registered, the Synlib program can refer to the window by the name "style" in all other functions. If it succeeds, the function returns the status "SYN_SUCCESS", otherwise some other status code would be returned. In this program we assume that the test agent is executed after the Style Manager window has been mapped on the display by invoking the stylemanager application and that the function will return SYN_SUCCESS.

SynSelectItem: The function computes the keystrokes needed to first set input focus to the object named by the FocusPath and then deliver the keystroke needed to select the item. The line:

```
SynSelectItem(display, "style", "MouseIcon")
```

is executed as follows. The string "MouseIcon" is assumed to be the alias of a FocusPath. Synlib searches the objects file and finds that the full FocusPath name for the object is: "StyleManager.Icons.Mouse". Next step is to validate the given FocusPath. Synlib searches its database for a FocusMap named "StyleManager". If found, it recursively follows children of the FocusMap to find if the given FocusPath leads to an valid item. In the process, Synlib determines the names and types of intervening focus elements. Consulting the description of the FocusMap named "StyleManager", Synlib finds that "Mouse" is the fifth child in the only FocusGroups "Icons" in this FocusMap. It now tries to compute the sequence of keystrokes needed to shift the input focus to the "Mouse" icon in the "style" window. This is the first time in the program, Synlib is being asked to set the focus in the "style" window. In absence of any other information, Synlib assumes that the input focus is currently at the item "Color" - which is the first child of the first FocusGroup and where the focus should be after the window is mapped. Since the focus is in first child and has to be moved to fifth child in the same focus group and since forward traversal within a FocusGroup is accomplished by pressing <DOWN_ARROW>, Synlib determines that this key needs to be pressed four times to move the focus to the object named by focus path. After pressing the necessary key strokes, Synlib updates its memory and remembers that the input focus in the "style" window is now at the object referred to by the focus path "StyleManager.Icons.Mouse".

The updated memory serves to provide the information about current location of input focus when Synlib is asked to select an object again in the "style" window. In this example the initial object where the input focus was and the destination object where the input focus was going to be moved to belonged to the same FocusGroup. So there was no need to press any <TAB> key. If however the initial and destination objects were separated by FocusGroups, then Synlib, after consulting the relevant FocusMap, would compute the needed number of <TAB> and <DOWN_ARROW> keys following the logic outlined here. If the final object was an earlier sibling in the list, then Synlib would generate needed number of <UP_ARROWS> or <SHIFT_TAB> keys or a combination of both type of keys. In short, when Synlib is asked to set focus in a window or is asked to select an object in a window, it looks up the FocusPath of the object currently having focus and with the help of supplied FocusMaps computes a navigation strategy using appropriate key strokes.

SynWaitWindowMap: Once the "MouseIcon" on the "style" window has been selected, the expectation of the test is that a dialog window will map on the display. So the program calls the function SynWaitWindowMap. This function blocks the execution of the program until a window maps on the display or a prescribed "time_out" period (in this example 30 seconds) expires. If a window maps within the "time_out" period, the functions registers the window in the Synlib's database of windows under the name "MouseDialog" and returns SYN_SUCCESS. Otherwise the function unblocks and returns the status code "SYN_TIME_OUT". In this example if the "MouseIcon" object in the Style Manager application is properly implemented this function will unblock and return SYN_SUCCESS.

SynGetWindowTitle: The test expects that the window mapped by selecting the "MouseIcon" shall have a specific title. To verify the title of a window, SynGetWindowTitle is called. This function returns the title of the named window.

The title string returned is then compared with the expected string. If the comparison fails then, the expectations set in the test are not being realized. In this example the test agent decides to quit. Otherwise the agent proceeds to verify the property of the "Cancel" object in this window. The "Cancel" object is accessed and selected by the function SynSelectItem() which has already been described. The expected result from this action is that the dialog window shall unmap. The function SynWaitWindowUnmap is used to verify this expectation.

SynWaitWindowUnmap : This function blocks execution of the program until either the named window unmaps or the prescribed time_out period expires. If the named window unmaps then the function return SYN_SUCCESS otherwise it returns SYN_TIME_OUT. By examining the return code, the program can decide whether selecting the "Cancel" button yielded expected behavior.

Rest of the program is quite self explanatory.

Experience and conclusion

Does this methodology work?

Synlib has been used in testing many GUI applications within the Hewlett-Packard Company including the company's desktop product "HP-VUE". Synlib and the testing methodology using FocusMaps and FocusPaths have been used to test for the Desktop product in the "Common

Desktop Environment" (CDE) jointly developed by : Hewlett-Packard, IBM, SUN Microsystems and Unix System Laboratories. Among others, the applications tested include: File-manager, Mail manager, Calender Manger, Window Manger , Editor and Help library. These are complex industrial strength applications. These applications present windows with complex assortment of focus elements. More than 1500 Synlib agent programs have been developed to test these applications. These programs uniformly use FocusMaps and FocusPaths to access the objects of interest. Such tests perform properly and reproducibly.

Are the tests portable?

The answer here is a resounding Yes! Synlib based tests are highly portable. The main reason for high portability is that the test programs themselves hardly ever contain any environment dependent or platform dependent information (as shown in the example). The scheme to name objects of interest is completely portable. The names of the objects do not refer to locations on the display; so they remain unchanged even if the tests are executed on displays of different resolution, different language environments or if the system is using different fonts. Since the naming scheme is independent of the internal names of the widgets implementing the objects of interest, the tests may not need to be changed even if the target application is redesigned or reimplemented using different widget hierarchy. It does not matter if the gadgets are being used; nor does it matter if the target application dynamically generate names for the widgets during execution. All test systems which use internal path names of widgets to identify objects of interest will fail in these situations. Even if the GUI interface of the target application were redesigned, the Synlib agents themselves need not necessarily be modified or recompiled. Assume that a redesign of the Style Manager application placed the "Mouse" icon as the last icon in the row after the "Startup" icon in the "Style Manager" window (Figure 2). If such rearrangement results in a different keyboard traversal model - then only the FocusMap need be edited and the FocusPath of the "Mouse" icon need be edited in the objects file. The actual test program itself need not undergo any change since it accesses the desired object through its alias and the alias as well as the FocusMaps are defined at runtime. They are not compiled into the program. The agent just needs to be executed with edited FocusMap file and edited objects file. These properties make Synlib agents themselves remarkably portable over many platforms, execution environments and application redesign cycles. This feature is attractive to software developers supporting products on many different platforms. About the only time it is necessary to modify a Synlib agent is when the semantics of the named object in the target application undergoes a change. For example, if the Style Manager application is so redesigned that the clicking the "Mouse" icon does not bring up the "Mouse Dialog" but brings up a dialog to select Fonts, changes in the test agent might be required. If the semantics of the target application is changed it is only natural that tests ought to be modified to fit new semantics of the target.

Ease of Use

The naming scheme described here is specially attractive because it does not create any external dependence in the testing process. Tests can be developed in parallel with the development of the application. Tests can be executed on the application "off the shelf". Testing does not require any "non-standard" vendor supplied code or library. This is a serious disadvantage in naming schemes where internal widget names are used to name the GUI object of interest. In the latter scheme the target application cannot be tested "as is". They must be specially prepared for testing; either the application must be mediative and recompiled or it must be relinked with some special library. This sort of preparation may require that the build environment of the application be accessible. This may not be possible in many testing situation.

To the user, a FocusMap is a considerable simplification of the complex widget hierarchy often required in building windows in Motif applications. There are many classes of widgets; some are visible to the user and some are not. FocusMap reduces them all to two visible types: child of a MenuGroup or a child of a FocusGroup. This simple model may be the reason why test engineers very easily adopt the idea of FocusMap and FocusPaths. Although the method of accessing objects via keystrokes is less natural than accessing them via keystrokes, the method of naming these objects via FocusMaps seem to be quite natural - perhaps because the user can easily correlate the FocusMap to the keyboard navigation of the contents of the window. Users have often come to regard the FocusMap as a specification of the window and indirectly as a specification of the target application.

Limitation

The ability of Synlib agents to drive and control a GUI application using FocusMaps, depends on the application providing keyboard traversal to and from the GUI object of interest. If an object is not traversable via keystrokes, then that object will not be accessible using FocusMaps. It should be noted however that such applications are not compliant with OSF/Motif style guide as well. Testing of GUI applications is such an expensive effort, that application developers would find it advantageous to improve the testability of their applications by providing keyboard traversal to all user accessible objects in a window.

References

[1] *OSF/Motif* Quality Assurance Test Suite Users's Guide (Revision 1.0).

[2] *Synlib User's Guide - An Experiment In Creating GUI Test Programs,* Sankar L. Chakrabarti, Hewlett-Packard Company (sankar@hp-pcd.cv.hp.com).

[3] *OSF/Motif Style Guide* Revision 1.1 - Prentice Hall, Englewood Cliffs, New Jersey.

Previewing PostScript over a Telephone in 3 Seconds Per Page

John M. Danskin[†]

Abstract

I have developed an X Protocol compression scheme called Higher Bandwidth X (HBX). This paper describes one aspect of HBX: POSTSCRIPT previewing. Using statistical models and arithmetic coding, HBX compresses the X protocol stream resulting from using ghostscript to preview documents by about 20:1, roughly 8 times the compression achieved by Xremote on the same stream. This is about 12 bits per source character after compression, implying a transmission time of about 3 seconds per page for normally formatted documents (3600 characters per page) using a standard 14400 bps modem.

Introduction

Higher Bandwidth X (HBX) is a compressed X protocol intended to provide improved interactive performance across low bandwidth interconnects such as serial lines. This paper describes the techniques used to achieve 20:1 lossless compression of the X protocol stream generated by the *ghostscript* POSTSCRIPT previewing program, when *ghostscript* is used to preview documents.

The technique used to achieve this compression is similar to program optimization: First, default compression methods are applied to the stream. Next, problem protocol streams are profiled to find resource intensive messages. Resource intensive messages are profiled to identify fields with poor compression. The programmer then analyzes and improves the statistical models used to predict these fields until satisfactory compression is achieved. The statistical models eventually used in this protocol stream use techniques reminiscent of text compression to predict the small images used by *ghostscript* to transmit character glyphs. The image size and coordinates are predicted using knowledge about how characters are usually positioned in documents (from left to right and

---

[†]*John M. Danskin is an Assistant Professor at Dartmouth College.*

roughly next to each other). These techniques are robust in the sense that poor predictions will lead to poor compression, but never incorrect results.

The compression technique used in HBX is called Structured Data Compression (SDC). Since SDC is amenable to optimization and tuning, it makes sense to ask what are the limits of compression for this application? A reasonable lower bound on message size for document previewing is the number of bits it would take to send the compressed unformatted ASCII document using state of the art text compression. This would be 2-3 bits per character: a quarter to a sixth the bits sent by HBX. I will show where the bits generated by HBX come from, and what might be done to move towards this lower bound.

Section 2 reviews some competing document transmission protocols. Section 3 is an introduction to HBX. Section 4 outlines tracing techniques. Section 5 introduces the *ghostscript* traces used to make the measurements presented in this paper. Section 6 discusses the predictive models used. Section 7 presents the compression results. Section 8 discusses the limits of compression and further opportunities for compression on this trace. Section 9 summarizes and discusses HBX. Finally, Section 10 contains a status report for the HBX project.

Competing Systems

Xremote

The compression system closest to HBX in design and purpose is the Xremote [Cornelius92] compression protocol for X. Xremote uses a two stage pipeline for compression:

Delta Compactor: Given a cache of the last 16 messages of 64 bytes or less and a new message to be encoded, builds a list of differing bytes for each of the cached messages of the same size, and forwards the smallest of these lists and the original message.

LZ78 Coder: implements the LZ78 dictionary based text compression algorithm [Ziv78] on the X message byte stream.

Both of these pipelined components work by removing repeated byte-strings from the input stream. They are very fast, and the LZ coder can be quite effective on the right kind of input. For the types of data streams considered in this paper, the Delta Compactor is ineffective, and the LZ coder delivers roughly 2.3:1 compression. For more details on Xremote performance see [Danskin4 94] or [Danskin2 94].

FAX

Fax protocols are not used to compress X, but they are used to transmit documents over phone lines, which is the application I am considering. Note that FAX compression ratios cannot be compared with X protocol compression ratios because the inputs are different. A more meaningful rate of effectiveness for comparison is the number of bits per printing character.

Essentially all modern FAX machines use an International Telegraph and Telephone Consultative Committee (CCITT) group 3 FAX protocol [McConnell92]. This protocol presently supports two compression options.

- The first group 3 FAX compression technique is one dimensional, running across scanlines. Each scanline is broken into runs of black or white pixels. The lengths of the runs are coded using a static Huffman table, mapping common run lengths onto short codes and rare run lengths onto long codes. This scheme achieves an average of about 8:1 compression across the 8 CCITT test documents [Netravali88], with a compression ratio as high as 16.7:1 for a nearly all white document (document 2), and as low as 4.9:1 for a document densely covered with text (document 4).

- The second group 3 FAX compression technique is two dimensional, running between scanlines. The first scanline is sent using the one dimensional technique described above. Afterwards, the locations of beginnings and endings of runs are tracked from one scanline to the next, with short codes for small displacements. There are special codes to deal with new runs, disappearing runs, and runs that move too far. For more detail, see [Netravali88] or [McConnell92]. This scheme achieves an average of about 12.9:1 compression, with a high compression ratio of 32.4:1 for the nearly all white document 2, and a low compression ratio of 6.5:1 for the densely formatted document 4. Document 4 has about 5000 characters, taking 175704 bits to send, for a rate of about 35 bits per character.

HBX Overview

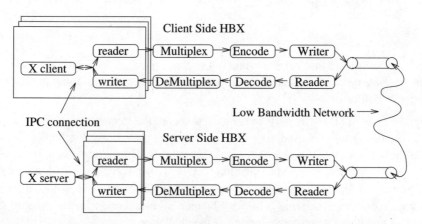

Figure 1: This is the HBX architecture, the multiple boxes on the client side show that there can be many clients, and reader/writer pairs. The multiple boxes on the server side show that although there is only one X server, there can be many connections and reader/writer pairs.

Figure 1 shows the gross architecture of HBX. HBX is transparent to both client and server. Inside HBX, traffic from multiple streams is parsed into messages, tagged by message type, and multiplexed together. The encode module compresses messages and precedes them with a length field, so that the decode module can be sure that it has a whole message before it starts decoding it.

Message length fields are statically coded to make it easy for the decoder to determine whether it has received the entire length field before it starts decoding it. Table 1 shows the sizes of HBX length fields as a function of compressed message size. These length code sizes very roughly approximate a static Huffman code for compressed message lengths.

Compressed message length	Size of length field
1-7 bits	1 bit
8-29 bits	3 bits
30 bits - 16 bytes	1 byte
17 bytes - 2048 bytes	2 bytes
2049 bytes - 2^{19} bytes	3 bytes

Table 1: Size of the length field for compressed HBX messages.

Compressed messages are padded to whole bytes and forwarded individually to the writer module, which buffers up all of the messages immediately available from the network and writes them out all at once to minimize network protocol overhead.

Note that the compression software operates on the multiplexed stream, not on individual streams. It would be easy to operate on individual streams instead, but memory requirements would be vastly increased, and individual streams would forfeit the possibility of learning from other streams.

Compression in HBX

HBX parses the X Protocol into messages and fields. Since padding does not transmit information, the data in padding fields is not usually transmitted. The rest of this discussion concerns fields which do transmit information.

HBX maintains a set of histograms which are used to record the frequencies of events in particular contexts. These histograms are used to generate an expected probability distribution for the values of fields in messages in the X protocol. Given a probability distribution and a value, HBX uses arithmetic coding (see [Bell90]) to produce $\log_2 p$ bits of output for each field, where p was the estimated probability of the field assuming the actual value. To the extent that the probability estimates are accurate, this scheme achieves Shannon's lower bound for the size of a message [Shannon48]. Finding good predictive models is the challenge.

HBX's predictive technique has two legs:

1. HBX maintains a set of histograms representing frequencies of values in various contexts. These histograms are indexed with context strings which are created by small registered state machines associated with fields in X messages. Histograms are created on demand. Unused histograms gradually get smaller and smaller and finally vanish. This is in order to prevent the histogram space from growing in proportion to the size of the input. The idea is to associate each message field with a registered state machine which will create a context string which indexes a histogram which will accurately predict the next value of the field. Relative histogram frequencies are used to estimate probabilities for arithmetic cod-

ing. The higher the probabilities estimated for actually occurring values, the lower the resulting bit-rate.

In practice, an ordered list of context strings is generated: each succeeding string referring to a less specific context. For instance: if I were compressing text, trying the predict the character after "aqu", the context strings might be ["TEXT,aqu", "TEXT,qu", "TEXT,u", "TEXT"]. "TEXT" is used to distinguish these contexts, and their associated histograms, from other contexts which might otherwise have the same byte strings even though they are used to compress different types of objects. This list of strings can be built in a straightforward way from the more compact list ["TEXT", "a", "q", "u"]. In the rest of the paper, when I say that I am using [*a, b, c*] for context, I will mean that my context strings are [*abc, bc, c*]

In this case, the last few characters are used to index a histogram to predict the next character in the input stream. The more specific the context is, the more likely its histogram is to make a very strong prediction, and the more likely it is not to predict our value at all. A zero probability prediction (*p=0*) for the actual next character would lead to an infinite number of bits transmitted (*log 0 = ∞*). This would not be productive, so an escape code with a non-zero probability is included in each histogram. The escape code is used to indicate a transition from a more specific context to a more general context. Escape code probabilities are estimated according to frequency of use as are other codes or values. In essence, escape codes are a simple way to represent the blending of probabilities from different histograms. So that histograms searches always terminate successfully, there is an implied fully populated byte level histogram which is used to encode values which were not found in more specific histograms.

The context string used for most message fields is simply a catenation of the message type with the field offset. This provides a unique identifier, and thus a unique histogram for each field. This context string is extremely effective for fields which are usually constant, like window IDs and graphics contexts. For other fields, context strings are carefully assembled from previously coded data to isolate appropriate histograms.

Details of histogram creation, deletion and pruning of predicted values are explained in more detail in [Danskin4 94]. The contexts used for predicting messages used by *ghostscript* are explained in Section 5. The escape code technique outlined here for switching between histograms is nicely described in [Bell90].

2. Some fields cannot be effectively predicted by histograms alone. For instance, sequence numbers and timestamp values do not often repeat and are thus very poor candidates for prediction with raw histograms.

HBX associates a predictive expression with every X message field. For fields which are already well predicted by histograms, this expression is a constant zero. For other fields, this expression is a guess at the new value of the field. At encoding time, the predictive expression is evaluated, and the difference between the guess and the field value is encoded using the histogram. Since a histogram is still used, the guess does not have to be accurate in order to improve compression. All that is necessary is that the difference between the predicted value and the actual value have less entropy than the actual value itself (where predictions are being made using a histogram). A trivial instance is where a constant field is being coded and the guess is always zero. The difference between zero and a constant is well predicted by a histogram and compression will be effective in this case.

In a more interesting example, HBX could improve on mouse position compression by predicting new mouse positions using the previous mouse position. This turns large random looking numbers (absolute mouse positions) into small random looking numbers (relative mouse positions), which are much more efficiently predicted by a histogram. By using linear extrapolation to predict mouse positions instead, HBX makes these numbers even smaller and more predictable [Danskin4 94, Danskin3 94]. (Quadratic extrapolation seemed promising, but turned out not to be an improvement over linear extrapolation in practice.)

Since encoding simply subtracts an actual value from a predicted value, actual values can be reconstituted in decoding by simply adding the transmitted value to the predicted value. There is no invertibility requirement for the predictive function.

Compression in HBX is based on predicting values of fields in X messages. Contextually indexed histograms and predictive expressions are used to make these predictions. Good predictions lead to low bit rates. Poor predictions may lead to higher bit rates, but will never lead to inaccurate results.

Tracing X

In order to make repeatable experiments, I needed to gather X protocol traces.

The tracing technique which I adopted was derived from work by Droms and Dyksen [Droms91]. They realized that if X clients and the X server converse using Berkeley sockets and TCP/IP, it would be easy to interpose a program between client and server which forwarded traffic in both directions while keeping a complete log. Complete data integrity is guaranteed at the price of a little performance. Droms and Dyksen used their traces to characterize the load on an Ethernet due to an X session. Another program which uses the interposition technique for snooping on X traffic is *xscope* by Peterson [Peterson89]. I used Peterson's table lookup technique for matching X queries with X replies.

On UNIX systems, X clients determine the address and method for connecting to the X server from an environment variable. The most common type of address is a machine name followed by a colon followed by a display number, for example "foo:0". To the X library, this address means to open a TCP socket to a machine named foo using port (6000 + *displayNumber*). Usually, *displayNumber* is 0. Most X servers only have one display and hence are not listening on ports 6001, 6002 etc.. It is easy to write a third program *XTee* which waits for new connections on one of these unused ports. When *Xtee* detects a new connection A, *Xtee* opens a new connection B to the X server. Input on A is forwarded to B, and input on B is forwarded to A. Input from both connections is logged (See Figure 2). To an X client, *Xtee* appears to be the X server, while to the X server, *Xtee* appears to be the X client.

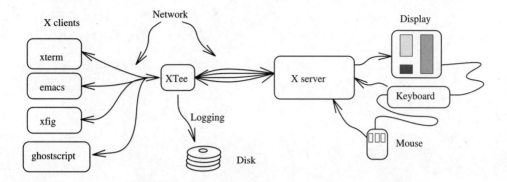

Figure 3: X clients attach to X server through logging process

Internally *Xtee* parses each client-to-server or server-to-client stream into separate messages, and then multiplexes the packetized half duplex streams into one half duplex stream going in each direction. Rather than annotate each message in the merged stream with a stream identifier, I pass a "ChangeStream" token down the merged stream whenever the current stream changes. New streams are identified with a "NewStream" token, and streams whose sockets have closed are shut down with "CloseStream" tokens. These three extra tokens provide enough information for demultiplexing and stream management. This multiplexing system is similar to the system used by Xremote which is discussed in [Cornelius92]. Messages in these two half duplex streams are logged into two files (client-to-server and server-to-client) with their length, a global sequence number, a unique timestamp, and a magic number which was used to increase programmer confidence in correct parsing of the logged data. The three stream management tokens are included in the logged data so that the streams can be isolated in later processing.

Since these traces are complete, the only way in which the collection of the traces can change the traces themselves is by degrading the performance of the system. In some cases a human subject might behave differently on a slower system, skewing results. For this paper, traces were gathered by running *ghostscript* non-interactively at full speed. Logging performance measurements suggest that tracing was not a bottleneck for this trace, so that the traces presented represent true system performance.

The performance impact of tracing with *Xtee* is discussed further in [Danskin4 94].

Ghostscript Traces

The experiments presented in this paper are based on two traces from the ghostscript application: ghostscript and ghost2. Images from these traces are presented in Figure 3. The ghostscript trace was generated by a short letter. The ghost2 trace was generated by a 7 page technical paper, which, as you can see, was densely formatted in two column mode with mixed fonts and a fair bit of mathematics.

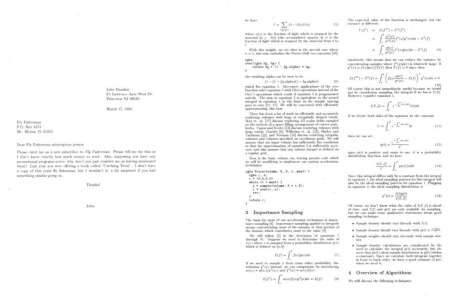

Figure 4: To the left is the ghostscript trace, a single page letter generated by LaTeX. To the right is a representative page from ghost2 trace, a seven page technical paper, also generated by LaTeX. Note the mixed fonts and complex formatting in the ghost2 trace. Pages in this trace average 4425 printing characters each.

A visualization of the X messages in these traces is presented in Figures 5 and 6. Measurements were made by running HBX on these traces in batch mode (as opposed to interactively with a real user). Batch mode experiments are repeatable and make it possible to accurately determine the value of individual modifications.

Predictive Models for Ghostscript

Figure 5: Model for predicting bits in bi-valued (bitmap) images: Pixels with known values have black dots. The values of the six pixels with circled dots identify a histogram for the next pixel to be encoded, which is identified with an 'X'.

Ghostscript draws text by sending each character as a small image using the X_PutImage command. This primitive is responsible for over 90% of the bits in my traces. Although compressing other primitives becomes important as X_Putimage is successfully compressed, I am only going to discuss this key primitive. Compression of other X messages is analogous.

The X_PutImage request, and the context strings and predictive expressions used for compression of this request are summarized in Table 2 and justified below.

Field	Bits	Guess	Predictive Model
		X_PutImage	
Opcode	8	0	Tag, Offset
Format	8	0	Tag, Offset
Length	16	0	Tag, Offset
Drawable	32	0	Tag, Offset
Graphics Context	32	0	Tag, Offset
Image Width	16	0	Tag, Length
Image Height	16	0	Tag, Width, Length
Dst-X	16	$PrevX + PrevWidth$	Tag, Offset
Dst-Y	16	$PrevY + PrevHeight - Height$	Tag, Offset
Left pad	8	0	Tag, Offset
Depth	8	0	Tag, Offset
Image	$w \times h$	0	Hash (Width, Height), Prev 3 Glyphs

Table 2: The model used for images depends on the size and depth of the image. Small bi-level images (width and height not more than 64) use a hash of the width and height fields and the previous three glyphs to predict the entire image as an atomic entity (as shown in the table). Larger bi-level images are predicted pixel by pixel using some of the previous pixels from the same image for prediction as shown in Figure 4. All of the images in the trace suite were bi-level.

- In HBX, a tag is transmitted before each X message. This tag serves to uniquely identify X messages (whose types are not always obvious) as well as HBX messages used to demultiplex multiple client streams. This meta-opcode or Tag is often used together with the offset of a field in a message to provide a unique identifier for that field. As shown in Table 2, this is the context used in histogram selection for the *Opcode, Format, Message Length, Drawable, Graphics Context, Left Pad*, and *Depth* fields. All of these fields except the *Length* field are usually constant. Associating a unique histogram with usually constant fields is very effective.

- The *Message Length* field is the first field which usually varies from message to message. It is not immediately clear what preceeding context we could use to get a better histogram for this field. However, there is an obvious correlation between image width, and the number of words in a packet, so the *Message Length* field can be used as context to select a histogram for the *Image Width* field. The combination of width and length constrain the *Image Height* field to just a few values (not just one value because the message length is in words and there can be several short scanlines packed into a single word).

- The location of the next character is specified by the *Dst-X* and *Dst-Y* fields. For a fixed width font, the value of the *Dst-X* field in the previous message would be a good prediction expression, because the difference in X positions for the two characters would be constant except in relatively unusual cases like the end of a line. Since POSTSCRIPT documents usually include varying width fonts we have to try harder. The value of the previous *Dst-X* field, plus the previous *Image Width* is a good guess for the new X position.

- If the *Dst-Y* field of the X_PutImage request specified the destination of the bottom edge of an image, then all of the characters in a line of text (except for those relatively rare characters with descenders) would start at the same Y position. Unfortunately, the *Dst-Y* field of the X_PutImage request specifies the top edge of the image, which depends on the height of the character. The value of the previous Dst-Y field minus the previous *Image Height* field plus the current *Image Height* field is a good guess for the current Dst-Y field, capturing the essential straight line along the bottom edge of a line of text.

  It is important to remember that even though the contexts and predictive expressions used for the *Dst-X* and *Dst-Y* fields are tuned specifically for document previewing, correct results will still be delivered to other applications, although with somewhat reduced compression performance. For most non-text imaging applications, the size of the images dominates the size of the coordinates, and coordinate compression is unimportant.

- When bi-level images are too big to be glyphs I use the pattern of bits in Figure 4 to predict bits one by one. This 6 bit pattern (similar patterns appear throughout the literature: see for example [Inglis94]), picks up both horizontal and vertical patterns in the input image, providing a kind of cheap 2D compression. I experimented with larger and smaller patterns, but this one seemed to give the best compression on my trace suite. I assign a third value to out-of-image pixels to account for image edges. This gives us 163 possible different contexts or histograms in which to predict a bit-value, each storing the relative frequencies (probabilities) of 0 and 1. These large images are not an important source of bandwidth in document previewing, however.

- Small bi-level images are remembered verbatim and predicted as indivisible values. I could use a single histogram for these images, and expect to achieve results comparable to an order-0 entropy coder for text, where characters probabilities are estimated according to their frequencies in text. A simulated arithmetic coder (SC) operating on the glyphs in the ghost2 trace with a single histogram achieves 6.4 bits per glyph and 5.3:1 compression. (The cost for missing all of the histograms in SC is the size in bits of the uncompressed glyph.)

  When encoding the image bits, the image width and height are already known. These fields significantly narrow the choice of glyphs, so I can use a hash of these values to index a histogram. Using this hash as a context, (with a single shared histogram as a backup) SC achieves 2.7 bits per glyph and 12.6:1 compression for a better than 2:1 improvement over just the single histogram.

Ghostscript sends characters in the same order as they appeared in the text. This means that the last few glyphs might be a good predictor of the current glyph. Using the last 3 glyphs and a hash of the width and height as context for predicting the next glyph, SC achieves 2.4 bits per glyph and 14.8:1 compression. This is the context used to predict the image field in the X_PutImage message in HBX.

Although this last technique is aimed specifically at text, many applications which draw lots of small images (icons for example) often repeatedly draw them in the same order, leading to good performance with HBX.

Fields in the X_PutImage request are predicted and encoded one by one in order. Any information that has already been encoded can be used to help predict new information. Coordinates values are predicted assuming even lines of text. Small images (character glyphs) are cached whole and predicted as if they were characters in English text.

Experimental Results

Figure 5 shows the performance of HBX on the ghost2 trace. Overall compression performance on this trace was 20.2:1. For reference, the Xremote compression protocol [Cornelius92] achieves 2.5:1 compression on this trace [Danskin4 94]. When I took the trace, the ghostscript program generated about 150K bits/sec. After compression, ghostscript generated less than 7.5K bits/sec which means that with the workstation I used to generate this trace, ghostscript could easily run at full speed over a 14.4Kbps modem. Overall, ghostscript is generating about 14 bits per printing character in this trace, which means that a reasonably full page with 3000 printing characters could be sent in about 3 seconds using a commonly available 14.4Kbps modem. This is roughly 3 times the performance of the 2 dimensional FAX compression algorithm.

Figure 6 shows the performance of HBX on the ghostscript trace. Overall compression on this trace was 10.1:1 while Xremote achieved 2.4:1. There are two reasons for the lower compression rates on this trace:

1. The trace is heavily influenced by startup messages. While these messages are compressible, HBX does not compress them as effectively as the image messages.

2. The trace is so short that the compression learning phase, where compression is relatively poor because many glyphs are being seen for the first time, is an important source of bits. If you look at the top of Figure 6, you will see how compression is improving over time. At the end of about one second's worth of X_PutImage messages, compression is in the 20:1 range achieved on the longer trace.

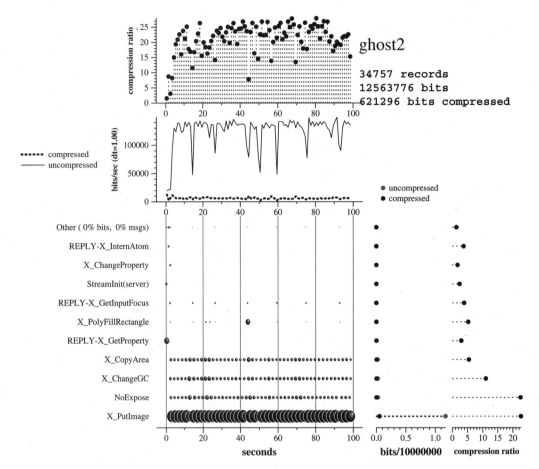

Figure 3: This graph shows the ghost2 trace. The X axis along the bottom of the central area is seconds since session startup. The Y axis in the main area is marked off by message type. The volume of spheres in the data area is proportional to the size of the messages which they represent (before compression). Spheres which are vertically stretched represent multiple nearly simultaneous messages, other spheres represent single messages. The dash-dot graph to the middle right shows the total number of bits for each type of packet. The dash-dot graph to the far right shows the compression ration for each type of packet. The line graph at the middle top shows the number of bits per second as a function of time. The integration interval is listed in the Y-axis legend. The dash-dot graph at the tip-top shows the compression ratio as a function of time.

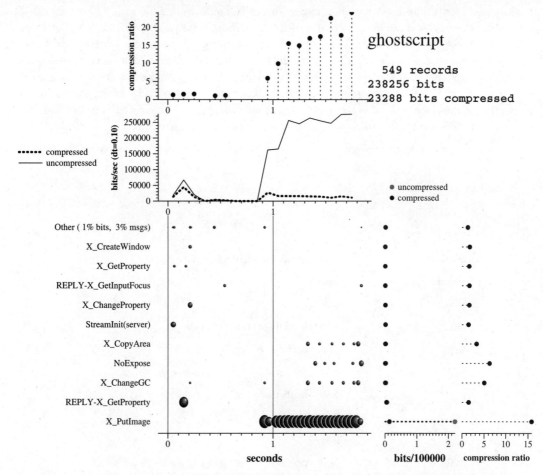

Figure 4: This graphs shows the ghostscript trace. For an explanation of this type of graph, see Figure 5. Note how compression improves over time, reaching 10:1 almost right away and 25:1 after about 200K bits of image transmission.

The Limits of Compression with HBX

Since HBX is amenable to optimization, it makes sense to ask what the limits of HBX compression are, and to measure HBX on this yardstick. Finding a reasonable upper bound for compression is easy for applications which only transfer text. For instance, *ghostscript* is a previewer for POSTSCRIPT files, which are usually derived from ASCII documents with embedded markup commands. It is reasonable to expect that the bitstream which *ghostscript* generates will not be compressed so that it is smaller than a compressed version of the original document with markup commands removed, as long as a good text compression algorithm is used on the original text.

The ghost2 trace is derived from a technical paper written using LaTeX. After the formatting commands have been removed with *detex*, the paper is 38625 bytes long. A simulated third order context based text compressor with lazy exclusions (STC) reduces this file to 11935 bytes or 2.47 bits per character, for a compression ratio of 3.23:1. *Ghostscript* generated 30976 X_PutImage messages in 1484196 bytes, essentially one for each printing glyph. There were 657 different glyphs from about 79 different printing characters in the source document. (The increase in the size of the character set presumably results from font changes.) HBX compressed these messages to 65630 bytes, or 13.59 bits per printing character. From the point of view of X, this is 22.6:1 compression. From the point of view of the compressed source file, we have a 5.5:1 expansion. The limits of compression for this trace will be somewhere between these points.

X_PutImage		
field	bits	comment
opcode	0.01	
format	0.01	
length	1.89	proportional to the size of the glyph
drawable	0.01	
gcontext	0.01	
width	1.81	partially predicted by the length
height	0.08	predicted by length and width
x	2.52	predicted by prev x and prev width
y	1.50	predicted by prev y and (prev height - curr height
pad	0.01	
depth	0.01	
image	3.00	predicted by prev 3 glyphs and width and height
total	10.86	

Table 3: Average number of bits generated for each field of the X_PutImage message by HBX in the ghost2 trace. HBX will average about 3 bits of message length information for messages this size, and messages are expressed in multiples of 8 bits, so the total number of bits sent for each message was 16.94. This is larger than the number of bits sent per character in the original source file because many of the characters in the original source file did not generate glyphs (space, newline, etc.).

Table 3 shows where the bits went in the X_putimage commands used to send glyphs in the ghost2 trace. Just under 11 bits were spent on overhead: the length field for the packet, and padding packets to an integral number of bytes. If HBX grouped messages on bit boundaries, and associated a single length field with a large number of messages, it might achieve about 8.7 bits per source character on this trace.

The next place to look for further compression on this primitive might be carriage return prediction (which is probably the major source of uncertainty in x) and glyph-with-descender detection, (probably the major source of uncertainty in y). Other fields like *width, height* and *length* could be determined from the glyph, but since these fields are used to help predict the glyph, it is not clear how much rearranging or grouping these predictions would help.

Incidentally, there are systems which extract fonts from scanned images, and match marks in scanned text to characters in the scanned font. This is a much harder problem than the one I have addressed here because of the noise and registration issues associated with scanning. A recent system, which achieved 37.8:1 lossless compression on a library catalog scanned at 400dpi was described in [Inglis94]. (The high compression ratio is because of all of the white space in a scanned document. HBX's compression ratio is lower because its input has denser content.)

In this example HBX has achieved a 5.5:1 expansion with respect to the compressed source text. We can see how to get to an expansion of only 3.5:1 over the compressed source with buffering, but further progress would probably require a deeper understanding of how characters are positioned.

Discussion

HBX exploits the separation of predictive model and coder in arithmetic compression to apply a custom compression technique to each field in each message in a graphics protocol, within a unified framework, and without wasting any bits in the transition from field to field. To the extent that the predictive models used accurately encapsulate all of the available knowledge about the fields in question, this technique is optimal. In practice, HBX achieved over 10:1 compression on a short ghostscript trace, and over 20:1 compression on a long trace. This was between 4 and 8 times the performance of the LZW-based Xremote protocol. This level of improvement is enough to transform phoneline POSTSCRIPT previewing from intolerable to pleasant.

I would like to improve POSTSCRIPT previewing compression performance by another factor of 2 by applying more sophisticated prediction techniques to this problem, and by removing some constraints from the HBX implementation. Currently fields must be predicted singly and in order. Hierarchical prediction, where some set of fields could be predicted together, and an escape code might mean breaking the fields up or switching to some other means of prediction altogether, might make it easier to achieve higher compression rates.

I am also interested in applying the techniques presented here to other application specific compression problems such as RPC.

HBX Status

HBX supports interactive sessions using Berkeley sockets for reliable stream transport. This means that HBX depends on an efficient underlying transport layer (like CSLIP or PPP, and not like SLIP) to achieve reasonable performance across a slow connection.

At this moment, HBX does not fully understand sessions involving machines with multiple byte orders. When this is fixed up and some documentation is written, HBX will be ready to release as research software. With any luck this will occur sometime this summer.

References

[Bell90] Bell, Timothy C., John G. Cleary, and Ian H. Witten, "Text Compression," Prentice Hall, Englewood Cliffs, NJ, 1990

[Cameron88] Cameron, R.D., "Source encoding using syntactic information source models," IEEE Transactions on Information Theory. (34)4 pp 843-850, July 1988

[Cleary84] Cleary, J. and I. Witten, "Data compression using adaptive coding and partial string matching," IEEE Trans. Communications, COM-32, No 4., 396-402 (1984)

[Cornelius92] Cornelius, David, "XRemote: a serial line protocol for X" 6th Annual X Technical Conference, Boston, MA, 1992

[Danskin1 94] Danskin, John and Pat Hanrahan, "Profiling the X Protocol,"*1994 SigMetrics conference on measurement and modeling of computer systems.* Full paper in Technical Report CS-TR-442-94, Department of Computer Science, Princeton University, Princeton, NJ, January 1994.

[Danskin2 94] Danskin, John and Pat Hanrahan, "Compression Performance of the Xremote Protocol," *1994 Data Compression Conference.* Full paper in Technical Report CS-TR-441-94, Department of Computer Science, Princeton University, Princeton, NJ, January 1994.

[Danskin3 94] Danskin, John, "Higher Bandwidth X," ACM Multimedia 94, Second ACM International Conference on Multimedia. 15-20 October 1994, San Francisco California. pp 89-96.

[Danskin4 94] Danskin, John, "Compressing graphics protocols for networks, or higher bandwidth X," PhD Thesis, Department of Computer Science, Princeton University, Princeton, NJ. Available as Princeton Technical Report CS-TR-465-94.

[Droms91] Droms Ralph and Wayne R. Dyksen, "Performance measurements of the X window system communication protocol," *Software Practice and Experience* vol. 20, no. S2, May 1991.

[Fulton93] Fulton Jim, and Chris Kent Kantarjiev, "An update on low bandwidth X (LBX)," Proceedings of the 7th Annual X Technical Conference, January 1993, O'Reilly and Associates.

[Gettys91] Gettys, James, Philip L. Karlton, and Scott Mcgregor, "The X Window System, Version 11," *Software Practice and Experience* vol. 20(S2), S2/35-S2/67, October 1991

[Guazzo91] Guazzo, M., "A general minimum redundancy source coding algorithm," IEEE Trans. Information Theory, IT-26 (1), 15-25, January 1980.

[Held91] Held, Gilbert. "The Complete Modem Reference," John Wiley & Sons, Inc. 1991

[Inglis94]   Inglis, Stuart, and Ian H. Witten, "Compression-based template matching," Proceedings 1994 Data Compression Conference, March 29-31 Snowbird Utah pp 106-115.

[Katajainen]   Katajainen, J., M., Penttonen, and J., Teuhola, "Syntax-directed compression of program files," Software-Practice and Experience, 16(3), 269-276

[McConnell92]   McConnell, Kenneth R., Dennis Bodson, and Richard Schaphorst, "FAX: digital facsimile technology and applications," Second Edition, Artech House, Boston, 1992

[Moffatt88]   Moffatt, A., "A note on the PPM data compression algorithm," Research Report 88/7, Department of Computer Science, University of Melbourne, Parkville, Victoria, Australia.

[Moffatt89]   Moffatt, Alistair, "Word-based text compression," Software-Practice and Experience, Vol. 19(2) 185-198 February 1989

[Netravali88]   Netravali, Arun, N. and Barry G. Haskell "Digital pictures, representation and compression," Plenum Press, New York, 1988

[Peterson89]   Peterson, James L., "XSCOPE: A debugging and performance tool for X11" Information Processing 89: Proceedings of the IFIP 89 Congress, August 1989, pp 49-54

[Rissanen79]   Rissanen, J. J., and G. G. Langdon, "Arithmetic coding," IBM J. Research and Development, 23(2), 149-162, March 1979.

[Rubin79]   Rubin, F., "Arithmetic stream coding using fixed precision registers," IEEE Trans. Information Theory, IT-25 (6), 672-675, November 1979.

[Scheifler88]   Scheifler Robert W., "The X Window System Protocol," M.I.T. Laboratory for Computer Science. 1988.

[Scheifler91]   Scheifler, Robert W. and Jim Gettys, "The X Window System," *Transactions on Graphics* 5(2), 79-109, April 1986, and *Software Practice and Experience* vol. 20(S2), S2/5-S2/34, October 1991

[Shannon48]   Shannon, C. E., "A mathematical theory of communication," Bell System Technical Journal, 27, 398-403, July 1948

[Storer88]   Storer, James A., "Data compression: methods and theory," Computer Science Press, Rockville Maryland, 1988.

[Thomas85]   Thomas, S. W., J. McKie, S. Davies, K. Turkowski, J. A. Woods, and J. W. Orost. "Compress (version 4.0) program and documentation," available from joe@petsd.uucp, 1985.

[Welch84]   Welch, T. A., "A technique for high-performance data compression," IEEE Computer, 17 (6), 8-19, June 1984.

[Ziv78]   Ziv, J. and Lempel, A. "Compression of individual sequences via variable-rate coding," IEEE Trans. Information Theory, IT-24 (5), 530-536, September 1978

Biography

John M. Danskin is an Assistant Professor of Computer Science at Dartmouth College. He is interested in application specific data compression and application specific channel coding. He can be reached at jmd@cs.dartmouth.edu.

D11: a high-performance, protocol-optional, transport-optional window system with X11 compatibility and semantics

Mark J. Kilgard[†]

Abstract

Consider the dual pressures toward a more tightly integrated workstation window system: 1) the need to efficiently handle high bandwidth services such as video, audio, and three-dimensional graphics; and 2) the desire to achieve the under-realized potential for local window system performance in X11.

This paper proposes a new window system architecture called D11 that seeks higher performance while preserving compatibility with the industry-standard X11 window system. D11 reinvents the X11 client/server architecture using a new operating system facility similar in concept to the Unix kernel's traditional implementation but designed for user-level execution. This new architecture allows local D11 programs to execute within the D11 window system kernel without compromising the window system's integrity. This scheme minimizes context switching, eliminates protocol packing and unpacking, and greatly reduces data copying. D11 programs fall back to the X11 protocol when running remote or connecting to an X11 server. A special D11 program acts as an X11 protocol translator to allow X11 programs to utilize a D11 window system.

1. Introduction

High-bandwidth services like audio, video, image processing, and three-dimensional graphics are at or coming soon to a desktop computer near you. Processors and graphics hardware continue to get faster. The increasing relative cost of cache misses, context-switching, and transport overhead give an advantage to greater system locality. Users desire slicker application appearances, better responsiveness, and seamless inter-application communication.

[†]*Mark J. Kilgard is a Member of the Technical Staff at Silicon Graphics, Inc. Mark believes software should get faster for more reasons than just that hardware got faster. Address electronic mail to mjk@sgi.com.*

What should window systems do to stay current with these trends?

This paper proposes a restructuring of the industry standard X Window System [Scheifler92] to answer these trends. This new window system architecture, called D11[†], provides higher performance local window system operations while preserving complete compatibility with X11 clients and servers. The system utilizes a new operating system facility similar in concept to the Unix kernel's traditional implementation but designed for user-level execution. Local D11 clients can execute within the D11 window system kernel without compromising the window system's integrity. The transport of protocol is eliminated for local window system interactions. Context switching and data copying costs are minimized.

The name D11 refers not to a new revision of the X11 protocol; indeed D11 aims to obsolete the local use of the X11 protocol. D11 is a new window system architecture but fully X11 compatible. X11 programs can be trivially recompiled to utilize D11 since the full Xlib application programming interface (API) is retained by D11. Existing X11 clients will continue to work with a D11 server by generating X11 protocol, and D11 clients will work with existing X11 servers by falling back to X11 protocol. D11 is not an extension or minor addition to X11. It is a reinvention of X11's fundamental architecture.

Section 2 motivates the new architecture for D11 by considering window system trends. Section 3 presents the means for better performance in D11. Section 4 contrasts D11 to other approaches. Section 5 describes the *active context* operating system facility that D11 utilizes. Section 6 considers the implementation of D11 and how to provide complete X11 compatibility in D11.

2. Window System Trends

The two dominant, standard window systems today are X11 and Microsoft Windows. X11 is the *de facto* window system for Unix workstations; Microsoft Windows is the Microsoft-imposed standard for PCs.

Network Extensibility Considered

X11 uses a network extensible protocol that allows cross-machine and even cross-vendor and cross-operating system interoperability of X clients and servers. X11's network extensibility is in high contrast to the lack of network extensibility in Microsoft Windows. Most X clients run reasonably well locally *and* remotely. In most cases, the user is unaware when a client is running remotely. The success of X's transparent network extensibility has even created an entirely new network device: the X terminal [Engberg91].

The X community often lauds network extensibility over PC users of Microsoft Windows, but Microsoft Windows has gained widespread usage despite the lack of network extensibility.

For most PC users, contemporary PC technology provides plenty of power for tasks such as word processing, spreadsheets, and electronic mail. The idea of remote execution of windowed

---

[†]*The D11 window system described in this paper is a proposal; an implementation of D11 does not exist nor do plans exist to implement D11 at this time.*

applications is considered interesting but frivolous. And in the homogeneous world of PCs, support for heterogeneous machines and operating systems is largely unnecessary.

For Microsoft Windows users, the network can be an important source of services (file systems, databases, and electronic mail) but the graphical front ends to such services can easily be implemented as a local Microsoft Windows program. Even when the storage or computational burden of an application like a database is beyond the capability of a desktop machine, the user's graphical application need be only an interface between the user and another computer managing the database. If services are sufficiently network extensible, a network extensible window system may not be necessary.

One should be careful not to draw the wrong conclusion. The point is not that network extensible window systems are unimportant, but that in a homogeneous environment using desktop computers with more than adequate power for common applications, network extensible window systems are not necessary. In a heterogeneous environment with users sharing computer resources beyond the capability of the machine on their desk, network extensible window systems have proven to be vitally important.

The important point is X11 is competing with window systems that are not network extensible but that derive important performance benefits from the optimization opportunities available to a purely local window system implementation.

Future Trends for High Bandwidth Applications

Future trends in computing suggest that local windowed applications may become more important. The bandwidth required for current and future interactive services such as audio, video, and three-dimensional graphics are difficult to meet without specialized protocols or workstation support. When an application requires the manipulation of huge quantities of video, audio, and graphical data at interactive and constant rates, distributing the application at the semantic level of window system operations may not be workable.

Future trends in the use of video, audio, image processing and three-dimensional graphics imply that the graphical and interactive components of applications using these capabilities will execute on the local desktop computer. Already most workstations and PCs have some capacity to handle high-bandwidth services; future machines will be even more capable. All these capabilities for video, audio, image processing, and 3D will still need to be networked, but specialized network protocols can be developed to meet the demands of these services.

If the local desktop computer is the most efficient location for the entire window system component of future applications, then a new window system must optimize the case of local window system applications. The effective division between client and server for future applications is less likely to be at the level of window system operations.

Protection and Reliability

An important benefit of client/server based window systems is the added protection and reliability that comes from isolating the window system server from the window system clients. A faulty client should not compromise the window system. Microsoft's Windows is moving in this direction. X has always had this type of protection.

Protection in X11 is achieved through isolating the window system server from its clients by putting the clients and server in separate address spaces. This isolation incurs a significant cost in cache misses, context switching, protocol packing and unpacking, and transport overhead.

A client/server architecture using separate processes is not the only means to achieve protection. D11 provides the same measure of protection as client/server based window systems but does so using the *active context* facility described in Section 3 and detailed in Section 5. D11 does not isolate the window system kernel from clients using isolated address spaces; instead D11 uses virtual memory techniques to allow the client to in effect *become* the window system kernel through controlled interfaces without a heavyweight process switch and change of address space.

X11 Compatibility

Considering future trends without regard to the past and present is dangerous. While X is not perfect [Gajewska90], one cannot deny the enormous success of the X Window System. The X Window System now claims over 3.5 million X capable seats [Auditore94]. X has well-established, portable APIs well known to workstation programmers. X is supported by nearly all workstation vendors worldwide. The number of X tools and applications grows daily.

A new window system standard in the X tradition should not abandon the existing base of applications, toolkits, programmers, and users. For this reason, D11 retains complete X11 window system compatibility.

3. Reinventing X11

D11 is about reinventing X11 for higher performance. This does *not* mean abandoning compatibility with the current X11 protocol or X11 semantics or network extensibility. Instead, D11 concentrates on optimizing the local window system interface. Programs compiled to support the D11 interface *will* operate with current X11 servers, *and* all X11 clients will operate *unchanged* with a D11 window system. The substantive difference is that D11 programs can achieve substantially better window system performance than equivalent X11 clients running locally.

The API for D11 is a superset of the X11 Xlib API. The D11 API is augmented with higher performance local interfaces for some existing Xlib operations. When a D11 program runs locally within the D11 framework, these interfaces allow window system operations to be performed in a manner optimized for the local case. When a D11 program runs remotely or connects to a local X11 server, the new D11 interfaces generate the X11 protocol to achieve the same effect at lower performance.

The D11 implementation does not structure the window system service as a separate process that clients communicate with via X11 protocol byte streams. Instead, the X server is reimplemented via a user-level kernel facility called active contexts. Instead of writing and reading X protocol through bytes streams, D11 programs call the D11 window system directly through a *protected procedure call* mechanism. A protected procedure call is a change of execution state into an active context where the program's address space is augmented by the memory regions for the active context and the process's identity (including all standard Unix resources like file descriptors and signal handlers) is transformed into that of the D11 window system kernel. On return from a protected procedure call, the program identity and address space are restored. Figure 1 shows the effect of a protected procedure call on a process's address space and identity.

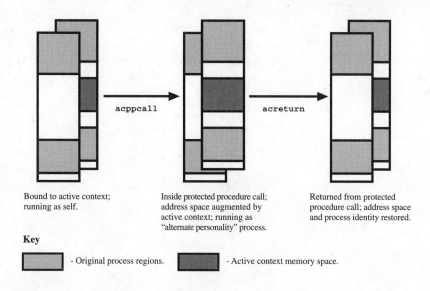

Bound to active context;
running as self.

Inside protected procedure call;
address space augmented by
active context; running as
"alternate personality" process.

Returned from protected
procedure call; address space
and process identity restored.

Key

- Original process regions.   - Active context memory space.

Figure 1: Calling and returning from a protected procedure call. The address space mapping on top indicates the current active address space mapping.

The active context facility is very much analogous to the Unix kernel's traditional implementation. In Unix, when a process traps into the kernel via a system call, the processor vectors to a well-defined kernel system call handler and then continues running at a higher privilege level with an address space augmented by the kernel's memory regions. An important distinction between a Unix kernel and the D11 active context is that threads of control within an active context execute in user mode like other Unix processes, not in kernel mode like the Unix kernel. Because of D11's kernel style architecture, what one would call the X server in X11 is called the window system kernel in D11.

Logically, a D11 program is subscribing to a *service* for window system functionality. Likewise, one could consider a Unix process to be subscribing to the Unix kernel for operating system services. While D11 does implement a service, we avoid the term "client/server" when describing D11 because it usually suggests an implementation style with the client and server implemented as distinct processes.

It is worth noting that many micro-kernel architectures have been implemented that take this notion of Unix as a service to the logical conclusion of implementing Unix as a server process and emulation libraries extracted from the kernel proper [Golub90, Khalidi93]. The advantage of a client/server structuring in separate address spaces is modularity and distributability. The advantage of kernel style structuring is less data transfer and lower context switching overhead for potentially better performance in tightly integrated systems (like local window systems) than a client/server implementation. The duality of client/server "message-oriented" structuring and kernel style "procedure-oriented" structuring has been recognized for some time [Lauer77]. Reimplementing X as D11 should provide further evidence of this duality.

Protocol Optional, Transport Optional

D11's most important optimization is making the packing and unpacking of X11 protocol and its transport optional in the local case. Standard implementations of Xlib and the X server work by writing and reading X11 protocol over a reliable byte-stream connection (usually TCP or Unix domain sockets). Excepting local optimizations to these underlying transport mechanisms [Ginsberg93], the local and remote case use essentially the same mechanism.

Operation	User CPU usage	Kernel bcopy CPU usage	Rate (ops/sec)	Protocol round trip
x11perf -getimage500	9.8%	25.3%	29	✓
x11perf -prop	19.4%	1.1%	1870	✓
x11perf -getimage10	33.3%	1.5%	1450	✓
x11perf -seg1	38.0%	22.6%	1,070,000	
x11perf -dot	38.2%	15.7%	1,840,000	
x11perf -putimage500	40.2%	22.2%	26	
x11perf -getimage100	40.7%	10.3%	421	✓
x11perf -rect1	51.9%	15.2%	899,000	
x11perf -putimage100	55.2%	16.5%	529	
x11perf -seg10	57.4%	15.0%	771,000	
x11perf -putimage	69.4%	6.5%	24,600	
11perf -rect10	76.7%	8.0%	404,000	
x11perf -ucirculate (4 children)	84.3%	3.2%	245,000	
x11perf -noop	86.3%	3.0%	431,000	
x11perf -seg100	86.7%[†]	3.8%	182,000	
x11perf -ucirculate (50 children)	91.6%	1.9%	125,000	
x11perf -rect100	95.9%[‡]	0.0%	25,400	

Table 1: Indications of processor utilization bottlenecks for assorted X operations. These results are generated by kernel profiling of an R4400 150 Mhz SGI Indy running IRIX 5.3. User CPU usage includes both client and X server CPU usage jointly. During the measurements, the CPU was never idle.

†. Includes 42.3% of time actually spent in kernel's stalling graphics FIFO full interrupt handler.

‡. Likewise includes 84.0% of time spent in FIFO full interrupt handler.

Consider the work that goes into this packing, transport, and unpacking process. The individual steps underlying a typical Xlib and X server interaction look like:

1. The client program makes an Xlib call.

2. Xlib packages up the call arguments into X11 protocol in an internal buffer.

   Steps 1 and 2 repeat until Xlib determines the protocol buffers should be flushed. This happens because a reply needs to be received, an explicit `XFlush` call has been made, the buffer is full, or Xlib is asked to detect incoming events or errors. Buffering X11 protocol is an important Xlib optimization since it increases the size of protocol transfers for better transport throughput.

3. When a flush is required, Xlib writes the protocol buffer to the X connection socket, transferring the data through the operating system's transport code.

4. The X server has an event dispatch loop that blocks checking for input on client sockets using the `select` system call.

5. `select` unblocks and reports pending input from a client that has written to its X connection socket.

6. The protocol request is read by the X server, the type of the request is decoded, and the corresponding protocol dispatch routine is called.

7. The dispatch routine unpacks the protocol request and performs the request. *If the request returns a reply, the sequence continues.*

8. Xlib normally blocks waiting for every reply to be returned.

9. The X server encodes a protocol reply.

10. The X server writes the reply to the receiving client's X connection socket.

11. The client unblocks to read the reply.

12. The reply is decoded.

There are a number of inefficiencies in the local case of the protocol execution sequence above. Table 1 shows that a number of important X operations can spend from 25% to 90% of their time within the operating system kernel. Clearly, operating system overhead can have a substantial impact on X performance.

There are three types of operating system overhead that are reduced by D11:

Protocol packing and unpacking. The protocol packing and unpacking in Steps 2, 7, 9, and 12 are done strictly according to the X11 protocol encoding. Unfortunately, the protocol encoding is designed for reasonable compactness so 16-bit and 8-bit quantities must be handled and packed at varying alignments that are often handled relatively inefficiently by RISC processor designs.

Using protected procedure calls, a process directly passes D11 API routine parameters to the window system, skipping the inefficient packing and unpacking of protocol.

Transport. Moving X protocol from one process to another in Steps 3, 6, 10, and 11 requires reading and writing protocol by the X server and its clients. Protected procedure calls and an active context augmented address space allow data to be passed to and from the D11 window system kernel without any reading and writing of protocol buffers.

The kernel `bcopy` CPU usage percentages in Table 1 provide a lower bound to the transport overhead of X protocol transport. The `bcopy` overhead is over 20% for some important X operations. The `bcopy` overhead counts only the raw data copying overhead and not the socket implementation and `select` overhead.

Context switching. Because the client process generating X requests is not the same process as the one executing X requests, there is context switching overhead for the completion of every X request. Fortunately, protocol buffering allows this cost to be amortized across multiple requests, but the overhead of context switching still exists. For X requests that generate a reply forcing a "round trip," the kernel overhead due largely to context switching is quite high as Table 1 shows (up to 80% for the `x11perf -prop` test that is mostly context switching overhead).

Beyond the cost of the actual context switch, there is a cost due to cache competition between the client and server processes [Chen94].

Execution of a protected procedure call is in effect a context switch, but is hopefully a lighter weight context switch than the typical Unix process switch between contexts. Among the advantages of a protected procedure call over a Unix context switch is that no trip through the Unix scheduler is necessary and that most processor registers do not need to be saved.

As an example of how the transport-less, protocol-less D11 window system improves performance, consider an `XGetImage` call. In X11, such a call is expensive because it requires a client/server round trip representing two heavyweight context switches, three copies of the image (an image copy from the screen to an X server reply buffer; a copy from the reply buffer to the kernel; and a copy from the kernel to the client), and the overhead of protocol packing and unpacking. In a local D11 program, the same `XGetImage` call is implemented with a single protected procedure call (two lightweight context switches), no protocol packing or unpacking, and a single copy directly from the screen to the D11 protocol buffer (because the caller memory space is directly available within the active context).

Private X Resources

All X resources (windows, colormaps, cursors, graphics contexts, etc.) exist in a global name space. This is natural when the entire window system exists within X server. A second D11 performance advantage accrues from supporting "private" graphics contexts and pixmaps.

Rendering to pixmaps within the X server is inefficient because X requests are being generated, transported, and executed to manipulate what are essentially arrays of pixels within the X server's address space. Efficiency of rendering to pixmaps would be greatly improved if the pixmap resided in the client's address space. But the major advantage of pixmaps is that they can be used efficiently to transfer pixels to and from windows and other pixmaps via `CopyArea` requests.

D11 supports a private pixmap resource created by `XCreatePrivatePixmap` that is accessible only to the local D11 program that created it. The memory for the pixmap resides in the

D11 program's address space, not within the D11 active context. Private pixmap rendering can be done without ever entering the D11 active context, greatly increasing the efficiency of pixmap rendering. The ease and efficiency of transferring pixels to and from other windows and pixmaps still exists because a D11 `CopyArea` request executing within the D11 active context can access the pixmap memory residing in the protected procedure caller's memory space. Use of private pixmaps by local D11 programs achieves both maximum rendering *and* `CopyArea` performance.

To support private pixmaps, private graphics contexts (GCs) are also provided by calling `XCreatePrivateGC`. Using public GCs with private pixmaps can work by reading the public GC state from the active context and using the public GC state as necessary.[†]

Remote D11 programs can always fall back to conventional "public" pixmaps and GCs with lower pixmap rendering performance, so support of private pixmaps and GCs does not compromise network extensibility.

Since most X11 clients would work fine if all their GCs and pixmaps are treated as private resources, a mode set by the D11 routine `XPrivateResourceMode` forces the standard `XCreatePixmap` and `XCreateGC` routines to create private resources. With a single new routine an X program recompiled for D11 could benefit from private resources.

Benefits

D11 optimizes local window system performance by reducing contexting switching overhead, eliminating transport overhead, eliminating packing and unpacking overhead, and improving pixmap rendering performance. Because D11 programs can fall back to X11 protocol for remote connections, network extensibility is preserved.

4. Other Approaches

The D11 architecture is not the only considered means of improving or reinventing the X Window System. We consider two other approaches and critically compare them to D11.

Shared Memory Transport

As previously discussed, the transport of X protocol between the client and server requires considerable CPU resources. A shared memory transport for X provides a faster means of transferring X11 protocol between local X clients and the X server by avoiding copying X protocol buffers. Many workstation vendors provide some sort of shared memory transport and typically report X benchmark results based on shared memory transport results.

Details on shared memory transport implementations are not well published because these transports often rely on proprietary operating system features and are treated as proprietary performance advantages.

In practice, the implementation of a shared memory transport is more involved than one might imagine. A simple reader/writer shared memory queue with semaphores is unacceptable because

---

[†]*The core X11 protocol does not allow the state of a GC to be returned to a client so special D11 support will be needed for this.*

the X server must not be allowed to hang indefinitely on a semaphore or spinlock used to arbitrate access to the queue. The X server must fairly service requests and timeouts from multiple input sources. It must also robustly handle asynchronous client death and corruption of the shared memory queue.

Other logistical problems exist. The reasonable assumption of the MIT sample X server [Angebranndt91] is that each request is dispatched from a complete and contiguous request buffer. The X server could construct a complete and contiguous request by coalescing partial buffers from the shared memory transport into a contiguous buffer, but this obviates much of the benefit of the shared memory transport for large requests (where a shared memory transport is most beneficial) since the request data must be copied. For this reason, a shared memory transport implementation is likely to allocate a shared memory queue as large as the largest X request (most servers support the X protocol limit of a quarter megabyte).[†] To obtain better performance, some vendors allocate even larger shared memory queues. The result is a transport that performs well for benchmarks but has poor locality of reference within the shared memory queue. In a benchmark situation where a single shared memory connection is in use, this is not a problem. But if every local X client on the system is cycling through their individual shared memory queues, the result is poor memory system behavior hindering overall system performance.

Excepting a few important requests like `GetImage` and `GetProperty`, the server-to-client direction is not as critical to X performance as the client-to-server direction. This makes it likely that a shared memory transport will use shared memory only for the client-to-server direction. The Xlib necessity for a `select`-able file descriptor and the need to detect transport failure makes the use of a standard TCP or Unix domain transport likely for the server-to-client direction. Such an implementation decision restricts the performance benefit of a shared memory transport to the (admittedly more important) client-to-server direction.

Aside from the implementation issues with a shared memory transport, the performance potential from a shared memory transport is limited. While a shared memory transport reduces the transport costs, it does not reduce the two other system costs of window system interactions: context switching and protocol packing and unpacking. A shared memory transport may also introduce new memory system strains.

Table 1 indicates a number of important performance cases that a shared memory transport does not address. Notice that operations requiring a reply have high operating system overhead (80% for `GetProperty`; over 90% for large `GetImages`). Such cases demonstrate the cost of context switching and sending data from server to client because each Xlib call waits for a reply, forcing a round trip between the client and server. Also notice that in no case is the kernel `bcopy` overhead larger than 25%. This places a fairly low upper bound on the performance potential of a shared memory transport because kernel data copies are the fundamental savings from a shared memory transport.

[†]*This approach is complicated by the Big Requests Extension introduced in X11R6 [Scheifler94].*

Direct Graphics Hardware Access

Support for local clients to directly send graphics rendering requests to the graphics hardware without interacting with the window system proper is a technique known as *direct graphics hardware access* (DGHA). DGHA mitigates both context switching and protocol packing and unpacking overhead for the execution of rendering requests to windows; such rendering requests can be executed directly by DGHA clients. While DGHA helps the performance of window rendering requests, non-rendering requests such as `CreateWindow` and `AllocColor` continue to be executed by the X server. Whether pixmap rendering requests use DGHA techniques depends on the DGHA implementation, though most implementations probably do not support direct pixmap rendering.

Many workstation vendors implement some form of DGHA, particularly to support 3D rendering when graphics hardware might otherwise be under utilized. The techniques used vary from software locking of graphics for multiple rendering processes [Boyton89] to utilizing asynchronously context-switchable graphics hardware [Tucker91, Kilgard93, Kilgard95] that virtualizes graphics rendering [Voorhies88].

Two major impediments to implementing DGHA for X are the global nature of X resources and the semantic restrictions of atomicity and sequentiality demanded by the X protocol.

The global nature of X resources greatly complicates DGHA for X rendering because X resources such as graphics contexts and pixmaps are allocated from a global name space accessible to all connections to the X server. Potentially, an X client can access the resources of any other client (in practice this is rare). This means DGHA implementations are violating the strict sense of the X protocol if they handle the state of X resources such as graphics contexts and pixmaps as local to their usage.

OpenGL's GLX extension for X [Karlton93] explicitly supports a form a DGHA known as *direct rendering* (as opposed to indirect OpenGL rendering that is executed by the X server). GLX provides this functionality by explicitly distinguishing direct resources that can be maintained within the client from indirect resources that are maintained globally within the X server. OpenGL rendering to pixmaps however *must* be done indirectly. This solution is unfeasible for X DGHA implementations because it is impossible to redefine the existing global nature of X resources.

X atomicity demands that "the overall effect must be as if individual requests are executed to completion in some serial order." X sequentiality demands that "requests from a given connection must be executed in delivery order."[†]

Strictly interpreted, the atomicity requirement would make virtual graphics techniques employing asynchronous context switches illegal because atomicity could not be guaranteed. The expense of the atomicity requirement for rendering operations is unfortunate since few tangible benefits derive from it.

It is entirely expected for X protocol requests within a connection to execute in their generated order. But this sequentiality requirement forces extra synchronization when rendering requests are

---

[†] *Found in the "Flow Control and Concurrency" section of X11 protocol specification [Scheifler92].*

executed separately from the non-rendering requests. Effectively, DGHA means rendering and non-rendering requests are executed in two distinct streams

Client trace	Requests	Reply %	Render %	Description
mwm startup	2,389	25.5%	7.2%	Generic Motif window manager starting with 10 pre-existing toplevel windows
4Dwm startup	3,362	26.8%	7.9%	SGI window manager starting with 10 pre-existing toplevel windows
xterm startup	74	24.3%	21.6%	Athena widget based terminal emulator
editres startup	143	16.8%	33.6%	Athena widget resource editor
apanel startup	799	20.9%	48.9%	Motif 1.2 SGI audio control panel startup
chost startup	1,047	21.39%	50.4%	Motif 1.2 SGI host management tool using enhanced Motif
glp startup	819	15.7%	55.2%	Motif 1.2 SGI printer graphical front-end
xrn-motif startup	608	3.9%	56.3%	Motif 1.1 news reader
MediaMail startup	2,414	7.1%	56.9%	Motif 1.2 SGI version of zmail GUI
xwsh startup	265	18.1%	59.2%	SGI terminal emulator
cdman startup	670	18.4%	66.3%	Music CD player using internal toolkit
xfig startup	1,718	4.9%	64.5%	xfig 2.0 public domain drawing program
desktopManager startup	2,675	13.4%	70.2%	Motif 1.2 SGI Indigo Magic file manager viewing home directory with many files
mwm startup, then usage	3,482	23.6%	14.9%	Generic Motif window manager starting with 10 pre-existing toplevel windows, then user interaction
4Dwm startup, then usage	6,391	15.9%	27.1%	SGI window manager starting with 10 pre-existing toplevel windows, then user interaction
xrn-motif startup, then usage	16,219	0.4%	77.4%	Motif 1.1 news reader news reading session

Table 2: X protocol request ratios for various X client protocol traces. A render request is a core protocol request potentially appropriate for DGHA use; that is, it manipulates graphics contexts or reads or writes pixels excepting ClearArea.

For example, a `MapWindow` non-rendering request could be generated to map an override-redirect pop-up menu, followed immediately by rendering requests to draw the menu. The X client must guarantee completion of the `MapWindow` request before using DGHA to execute the rendering requests or else the rendering will likely be done to an unmapped window. This implies an X11 protocol round trip must be performed after the `MapWindow`. The reverse guarantee (that non-rendering requests must not execute before rendering requests) must also be made, but it is easier for a client to know a DGHA rendering request has completed.

9TH ANNUAL X TECHNICAL CONFERENCE

OpenGL's GLX explicitly distinguishes the OpenGL rendering stream from the X protocol stream, in effect relaxing X protocol semantics for OpenGL rendering. The `glXWaitX` and `glXWaitGL` routines allow a user to explicitly synchronize the streams.

For OpenGL, this explicit solution for supporting DGHA is reasonable, but for core X rendering the solution is unworkable because X programs implicitly rely on non-rendering and rendering requests executing sequentially as expected.

Contrasting D11 to DGHA approaches, D11 requires no semantic changes to the X11 model (though relaxing the atomicity requirement for rendering is probably useful) and, unlike DGHA, D11 does not segregate the execution of rendering requests from non-rendering requests so no extra synchronization is needed between the two requests types. DGHA helps only DGHA-capable rendering requests while D11 helps all classes of requests. Table 2 shows that X clients combine rendering and non-rendering requests, particularly during program startup. The results show that for many clients, more than 40% of the requests are non-rendering requests that DGHA will not improve. It also indicates the likely cost associated with synchronizing DGHA requests with non-DGHA requests. The ratio of replies to requests indicates that up to 25% of requests require replies, generally each necessitating a client/server round trip, an expensive operation that gets no benefit from DGHA. The percentage of rendering requests is *overstated* because it also includes pixmap rendering and `CopyArea` that many DGHA implementations will likely not improve.

5. The Active Context

The active context is the operating system facility that underlies the implementation of D11. D11 requests from local D11 programs are translated into protected procedure calls that enter the D11 window system kernel. Because protected procedure calls can be implemented so that they are inexpensive relative to a standard Unix context switch and no protocol needs to be packed, sent through a transport, and unpacked, D11 protected procedure calls should be a net win over local use of the X11 protocol using conventional transports. This section details the working of active contexts and protected procedure calls for a Unix style operating system.

Initiating an Active Context

To initiate the D11 window system, a standard Unix process "bootstraps" the active context for the D11 window system kernel. The process requests that the operating system create the D11 active context. The active context is a reserved range of user-space memory. The call to create an active context looks like:

```
fd = acattach("/tmp/.D11-ctx:0", AC_CREATE, 0x50000000, 0x10000000);
```

This call creates an active context, "attaches" the active context to the calling process, and reserves a 256-megabyte range of virtual memory in a normally unallocated region of user address space. File system path names provides a convenient name space for active contexts, but active contexts are not otherwise reliant on the file system. Only privileged processes may create an active context.

The creator of an active context or a process running inside the active context can use the `mmap` family of system calls [Joy87] to allocate, deallocate, and control memory within the active context. The effect of these calls is seen by all users of the active context. After an active context is created, the creator is expected to "populate" the context with text, read-only data, and writable data before enabling protected procedure calls to enter the active context.

The D11 bootstrap program `mmaps` the text and static data of the actual D11 window system kernel. The bootstrap program also establishes file descriptors, synchronization primitives (such as semaphores and spinlocks), and memory mappings for the graphics hardware and input devices.

The *entry point* for an active context is the address of initial execution when a process enters an active context via a protected procedure call. Initially, there is no entry point. The entry point to the active context is set by calling:

```
accontrol(fd, AC_SET_ENTRY, entry_func);
```

`entry_func` is the address of the routine within the active context to be used as the active context entry point.

To make it possible for other processes on the system to attach to and make protected procedure calls into a newly created active context:

```
accontrol(fd, AC_ALLOW_ENTRY, /* true */ 1);
```

must be called and an entry point must be established. The `accontrol` can be called only by the creator of an active context.

Protected Procedure Calls

Once an active context is set up and entry by other processes is allowed, other processes can call `acattach` (without the `AC_CREATE` flag) to attach to the active context. For example:

```
fd = acattach("/tmp/.D11-ctx:0", 0, /*ignored*/ 0, /*ignored*/ 0);
```

Attaching to an active context creates an "alternate personality" process (with a slot in the system process table). This *alternate personality process* (APP) exists as a standard Unix process and is a child of the active context creator (*not* the process attaching to the active context). An APP inherits file descriptors, signal handlers, the effective uid, and other Unix process attributes from the active context creator. In many ways, the APPs associated with an active context are similar to IRIX *process share groups* [Barton88, Sgi93] to the extent that they share Unix system resources with one another in a way consistent with expected Unix operating system semantics.

A process attached to an active context can initiate a protected procedure call to "switch personalities" to the process's APP by calling:

```
status = acppcall(fd, op, ...);
```

The result of `acppcall` is that the calling process is suspended and execution is handed off to the process's APP which begins execution at the active context entry point. The entry point is called with the following parameters:

```
entry_func(app_id, op, ...);
```

The `app_id` is a small unsigned integer indicating what APP is running. The `entry_func` uses this parameter to determine the identity of the APP within the active context. The `op` parameter is an integer indicating the operation to perform.

An APP returns from a protected procedure call by calling:

```
acreturn(status);
```

Returning from a protected procedure call suspends the APP and resumes the process initiating the protected procedure call. `status` is an unsigned integer returned as the successful return value of `acppcall`.

Multiple APPs can enter the active context simultaneously, so shared synchronization mechanisms within the active context should be used to coordinate execution within the active context.

Augmenting the Address Space

While most Unix process resources of an APP are inherited from or shared with the active context creator, the address space of an APP is the caller's address space augmented by the active context memory range. The benefit of this augmentation is that data can be read and written directly into the caller's address space during a protected procedure call.

The active context memory range is mapped in a fixed address space range for all APPs using the active context. This means the code within the active context can be position dependent and pointers to data within the active context need no translation. The active context address range can be thought of as a *sub-address space* shared by all APPs.

For D11, protected procedure calls into the D11 active context mean that no protocol packing, transport, or unpacking is necessary for local D11 programs entering the D11 window system.

The augmented address space does mandate a number of rules for writing code running within an active context to ensure robustness. These rules are analogous to the rules Unix kernel programmers follow to ensure robustness in the kernel. Active context code should *not* call routines in the non-active address space range. Reads and writes through pointers supplied by the protected procedure caller *must* be verified as outside the active context address range. Signal handlers must be established to trap memory access violations due to accessing memory outside the active context address range and remedy the situation.[†]

Active Context Notification

The signals delivered to an APP are distinct from signals delivered to the calling process. While running in a protected procedure call, Unix signals posted for the calling process that would not result in immediate process death are not delivered until `acreturn` is called. If a signal resulting in immediate process death such as `SIGKILL` is posted for a calling process, the calling process dies immediately, but the APP continues running until `acreturn` is called at which point the

---

[†]*Windows NT style structured exception handling language support [Custer93] might be useful to make explicit in the code handling of memory access violations when accessing memory outside the active context.*

APP terminates. One ramification of this is that protected procedure calls should not block indefinitely within the active context. For this reason, some means must exist for active context users to block on events occurring within the active context.

The file descriptor for the active context is not usable for I/O operations but is `select`-able and can be used to receive notification of state changes within the active context. Any process running within an active context can call:

```
acnotify(app_id);
```

to cause `select` to indicate that the active context file descriptor of the specified APP is "readable." Calling `acnotify` is usually preceded by some indication in a shared data structure within the active context of why the notification was delivered. In response to an `acnotify`, a process should perform a protected procedure call into the active context to determine why the signal was delivered. The call:

```
acack();
```

will acknowledge a posted active context notification for the calling APP.

Implementation Issues for Active Contexts

The `acattach` family of routines can be implemented as new Unix system calls. The most critical aspect of implementing active contexts is ensuring protected procedure calls are as fast as possible. Techniques for fast, local cross-address space communication such as *lightweight procedure calls* [Bershad89] are readily applicable to optimizing active context protected procedure calls. The most important difference between a protected procedure call and other cross-address space procedure call mechanisms is the augmented address space.

Because APPs exist as distinct process table entries within the Unix kernel, current Unix semantics can be cleanly mapped to APPs. Most areas of the Unix kernel can be completely unaffected by the introduction of active contexts.

Current RISC processors supporting a *virtual cache with keys* [Schimmel94] should make possible efficient address space augmentation for protected procedure calls. The protected procedure caller and its APP can each maintain distinct *address space ids* (ASIDs). The `acppcall` and `acreturn` operations need to change the ASID appropriately.

This scheme treats the augmented address space as a completely distinct address space which is somewhat inefficient in translation lookaside buffer (TLB) entry usage. Processor support for distinct user and kernel modes is very similar to the address space augmentation needs of protected procedure calls. Unfortunately, kernel mode is quite inappropriate for the user-level execution of active contexts. Some processors like the MIPS R4000 [Mips91] do provide a *supervisor* mode with more limitations than kernel mode. But MIPS supervisor mode enables access to memory outside the typical user range and is probably still too permissive for use in implementing active contexts.

The reservation of a large chunk of user address space for the active context memory range may be an issue for 32-bit processors that are limited to two gigabytes of user address space. Support for 64-bit address spaces obviates this problem. Also in such systems, support for *protection domains* [Koldinger92] may also reduce the cost of address space augmentation by treating protected procedure call exit and entry as a lightweight protection domain switch.

6. Implementing D11

We begin by discussing D11's implementation for local D11 clients; support for remote D11 programs and X11 clients is discussed afterwards.

Within the D11 Active Context

The D11 window system kernel is implemented as an active context and bootstrapped as described in the previous section. The executable code for the D11 kernel can be largely reused from the X11 server's implementation. Code that needs to be reimplemented for D11 includes initialization, the main event loop, and client I/O code. The vast bulk of the X server code such as machine-independent and device-dependent rendering code, font handling code, etc. can be identical to the X11 server's implementation.

Once the active context creator "populates" and activates the active context, it takes the role of a housekeeper for the active context. It manages window system kernel tasks that are not initiated by D11 program requests. For example, reading input events, handling the screen saver, managing window system reset, and reaping terminated APPs are all done by the D11 kernel housekeeping thread.

D11 programs attach to the D11 active context during `XOpenDisplay`. The first "establish connection" protected procedure call enters the D11 kernel and establishes the data structures for the new D11 connection. Within the D11 active context is a global locking semaphore that is acquired whenever a process running within the active context manipulates global data structures. Acquiring this semaphore while executing requests satisfies the X atomicity requirement. While a global lock may seem too coarse, the request dispatch loop of current single-threaded X servers is logically equivalent to a global lock.

Once a connection is established, the D11 program can make protected procedure calls. Based on the `op` parameter to the `entry_func`, the D11 kernel executes the correct code to handle the D11 request. When executing a request, the APP may directly manipulate the caller's address space to read arguments and return data (such accesses must be correctly protected against memory violations).

Because multiple processes may run in the active context at one time, code within the D11 active context must correctly lock accesses to data structures. Because of the use of a single global lock, most locking concerns are straightforward. Existing X server code for executing requests can generally assume the global lock is already acquired and so existing code does not need any special locking. Inexpensive locking around the global memory allocation pool is necessary. Multi-threaded and multi-rendering X servers [Kilgard94, Smith92] already abide by this requirement.

So a typical D11 request is executed by generating a protected procedure call that enters the D11 active context, acquires the global lock, calls the appropriate request execution code, releases the lock, and returns from the protected procedure call. In the process of executing a request, data may be transferred from the caller's memory space; and if the request returns a reply, data may be written into the caller's memory space.

As mentioned earlier, the D11 active context creator is watching for asynchronous events such as mouse or keyboard input. When such input arrives, the housekeeping process will acquire the global lock, determine how to handle the input, generate events to be sent to D11 connections if necessary, and release the global lock. Generating events for a D11 connection is done by placing events in the connection's pending event queue. Each queue has a lock that arbitrates access to the queue. Any D11 active context process can send events by acquiring the lock for a D11 connection's event queue, appending the events to the queue, and calling `acnotify` for the APP owning the queue, then releasing the queue lock. Errors are also placed in the queue. But replies are returned synchronously.

The D11 Interface Library

In the local case, the D11 interface library (essentially Xlib for D11) translates D11 requests into D11 active context protected procedure calls. In the case of a remote D11 kernel or X11 server, the D11 interface library uses the X11 protocol. A per-connection local or remote jump table is used to vector D11 request generating routines to the correct local or remote request generator.

A D11 program can use its active context file descriptor to determine when events or errors have been placed in its D11 connection event queue. By using the `select` system call on the D11 program's active context file descriptor, the program can determine when events are pending because `acnotify` is called whenever events are appended to a D11 program's event queue. `XNextEvent` and `XPending` can block and poll for events respectively using thi mechanism. A "return events and errors" protected procedure call copies all the events and errors from a D11 connection's event queue into the caller's memory space. `acack` acknowledges active context notification. This is actually more efficient than Xlib's event reading strategy that requires a 32-byte `read` system call per event, reply, or error received to ensure the length field is decoded before any more data is read so variable length replies can be read into contiguous buffers. D11 makes the returning of events and errors more efficient than in X11.

Handling Client and Server Termination

If a D11 program terminates, its associated APP is terminated cleanly. If the APP is currently executing when its associated D11 program terminates, the protected procedure call executes to completion before the APP terminates. If the APP terminates unexpectedly (because of a memory fault or termination by a signal), the `acppcall` returns with an error indicating the active context has become unattached (the window system has crashed). When the APP terminates (because of D11 program death or a software fault), the active context creator is notified it should reap the APP. If the APP died cleanly (because its associated process terminated), the housekeeping thread will clean up the data structures associated with the APP's D11 connection. If the APP died of a software fault, the reaper will generate a fatal window system error.

X11 Protocol to D11 Conversion

A critical compatibility concern is how to make old X clients (and remote D11 programs) that generate X11 protocol work with the D11 window system. The solution is an X11-to-D11 gateway process that converts X11 protocol requests to the X server's standard ports (such as TCP port 6000) into D11 protected procedure calls. This gateway process is a standard Unix process that attaches to the D11 active context. The process makes "raw protocol" protected procedure calls that pass raw protocol buffers to the D11 kernel to be unpacked and executed. A single gateway process could broker multiple X11 protocol connections simultaneously, with each connection having its own associated APP. The gateway process is also responsible for correctly returning events, replies, and errors to the appropriate X11 protocol connections.

One might think the X11-to-D11 gateway would be inefficient relative to a traditional X server. This does not have to be the case. Because D11 protected procedure calls require no copying in passing protocol to the D11 kernel, there is no more protocol copying than when using a traditional X server.

Implementation Concerns

Several concerns about D11 usage must be addressed by a real implementation. D11 requests are executed synchronously. A multiprocessor workstation could *potentially* achieve a performance benefit from the current client/server implementation of X11 because an X client and the X server could run in parallel on different processors. Potentially, D11's lower operating system overhead could make up for the advantage of X11's client/server parallelism.

A given implementation of protected procedure calls may not be fast enough. Xlib's buffering of protocol allows the operating system overhead to be amortized across several Xlib calls. If protected procedure calls are too expensive to be done per D11 request, a similar buffering scheme may be necessary for D11 requests. This reintroduces the cost of protocol packing and unpacking but retains the other performance benefits of D11.

An APP per window system connection may be rather expensive in terms of the APP's associated kernel data structures. The cost of APPs should be minimized.

7. Conclusions

D11's kernel style window system architecture promises significant performance benefits over X11's current client/server architecture involving clients and servers running in separate address spaces. The performance benefits of D11 come from reduced context switching overhead, the elimination of local protocol packing and unpacking, the elimination of local transport overhead, and more efficient support for pixmap rendering.

D11 does require significant operating system support for active contexts, alternate personality processes, and protected procedure calls. The performance of protected procedure calls is vital to fulfilling D11's promise. Implementing the window system component of D11 is eased because most of the existing X11 client and server code can be reused in a D11 implementation.

Comparing D11 with other methods for improving window system performance, D11 reduces system overhead for local window system usage in all significant areas. D11 can be considered a logical extension of DGHA techniques to encompass the full range of X requests, not just rendering requests. D11 can also be considered the next logical step beyond a shared memory transport, where not only is the copy of data from the transport buffer eliminated, but so is the copy into the transport buffer and all associated protocol packing and unpacking.

No compromises in network transparency, X11 compatibility, or protection and reliability are made by D11. D11 favors local window system usage at a time when trends for high-bandwidth applications will likely result in greater reliance on and need for local window system performance. D11 optimizes local window system performance currently unharnessed by X11.

References

[Angebranndt91]   Susan Angebranndt, Raymond Drewry, Phil Karlton, Todd Newman, Bob Scheifler, Keith Packard, Dave Wiggins, "Definition of the Porting Layer for the X v11 Sample Server," *X11R6 documentation*, April 1994.

[Auditore94]   Stephen Auditore, "The Business of X," *The X Journal*, March 1994.

[Barton88]   Jim Barton, Chris Wagner, "Enhanced Resource Sharing in Unix," *Computing Systems*, Spring 1988.

[Bershad89]   Brian Bershad, Thomas Anderson, Edward Lazowska, Henry Levy, "Lightweight Remote Procedure Call," *Proceedings of the Twelfth ACM Symposium on Operating System Principles*, December 1989.

[Boyton89]   Jeff Boyton, et.al., "Sharing Access to Display Resources in the Starbase/X11 Merge System," *Hewlett-Packard Journal*, December 1989.

[Chen94]   Bradley Chen, "Memory Behavior for an X11 Window System," *Usenix Conference Proceedings*, January 1994.

[Custer93]   Helen Custer, *Inside Windows NT*, Microsoft Press, 1993.

[Engberg91]   Björn Engberg, Thomas Porcher, "X Window Terminals," *Digital Technical Journal*, Fall 1991.

[Gajewska90]   Hania Gajewska, Mark Manasee, Joel McCormack, "Why X Is Not Our Ideal Window System," *Software Practice and Experience*, October 1990.

[Ginsberg93]   Michael Ginsberg, Robert Baron, Brian Bershad, "Using the Mach Communication Primitives in X11," *Usenix Mach III Symposium Proceedings*, April 1993.

[Golub90]   David Golub, Randall Dean, Alessandro Forin, Richard Rashid, "Unix as an Application Program," *Usenix Conference Proceedings*, June 1990.

[Joy87]   William Joy, et.al., "Berkeley Software Architecture Manual 4.3BSD Edition," *Unix Programmer's Supplementary Documents*, Volume 1, 1987.

[Karlton93]   Phil Karlton, *OpenGL Graphics with the X Window System*, Ver. 1.0, Silicon Graphics, April 30, 1993.

[Khalidi93]   Yousef Khalidi, Michael Nelson, "An Implementation of Unix on an Object-oriented Operating System," *Usenix Conference Proceedings*, January 1993.

[Kilgard93]   Mark Kilgard, "Going Beyond the MIT Sample Server: The Silicon Graphics X11 Server," *The X Journal*, SIGS Publications, January 1993.

[Kilgard94]   Mark Kilgard, Simon Hui, Allen Leinwand, Dave Spalding, "X Server Multi-rendering for OpenGL and PEX," *Proceedings of the 8th Annual X Technical Conference* appearing in *The X Resource*, January 1994.

[Kilgard95]   Mark Kilgard, David Blythe, Deanna Hohn, "System Support for OpenGL Direct Rendering," submitted to *Graphics Interface '95*, May 1995.

[Koldinger92]   Eric Koldinger, Jeffrey Chase, Susan Eggers, "Architectural Support for Single Address Space Operating Systems," *Proceedings of the Fifth International Conference on Architectural Support for Programming Languages and Operating Systems*, October 1992.

[Lauer77]   Hugh Lauer, Roger Needham, "On the Duality of Operating System Structures," *Proceedings of the 2nd International Symposium on Operating Systems*, October 1978, reprinted in *Operating Systems Review*, April 2, 1979.

[Mips91]   MIPS Computer Systems, *MIPS R4000 Microprocessor User's Manual*, 1991.

[Scheifler92]   Robert Scheifler, James Gettys, *X Window System*, 3rd edition, Digital Press, 1992.

[Scheifler94]   Robert Scheifler, "Big Requests Extension," Vesion 2.0, *X11R6 documentation*, 1994.

[Schimmel94]   Curt Schimmel, *Unix Systems for Modern Architectures*, Addison-Wesley, 1994.

[Sgi93]   Silicon Graphics, *Parallel Programming on Silicon Graphics Computer Systems*, Version 1.0, Document Number 007-0770-010, December 1990.

[Smith92]   John Allen Smith, "The Multi-Threaded X Server," *The X Resource: Proceeding of the 6th Annual X Technical Conference*, O'Reilly & Associates, Winter 1992.

[Tucker91]   C. H. Tucker, C. J. Nelson, "Extending X for High Performance 3D Graphics," *Xhibition 91 Proceedings*, 1991.

[Voorhies88]   Doug Voorhies, David Kirk, Olin Lathrop, "Virtual Graphics," *Computer Graphics*, August 1988.

XVE: X Visual Effect Extension

User Interface Design with Visual Effect Techniques

Hajime Takano
Hiroshi Matsuura
Hiroshi Matoba[†]

Abstract

XVE (for X Visual Effect Extension) provides new types of user-interface "look & feel", using visual effects such as fade, wipe, zoom, and slide. This look & feel produces continuous visual change of display image from previous state to current state, when user requests to operate a window are occurred.

XVE Server includes Visual Effect (VE) Routines and Effect Contexts (ECs). Each VE Routine is implemented in DDX layer, and produces an appropriate visual effect. Its parameters are stored in a EC, which is implemented in DIX layer as a new server resource. Each visual effect is activated by conventional requests for window operations. Therefore, every X Client can handle visual changes without any modification to them.

XVE prototype is currently running on NEC EWS4800/330 workstation, and it has demonstrated the useful of visual effects that have a more familiar "look and feel" than the conventional X.

Introduction

Recent multimedia technology offers a great potential for increased application in the areas of both business and engineering (e.g., desktop presentation, hypermedia, CAD/CAM, etc). The potential for rapid growth in these fields has been somewhat limited, however, by the fact that design

---

[†]Hajime Takano is a researcher at NEC Corporation. Hiroshi Matsuura is a software engineer at NEC Informatec Systems, Ltd. Hiroshi Matoba is an assistant manager at NEC Corporation.

considerations for user interfaces have tended to focus most heavily on operation flow, at the expense of user interface "look & feel."

In typical multi-window based applications, for example, almost every user interaction results in a visual change in display state. Such changes can often be so unexpected or startling as to cause users to lose track of what is happening in the application itself.

Sudden, instantaneous screen changes can be particularly distracting to users and, in the case of presentations, distracting to an audience. Such distractions might be eliminated with the use of such conventional video and film editing effects as fade in, fade out, zoom, wipe, etc. [SON89] These sorts of non-instantaneous changes have a more natural feel and, because they are performed over time, are significantly easier for users and viewers to absorb and appreciate.

This is the approach we have taken in our current study, in which we have developed an extension of the user interface in the X-Window System. We refer to this extension as XVE (for X Visual Effect Extension). Let us consider, for example, the use in the X-Window System of icons to represent windows. In the conventional X-Window interface, the icon disappears the instant that it is clicked, the same instant in which a new window appears. The feeling of this change might be improved if the icon itself were to expand gradually, steadily growing to become the actual window that it represents, and this is in fact precisely what XVE accomplishes.

Or, we might also consider the moving of a window from one location to another. Conventionally, after we have moved an outline to a desired position, we make the window at the old location disappear and a new one appear, in the same instant, in the new location. With XVE, we can drag the window itself across the screen to wherever we wish -- a process less visually abrupt and easier to follow in its entirety. Additionally, for full window changes, XVE makes use of a fade in and a wipe for a generally more user-friendly interface.

XVE is based on a server extension consisting of the following three parts: 1) **Visual Effect (VE) Routines** added in the DDX layer (new *wrapper* routines which replace core wrapper routines); 2) **Effect Context (EC)**, a new server resource introduced to improve reusability and flexibility (EC is a set of visual effect attributes identified as being executable by an individual application); 3) **XVE API**, i.e., XVE extension protocol, defined to provide compatibility to the core X protocol and to manage EC operations. In XVE API, core requests for drawable operations (e.g., `MapWindow`, `ConfigureWindow`, etc.) are also available to handle visual effect routines. In addition, we have developed XVE Library to handle XVE API in applications.

In test runs of XVE Server and XVE Client with XVE Library on our workstations (NEC EWS4800 model 330 (CPU: MIPS R4000), the XVE Client has demonstrated the value of visual effects that have a more familiar "look and feel" than the conventional X. Further, XVE can be used with existing applications without any modifications to them.

Definition of Visual Effects in XVE

This section describes the types of visual effects handled in XVE and the relation between those visual effects and window operations.

Visual Effect Types

The following are the main visual effects we will be concerned with in this study:

Fade: Gradual change in the visibility of a window. "Fade in" gradually increases the visibility of an image, and "fade out" gradually causes that visibility to decrease, and eventually to disappear.

In fading, the colors of an obscured background image are gradually blended with the colors of the obscuring foreground image, and as the ratio of this blend changes, the obscured image gradually comes into view.

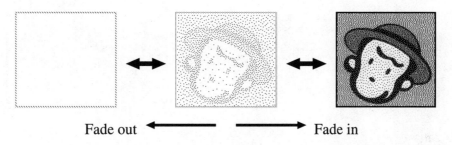

Fade out ⟵   ⟶ Fade in

Figure 1: Fade

Wipe: A gradual change in the visible area of a window. "Wipe in" replaces a background image with a new image, and "wipe out" progressively removes image area until, eventually, the entire image has been eliminated.

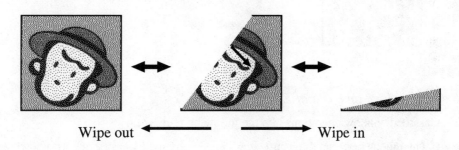

Wipe out ⟵   ⟶ Wipe in

Figure 2: Wipe

Zoom: A gradual change in the size of the visible portion of a window. That is to say, in this study we use "zoom" to refer to the gradual expansion or contraction of the visible portion of a window; the size of the image it contains remains unchanged.

Slide: The smooth, constantly visible 2-dimensional movement of a window from one location on the display to another.

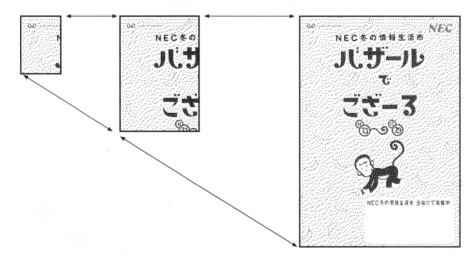

Figure 3: Zoom

Figure 4: Slide

Window Operations and Visual Effects

We have classified window operations into the following four types:

APPEAR: Operations performed to cause a previously obscured window or part of a window to become visible, or to present an entirely new window. It includes, then, the opening of a new window by the XMapWindow() function, or the exposure of a previously obscured window or part of a window by bringing that window into the foreground by means of the XRaiseWindow() function.

DISAPPEAR: Operations performed to cause a previously visible window or part of a window to become no longer visible. It includes, then, the removal of a previously visible window by the XUnmapWindow() function, or the obscuring of a previously visible window or part of a window by putting that window into the background by means of the

`XLowerWindow` function.

RESIZE: Operations performed simply to change the size of a window, e.g. by means of the `XResizeWindow()` function, etc.

MOVE: Operations performed simply to relocate a window, e.g. by means of the `XMoveWindow()` function, etc.

The window operations listed above can be carried out in XVE by means of the following visual effects:

1. Fade in and wipe in for APPEAR

2. Fade out and wipe out for DISAPPEAR

3. Zoom for RESIZE

4. Slide for MOVE

Table 1 lists Xlib functions and their corresponding visual effects.

Xlib Function	Visual Effect
XMapWindow()	Fade in and wipe in
XRaiseWindow()	Fade in and wide in
XUnmapWindow()	Fade out and wipe out
XLowerWindow()	Fade out and wipe out
XResizeWindow()	Zoom
XMoveWindow()	Slide

Table 1: Window operations and visual effects

XVE Design Requirements

In this section, we describe problems encountered in the conventional X when trying to produce certain visual effects with Xlib, and we discuss the ways in which XVE has addressed these problems.

Visual Effects in the Conventional X

Among the problems encountered when attempting to produce certain visual effects in the conventional X with Xlib functions, the followings are particularly significant:

1. Xlib lacks the functions and performance capability to display either fade or wipe effects.

2. There is excessive communication overhead between X Client and X Server because the X Client must repeatedly send requests to for display changes, e.g., thirty times per second. Further communication overhead is created when X Server sends EXPOSE Events to other windows affected by a certain window operation.

3. When executing visual effects in an application which has no visual effect library, it becomes necessary to modifying the application itself.

Requirements

In designing XVE, we considered the following to be requirements for solving the problems noted above:

First, in order to achieve the performance necessary to accomplish fade and wipe, the routines for producing those effects must be able to access video RAM devices directly, which means that visual effects applied to a window must be executed in X Server rather than X Client, and that the functions required for accomplishing fade and wipe effects must be contained in X Server. This also has the important advantage of eliminating the problem of excessive communications overhead. Finally, in order to avoid the necessity of modifying applications that have no visual effect libraries, it is necessary for existing window operation protocols to be able to call up the routines that are used to produce desired visual effects.

XVE Configuration

XVE consist of XVE Server and XVE API. The extension portion of the XVE Server consists of Effect Contexts (ECs) and VE Routines. Figure 5 illustrates its configuration.

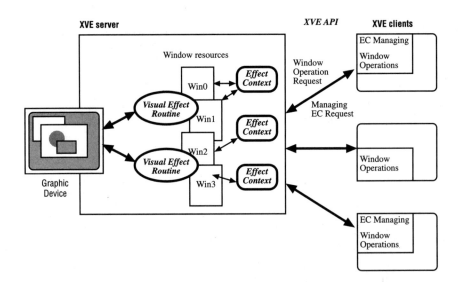

Figure 5: Overview of XVE configuration

"Effect Context" are similar to Graphics Contexts. Each EC represents a set of parameters and their values as they have been determined with respect to each window operation (Appear, Disappear, Resize, Move). Each window is assigned one EC by which these respective operations will be executed. When the XVE Server receives an request from a Client for a specific operation to be performed on a specific window, it checks to see which EC has been assigned to that window and orders the execution of the appropriate VE Routine, each of which provides a single VE, to accomplish that operation in the manner prescribed in the EC. Since the order itself from the Client does not need to contain any specific parameter information, communication overhead between Server and Client can be kept low.

ECs are sharable, i.e. a single EC can service multiple windows and it is unnecessary to make copies of them even when most windows in the resource set will be set to make the same types of visual changes.

The XVE API consists of two types of protocols; core X request protocol [Sch89] and XVE extension protocol. The core X request protocol is used to relay requests for window operations. XVE extension protocol is used to relay requests for EC operations, i.e. `CreateEC`, `DestroyEC`, `CopyEC`, and `ChangeEC` (for changing the parameters in an EC). `BindEC` assigns an EC to a window, and `UnbindEC` releases an EC from a window. These EC operations can be applied to a window by any applications, such as a window manager.

General Implementation Issues of XVE

This section describes some issues in the prototype implementation.

Visual Effect Routines

In this section, we explain a sample algorithm for each visual effect routine, e.g., fade, wipe, zoom, and slide. In addition, we describe the mechanism to solve the problem which a visual effect routine blocks another request routine.

Sample Algorithms

A visual effect is produced by iterative processing[†] of a primitive operation which changes the screen image step by step. A types of a visual change is defined by an algorithm of the primitive operation in a VE routine. The followings describe some sample algorithms for each visual effect routines, i.e., fade, wipe, zoom, and slide.

Fade

Fade needs to produce an image which blends a target window with a background image obscured by the window, which we call *alpha blending*. A clearness of a target window in the produced image is defined with a *blending parameter*, which is changeable from 0% (a target window is disappeared) to 100% (a background image is perfectly obscured). Fade in is organized by changing the blending parameter of the foreground window from 0% to 100% , and fade out is organized by changing it from 100% to 0%.

In the current workstations, however, the calculation of the alpha blending needs much CPU power and wide bandwidth of a system bus, because this calculation should be executed for more than ten thousands of pixels at each step. Therefore, when we produce effective visual changes with fade in/out, a special hardware is necessary to calculate repeatedly an alpha blending.

[†]*For example, each step occurs at most sixty times per second in most available UNIX workstations.*

If we execute the calculation only by using software, we have to handle a pseudo algorithm for alpha blending[†]. The pseudo algorithm uses the *pixel density* instead of the alpha blending parameters. The pixel density means the ratio of the number of pixels in a foreground target-window image to that in a background image obscured by the window. For example, low pixel density means that the number of pixels in an image obscured by a foreground image is more than that in a foreground image. It looks that a background image is more clearly displayed than a foreground image is (see Figure 6(a)). On the contrary, high pixel density looks that a background image is hardly displayed in comparison with a foreground image(see Figure 6 (b)).

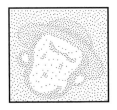 

(a) Low Pixel Density   (b) High Pixel Density

Figure 6: Example of low and high pixel density

Wipe, Zoom, and Slide

Lots of various wipe patterns are available, so that we can't describe a general algorithm for all of them. Instead, we have to provide a VE Routine for each corresponding wipe pattern[‡].

We explain `RadialWipe` as an example of wipe patterns. In a `RadialWipe`, a diagonal line sweeps to reveal the foreground target window from the background image obscured by the target window. The `RadialWipe` repeatedly set a current angle of the sweep line and changes the angle from 0 degrees to 90 degrees (See Figure 2).

An essential step of Zoom in/out is to expand or reduce the size of a window. When Zoom in operation is applied to make a window twice as large, the size of the window is expanding from current size to destination size (twice as large as the original size) step by step, and a size of the window in each step is calculated by interpolation between the original size and the destination size.

Slide displays a window moving over a screen, which primitive step is a relocate the window position. A position in each step is calculated as a interpolation between the source position to the destination position, and the path of the interpolation is, for example, linear, arc, etc. User can define the path of the interpolation by setting several sample points.

[†]*Alternatively, there is a way to change color values of a LUT. However, we don't adopt the way because it may destroy colors of the other images at the same time.*

[‡]*In the current test, we provide fifteen wipe patterns of Visual Effect routines.*

Non-Blocking Request Mechanism

While a VE Routine is executing, any other requests must be waiting for a long time in the request queue. This problem is caused by the request dispatch mechanism in the conventional X server. The mechanism can't start processing the next request in the request queue until the executing request is finished.

To solve this problem, we minimize a time between entering to a request processing routine and returning to the dispatch loop. We have divided a Visual Effect Routine into the *initializing part* and the *runtime part,* so as to reduce this turn around time. The initializing part returns to the request dispatch loop immediately after only initializing parameters of a Visual Effect Routine.

The runtime part executes repeatedly each essential step of a visual effect, and it is asynchronous to the request dispatch loop. To support the runtime part, *Wakeup Handler* and *Visual Effect Tables* are introduced. In each step, the runtime part executes the following four procedures:

1. Set next wakeup time to the Wakeup Handler

2. Read a parameter from the Visual Effect Table

3. Execute the step in visual effect according to a value of a parameter

4. Sleep

where the Visual Effect Table stores parameters of the VE Routines running currently, and the Wakeup Handler wakes up periodically the runtime part at each step.

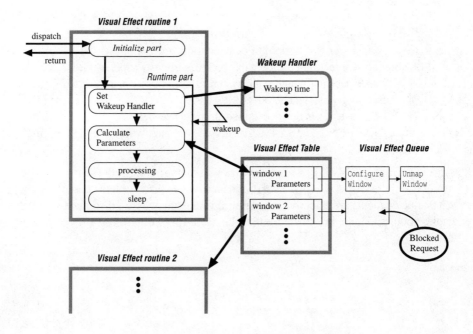

Figure 7: Non blocking Mechanism in Visual Effect Routines

In addition, we implemented *Visual Effect Queue* to block such inconsistent request that `UnmapWindow` request to a window is accepted while fade-in presentation is produced on the same window by `MapWindow` request. Figure 7 illustrates the configuration of the non-blocking mechanism.

Effect Context

This section describes the data structure of EC.

EC Structure

EC is implemented as `XECValue` structure in DIX layer as shown below. In the XECValue structure, a type of `TIME` is a dimension of time.

```
/* Values */
typedef struct{
    TIME duration ;
    unsigned char fade_style ;
    TIME fade_delay ;
    TIME fade_advance ;
    unsigned char wipe_style ;
    TIME wipe_delay ;
    TIME wipe_advance ;
    unsigned char zoom_style ;
    TIME zoom_delay ;
    TIME zoom_advance ;
    unsigned char slide_style ;
    TIME slide_delay ;
    TIME slide_advance ;
} XECValue ;
```

The element `duration` specifies the length of execution time. `wipe_style` specifies which wipe is used or not, and it selects a type of wipe patterns in case wipe is used. Each of {`fade`, `zoom`, `slide`}`_style` specifies which each visual effect is used or not. Each {`fade`, `zoom`, `slide`}`_style` has two types: `LINEAR`, `NONLINEAR`. `LINEAR` changes linearly display image, and `NONLINEAR` uses user-defined transition rule(See below). `wipe_style` selects a wipe pattern among `NORMALWIPE`, `BANDSLIDE`, `SPLIT`, etc., which are already implemented in the XVE server.

The {`fade`,`wipe`,`zoom`,`slide`}`_delay` specifies a delay time from the start of a visual effect. The {`fade`, `wipe`, `zoom`, `slide`}`_advance` is an advance time from the end of a visual effect. These XECValue elements are effective when plural visual changes are displayed simultaneously. For example, zoom and slide are carried out at the same time. Figure 8 shows a example of the `XVEValue`.

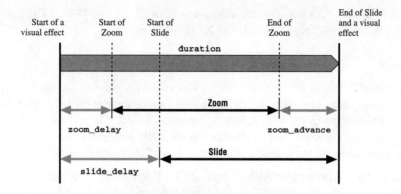

Figure 8: Example of the EC parameters

Transition Rule

Transition rules enable users to specify user defined visual effect parameters. For example, a transition rule for fade is to specify the set of time and alpha blending parameters. A transition rule for zoom is to specify the set of time and both width and height of a window. A transition rule for slide is to specify the set of time and location parameter (x, y). For each transition users have only to specify several sample points for interpolation. A transition rule is effective only when the value of {fade,zoom,slide}_style is NONLINEAR.

Modification to the Original Source Code

We developed about 10K lines of additional codes for XVE. Table 2 shows the number of lines for each function blocks newly implemented in the XVE server. In addition, we modified at most fifteen portions in the conventional part of the XVE server. This modification is based on the extension support routines and the wrapper techniques.

Functions	Server Layer	Numbers
Initialize	DIX	14
Dispatch	DIX	1 K
EC Management	DIX	2 K
Wrapper install	DDX	2 K
Visual Effect Routines	DDX	5 K

Table 2: Number of lines in the XVE codes

Future Work

The future work regarding XVE is as follows:

1. Redesign of non-blocking request mechanism in the multi-thread X server [Smi92].

2. Implementation of the window manager corresponding to XVE

3. Integration of the XVE with other extensions of the X such as "Shape Extension"[Pac89], "MVEX: Minimal Video Extension to X" [Bru91], etc.

Conclusion

We have proposed X Visual Effect extension (XVE) which provides visual changes to a window such as fade, wipe, zoom, and slide, to become a user interface more friendly. XVE is based on a server extension consisting of Visual Effect Routines, Effect Context, and XVE API. Non-blocking request mechanism is implemented to solve such problem that a visual effect routine blocks other routines in the request dispatch mechanism of the conventional X.

In the test runs of XVE server and XVE clients, the XVE application has demonstrated the value of visual effects that have a better "look and feel." Further, XVE can be used with existing applications without any modifications to them.

We believe that the user interface based on XVE will become more important in particular for the multimedia application systems in the near future.

Acknowledgments

We would like to thank Yoshinori Hara for his discussions and encouragements, and also thank Rei Hamakawa, and Shiro Sakata for their helpful comments. We appreciate our colleagues in C&C Research Laboratories and Information Technology Research Laboratories, NEC Corporation for their supports.

References

[Bru91]   Todd Brunhoff. *MVEX: Minimal Video Extension to X Version 6.2.* Tektronix, Inc., 1991.

[IF92]   Elias Israel and Erik Fortune. *The X Window System Server.* Digital Press, 1992.

[Pac89]   Keith Packard. *X11 Non-Rectangular Window Shape Extension.* X Consortium, Laboratory for Computer Science MIT, 1989.

[Sch89]   Robert W. Scheifler. *X Window System Protocol.* MIT X Consortium Standard Version 11, Release 5. Massachusetts Institute of Technology Laboratory for Computer Science, 1989.

[Smi92]   John Allen Smith. *The Multi-Threaded X Server.* The X Resource, Vol. 1, pp. 73-89, Winter 1992.

[SON89]   SONY Corporation. *DME-450 Users Manual*, 1989. (in Japanese).

Help! There's a Spy in My Code

Ian Elliott[†]

Abstract

To reduce the RAM requirements of a particular piece of code, its *working set* must reduced. This means doing such things as reducing the working set's size (code and data) and improving locality. However, reducing a working set is difficult if it can't be identified in terms of frequently accessed code and data structures.

A method and tools are presented that tie a process's heap working set to *C* data structures and the procedures that accessed those data structures. Using a modified libc, a slightly enhanced kernel, a data logger, and a data analysis tool, called MemSpy, insights can be gained into the heap's actual working set--the frequently accessed *C* data structures and their accessing procedures. Examples are given of improvements made to HP's X server using MemSpy.

Introduction

Over the years, system RAM requirements have grown exponentially. Once, PDP-11 minicomputers ran Unix with only 64 KBytes. Some of the early workstations were hard-limited to a maximum of 2 MBytes. These days, entry-level workstations with 16 MBytes may seem sluggish when running modern desktop software.

While much of this extra RAM is consumed by additional functionality, much of it is simply wasted as a result of "poor programming practices." This wasted RAM can be reclaimed. However, memory tuning efforts tend to be very difficult. This is due to a lack of insight regarding what makes up the *working set* of a given piece of code. There are few tools that can give such insights.

It may be tempting to simply dismiss memory tuning as unnecessary. After all, RAM prices continue to fall. However, system prices also continue to fall. Given the relative ratios of RAM requirement increases, RAM price reductions, and system price reductions, RAM continues to represent a significant portion of system cost. In addition, in todays competitive environment, if

---

[†]*Ian Elliott (ian@elliott.fc.hp.com) is a Technical Contributor for Hewlett-Packard Company.*

one set of software requires more RAM, and as such, requires a more expensive system than another set of software, sales of the former may suffer.

Too often, modern software has grown obese. It's time to put it on a diet! But how? This was the situation a group of engineers confronted in 1992. Given the "diet" theme just mentioned, the effort was code-named *Ultra-Slim Fast* (*USF*).

This paper discusses a subset of the USF focus; specifically *how* to reduce the working set of heap (a.k.a. malloc'ed) memory. First, a brief review of virtual memory and working set theory is presented. Then, a methodology will be given for approximately identifying the *actual working set* of a process's heap--frequently used *C* data structures. After that, the design of a tool called MemSpy, and it's associated data logging tools, will be presented. Then, a case study will be discussed--reducing the working set of the HP-UX X server. Finally, future opportunities will be discussed.

Virtual Memory and Working Set Basics

Why does a fast computer slow down when it doesn't have enough RAM? It all has to do with the virtual memory (VM) system. This section presents a brief review of VM concepts.

Virtual Memory Refresher

A virtual memory system gives computer processes the illusion that a computer has more memory than it actually has. Every process can have a virtual address space that's much larger than the amount of physical memory (RAM) installed in the system. VM systems give this illusion in a complicated manner. For the purpose of this paper, the following, simplified model will be employed:

- Both the virtual and the physical address spaces are divided into chunks, called *pages*. Pages are typically a few KBytes in size.

- Each page is actually located in either RAM or in *swap space* (typically a portion of a hard disk).

- The VM system maintains a mapping between each virtual page and it's actual location. Part of this mapping is stored within special *memory management* hardware within the CPU. Each virtual memory access goes through this memory management hardware. If the memory location's page is located in RAM, the correct physical address is used for the memory access. If the memory location's page is located in swap space, a *page fault* occurs whereby the page is loaded into RAM before the memory access occurs.

- When the RAM is full, before a page is brought into RAM, another page must be sent to swap space (*paged out* or *swapped out*). The VM system tries to use a fair policy for determining which page to swap out.

- It takes a relatively long period of time to perform the paging activity described in the previous two bullets. The exact time will depend upon various factors (e.g. the relative speeds of the swap disk and the computer), but will be so lengthy that when a process takes a page fault, it will be suspended until after the page has been brought into RAM.

A simple example is in order. Let's say that each page size is 4 KBytes, that a computer has 64 KBytes of physical RAM, and that a particular process uses 128 KBytes of virtual memory. Thus, the system has 16 pages of physical memory and the example process has 32 pages of virtual memory. Let's say that the first 16 pages of the process are currently residing in RAM when the process wants to access an address in the 17th page. The VM system takes a page fault on the access in the 17th page. In order to page in the 17th page from the swap disk, one of the first 16 pages must be swapped out to disk.

In this simple example, if the process keeps most of its memory accesses within the same 16 pages, it will seldom take a page fault, and as such have excellent performance. However, if the process accesses all 32 pages in a round-robin fashion, it will be suspended most of the time. When this occurs, a process is said to be *thrashing*. When most active processes are experiencing excessive paging, the system is said to be thrashing. Little visible progress occurs, because the "active" processes are suspended most of the time. This is why a "fast" computer can appear to be "slow" when it doesn't have enough RAM.

Working Set Model

The previous paragraphs presented a deliberately simple view of virtual memory systems. Modern, multi-tasking operating systems, such as HP-UX, use much more complicated VM systems. A few examples are relevant to this paper.

First, since the kernel is trying to time-slice several processes at the same time, it seldom devotes all of the computer's RAM to one process. The RAM will contain virtual pages from multiple processes.

Second, modern kernels employ sophisticated algorithms to reduce the number of page faults. For example, when certain page faults occur, the HP-UX kernel will determine if surrounding pages should be brought in at the same time, in case they will be accessed soon. This kernel also keeps various metrics to determine which pages to swap out (i.e. those unlikely to be brought back in again soon). A kernel never wants to page out memory in a process's *working set*.

The *working set* model, introduced by Denning [1][2], helps understand VM activity in a multi-tasking operating system. The basic idea is that a process will frequently access a subset of its pages. These pages are called the process's *working set*. The working set pages must remain resident in order for the process to not thrash.

A process's working set will tend to vary over time. For example, at start-up time, a process's working set may be much larger and much different than the process's steady-state working set. Also, the working set of a menu-driven program may vary as a user chooses different menu items.

If the virtual memory sizes of all processes fit within the available RAM, page faults will only occur when a process accesses a page for the first time. In such cases, system performance will not suffer from thrashing.

Thrashing occurs when the sum of the working sets of all active processes exceeds available RAM. In such cases, in order to page in one process's working set, another process's working set must be paged out.

When a kernel detects that thrashing is going on, it may start taking drastic measures. For example, a kernel may swap out entire processes to increase the number of available pages for the remaining process(es). Of course, when the swapped out processes finally get to run again, all of their working set pages must be brought back in, causing other processes to be swapped out.

A lot of research and engineering work has been done [3][4][5] to improve VM paging algorithms to increase overall system performance, to reduce the likelihood of thrashing, and to reduce the ill-effects of thrashing when it does occur. While these improvements are important, they don't seem to make up for the continual growth in memory usage. Thus, system RAM requirements continue to increase.

Memory Tuning

An understanding of the working set model can lead to insights that make it possible to "tune" (i.e. shrink) the memory usage of a process or set of processes. This section will present a high-level model for memory tuning. Engineers who do memory tuning are called *memory tuners*.

Obviously, it doesn't help to tune non-working-set memory. Going back to the simple example from above, assume that the working set is 17 pages while the entire virtual size of the process is still 32 pages. Again, the system only has 16 pages. According to the working set model, the computer will thrash. If a memory tuning effort trimmed away 8 pages (easily measured with generally available tools), none of which were in the working set, the computer will still thrash even though 1/4 of the process's pages were trimmed. If, instead, one of the working set pages is trimmed, the computer will no longer thrash.

Working Set Model Refinement

Before further memory tuning discussion, some refinement is needed in our understanding of working sets. Until now, our usage of the term working set has been very focused on virtual memory system pages. However, memory tuners deal with code and data structures. From the perspective of the VM system, an entire page may be in a process's working set. However, the program may only be using a small part of that page.

The actual memory that a process frequently uses is called the process's *actual working set* (*AWS*). The frequently used pages are called the process's *VM working set* (*VWS*). For the benefit of memory tuners, who generally use high-level languages (e.g. *C*, *Fortran*), the AWS is expressed in terms of procedures and data structures. The VWS (i.e. traditional working set) is expressed in terms of pages.

In most situations, the AWS will always be smaller than the VWS. This is because of differences in granularity. The granularity of the AWS can be measured in bytes, where the VWS is always measured in the size of each page (typically a few KBytes). This difference in size presents an opportunity for memory tuning.

Let's go back to the simple example from above. Again, assume that the VWS is 17 pages. However, this time, let's look a little deeper. Assume that the program's code occupies just one page (the first), and that the program constantly accesses two sets of variables. The first set occupies roughly 1/2 of the second page. The second set is a 16-element linked list where each element's size is 24 bytes, and where each element lives in a different page.

In this particular case, instead of thinking of the working set as 17 pages (i.e. the VWS), we can see that the actual working set (the particular data structures being frequently accessed) is very small. Careful programming can allow the linked list to live within the second page, and the VWS will be just two pages (closer to the size of the AWS).

How to Memory Tune a Process

Memory tuning is the process of reducing a process's VWS. If done to a process that contributes to thrashing, thrashing will be reduced or eliminated (depending on how much reduction is done). Memory tuning is generically described as doing one or more of the following types of tasks:

1. Improve locality. Frequently accessed items that are relatively small and live in different pages make the VWS unnecessarily large (as in the simple example above). If possible, allocating the items next to each other will result in a smaller VWS (closer in size to the AWS) and fewer page faults. This rule applies to code as well as to data. For example, grouping frequently-used procedures can reduce the AWS of the code. Some compilers (e.g. the one sold for HP-UX) help automate this task for code.

2. Reduce heap *fragmentation*. Fragmentation occurs when memory is allocated and freed in patterns that leave unused holes in the heap. Fragmentation reduces the locality of the AWS, thus needlessly increasing the VWS.

3. Eliminate *memory leaks*. A memory leak occurs when a piece of allocated memory is no longer used, but not freed. Memory leaks also reduce the locality of the AWS, thus needlessly increasing the VWS.

4. Reduce the size of code and data structures. The idea here is to shrink the actual size of something (i.e. make the AWS and VWS smaller). For example, if a structure contains multiple 32-bit fields for each of several boolean values, it can use a group of 1-bit fields instead. Sometimes 16-bit integer fields can by substituted for 32-bit integers. Sometimes infrequently used code/data can be pulled out of the midst of frequently used code/data (e.g. the X server's WindowOptRec).

5. Re-use memory. For example, assume that a procedure allocates one or more temporary items each time it is invoked, uses them, and then frees them. By allocating the items once and keeping them around for the future, absolute performance can be gained (malloc and free are expensive procedures) and fragmentation of the heap is reduced (which can improve locality for other malloc'ed data structures).

6. Schedule working set growth. A simple example illustrates this. The VWS of a process is often very large at start-up time. Starting up several processes at the same time can result in a temporary thrashing situation. By synchronizing the starting of the processes, the sum of the working sets won't get large enough to cause thrashing. This is a system-level example, but similar examples can be found within code.

From the above list, it appears that reducing a process's VWS is relatively straight-forward. However, experience has shown that determining a process's AWS is the most difficult part of memory tuning. If one person, or a group of individuals fully understands a piece of code, intuition can help. However, effective memory tuning requires the use of tools that determine the AWS of a piece of code, expressed in the high-level language procedures and data structures with which the code is written. Going back to the simple example from above, if a tool showed that most of the page faults were caused by the linked list, and showed that each element of the list was in a different page, memory tuning that program would be easy.

Determining the Actual Working Set

This section describes a novel method for approximately determining the AWS of a process's *heap* (i.e. malloc'ed memory) for a given benchmark run. This method is referred to as the *AWS-determination method* (*ADM*). The methods for determining the AWS of other portions of a process (e.g. code and global variables) is analogous, but outside the scope of this paper.

The basic approach of the ADM is to observe which data structures cause page faults when the targeted process is severely thrashing. The ADM is specifically discussed in the context of the *C* programming language, but the ADM can be adapted and applied to any programming language. The ADM consists of the following characteristics and steps:

- Be able to consistently, and repeatedly run the same set of processes doing the same operations, while instrumenting the process of interest for the following data-collection steps.

- Maximize the number and granularity of heap page faults for the process of interest. This can be done by reducing system RAM or other clever methods.

- Build a time-ordered, time-stamped list of all heap page faults, including all relevant information for each fault (i.e. address that caused the fault and the program counter at the time of the fault).

- Build a time-ordered, time-stamped list of all *heap transactions* (i.e. calls to *malloc()*, *calloc()*, *realloc()*, and *free()*), including all relevant information for each transaction (i.e. size allocated, address allocated, address freed, and procedure call traceback).

- Correlate heap transactions to *C* data structure types.

- Cross-reference and penalize the information from the previous steps, to gain insights about the AWS.

The remainder of this section provides more detail about the ADM. The next section provides detailed information about the tools which implement the ADM.

Consistent Benchmark Runs

To objectively measure the progress of any tuning project, a consistently repeatable benchmark is required. ADM benchmarks are different than other types of benchmarks. Many benchmarks deal with one or two processes (e.g. the X server and x11perf) where ADM benchmarks involve multiple processes which must always perform the same operations in the same inter-process order (to minimize run-to-run page fault variations).

In an X11 environment, a recorded user session can serve as an ADM benchmark. The playback tool must replay the session very precisely. All user input and X server events must be well-timed requiring the playback tool to actively monitor client behavior, not just passively send events to the X server.

The requirement to maximize page faults makes for a demanding playback environment, and for a poor recording environment. Therefore, benchmark recording must be done when few page faults are occurring, and playback must be done when many page faults are occurring. It is important to playback the session as fast as possible, compressing gaps in user input, and preserving the order of inter-process actions.

Maximizing Page Faults

Maximizing the number and granularity of page faults increases the accuracy of the ADM, which makes its determinations based upon observed page faults. If few faults are observed, there is little data to go on.

In many cases, multiple data structures occupy the same page. If such a page is faulted only once, only one structure will be seen and the rest will be hidden. The more times a page is swapped in and out, the higher the probability these hiding structures will be seen.

For example, assume that two data structure types, *A* and *B*, are frequently accessed, are both spread throughout memory (i.e. have poor locality), and, for a particular benchmark, occupy the same set of pages. If page faults aren't maximized, different scenarios can occur depending upon the access patterns of the benchmark:

- Both structure types will split the faults for their shared pages.
- One of the two will consume all of the faults.
- Some other structures will consume all of the faults.
- Some combination will occur.

Some of these scenarios limit a memory tuner's effectiveness, because the tuner won't know to tune for the hidden structure types during the first tuning attempt.

In other cases, only one structure occupies each page. If these pages are always swapped out soon after their use, then the number of faults these structures receive will indicate how frequently they are used. For example, assume that two structures, *C* and *D*, each receive just one page fault during light paging, but during heavy paging, *C* receives 2 page faults and *D* receives 20. Obviously, *D* is more important to memory tune than *C*.

Several approaches can increase the number and granularity of page faults during an ADM benchmark run. The easiest is to reduce the amount of system RAM. The simplest way to do that is to turn off the system and pull out SIMMs. However, this can be time consuming and probably won't yield enough granularity to zero-in on the *optimal* amount of page faults (enough that a relatively accurate AWS-determination can be made, but not so many that the benchmark runs unacceptably long). A better way is to use an enhanced kernel which allows a user to specify, in relatively small increments, the amount of RAM the kernel thinks is available.

Another approach is to turn off special VM system *prepaging* features. For example, a kernel may bring in the surrounding pages of a page which receives a fault, in anticipation that those pages will be accessed soon. Prepaging is an excellent feature, except during an ADM benchmark. This is because the purpose of prepaging is to effectively hide data structure accesses.

One of the best approaches is to use a special kernel which targets a particular process. Instead of reducing system RAM, which slows down all processes, consider a kernel which puts just one heap page into the CPU's memory management unit. The targeted process will fault every time it accesses a different heap page. Not only will most hiding data structures be found, but the observed frequency of each data structure's usage will be relatively accurate. To maximize performance, the kernel must keep the process's heap pages in RAM, and service each page fault very quickly.

Another valuable approach is to direct page faults at specific data structures. One way to do this is to modify the malloc library so that no two data structures ever share the same page. When used in conjunction with the enhanced kernel, described in the previous paragraph, the ADM's accuracy becomes near perfect.

Logging Page Faults

As discussed above, the ADM observes (i.e. logs information about) page faults when a process is severely thrashing. For each page fault, the following relevant information is logged:

- The address that caused the page fault.

- The program counter value (address) which shows what procedure caused the page fault.

Logging Heap Transactions

For each call to *malloc()*, *calloc()*, *realloc()*, and *free()*, the following relevant information is logged:

- Whether memory was allocated or freed.

- The size of block allocated (if appropriate).

- The address(es) allocated and/or freed.

- The procedure call traceback (e.g. *malloc()* was called by *Xalloc()*, which was called by *AllocateWindow()*, which was called by *CreateWindow()*, etc.). For each *traceback line* (i.e. a particular *called by <procedure>*), log the procedure's name, the offset from the beginning of the procedure (to differentiate one procedure call from another) and the procedure's source file (if possible).

There may be other ways to correlate heap addresses with *C* data structure types, but in the context of ADM benchmarks, the method described in this section has proven very workable and relatively unobtrusive.

Correlating Heap Transactions To C Data Structure Types

Given the information logged for each heap transaction, it is easy to correlate each block of heap memory to a particular *C* data structure type. This correlation is accomplished by comparing the logged information against a set of rules.

An example will demonstrate the basic approach. One of the most important data structure types in the sample X server is the *WindowRec* (or simply the *Window*) structure. While the size of *Window* structures can vary in a multi-screen X server, there are only two unique procedure call tracebacks used to create *Window* structures. The first is for creating the root window:

- *malloc( )* was called by ...

- *Xalloc( )* was called by ...

- *AllocateWindow( )* was called by ...

- *CreateRootWindow( )* was called by ...

- *main( )*

The second is for creating client windows:

- *malloc( )* was called by ...

- *Xalloc( )* was called by ...

- *AllocateWindow( )* was called by ...

- *CreateWindow( )* was called by ...

- *ProcCreateWindow( )* was called by ...

- *Dispatch( )* was called by ...

- *main( )*

Often, each *C* data structure type will have just one unique allocating traceback. In this example, there are only two.

Notice that the first three procedures in each traceback are the same. In fact, the first two and the last two procedures are often identical for most X server data structure types. Thus, the procedures in the middle of the traceback are generally more interesting. In this example, *AllocateWindow( )* is in both tracebacks. A quick perusal of *AllocateWindow( )* reveals that it only makes one call to *Xalloc( )*. Therefore, any heap transaction with *AllocateWindow( )* in the traceback is a *Window* structure.

The way *C* data structure types are identified is with one or more *rules*--specifications of what the type's allocating or freeing transactions look like. A set of rules is given a name (typically, the structure type name). These rules are compared with each heap transaction. When a rule matches a transaction the corresponding heap block is identified.

Rules should allow each data structure to be identified more than once. Sometimes it is useful to have a hierarchy of structure type names. For example, pixmaps are used for a variety of purposes (e.g. backing store, tiles, stipples). Therefore, one set of rules can identify all pixmaps, and other sets of rules can identify particular types of pixmaps.

Information Processing

Given the information collected and correlated in the above steps, it is possible to make an approximate determination of the targeted process's heap AWS. This section describes the general algorithm for processing the logged and correlated information.

First, each freeing transaction is matched with its corresponding allocating transaction. If no freeing transaction was logged that matches an allocating transaction, the corresponding memory block is a potential memory leak.

Next, each page fault is correlated with the *C* data structure that caused it. This is easy given the above information. All heap transactions are time stamped, freeing transactions are matched with allocating transactions, and each heap memory block can be correlated with a *C* data structure type. Each page fault is also time stamped. Therefore, the address that caused each fault is compared with the heap information until it is matched with a particular data structure.

For example, assume that a particular fault occurs 13 minutes into a benchmark run. The address that caused the fault (0x400ab340) falls within the address range of 3 different pairs of heap transactions. After comparing time stamps, it becomes obvious which pair corresponds to the page fault.

All of this newly cross-referenced information can now be analyzed to gain insights about the AWS. Analysis examples have been given throughout this section. Additional examples are given in the section that discusses memory tuning HP's X server.

The MemSpy Tool

This section provides information about the MemSpy tool and its corresponding data gathering tools. These tools implement the AWS-determination method (ADM) described in the previous section.

MemSpy is an interactive, Motif-based, information processing tool. It attempts to efficiently process the large amounts of data logged during an ADM benchmark run. It also allows users to interactively explore the processed data, to gain insights into a process's heap AWS.

Repeated Running of a Test Run

In the previous section, several criteria were outlined for a benchmark playback tool. Several commercially- and privately-available tools exist which meet some, but not all of these criteria. Most either weren't designed for the demanding criteria, or were stretched past their quality limits. What proved most difficult, was accurately playing back a session when the benchmark system was severely thrashing. Because of this limitation, the USF team couldn't decrease system RAM to an optimal level, which limited the accuracy of the ADM.

Maximizing the Number and Granularity of Page Faults

In the previous section, the importance of increasing the number and granularity of heap page faults was stressed. Several approaches were outlined. The USF team used an enhanced kernel which allows a user to: 1) specify the amount of RAM the kernel thinks is available; 2) turn off the special VM system *prepaging* features. The USF team found both of these to be very valuable. The last two approaches mentioned in the previous section (a kernel which targets a particular process, and a malloc library which doesn't allow structures to share pages) would have been extremely valuable, but weren't done.

Logging Page Faults

It was relatively easy for the USF team to construct a tool that logged page fault information. The HP-UX kernel already provided this information in a special measurement information buffer, and a data logging tool already existed. Some modifications were necessary, but were very straight-forward. It should be noted that this logging tool is relatively small and unobtrusive.

Logging Heap Transactions

Difficulties were encountered in accurately and efficiently logging heap transaction data. Each problem was solved, and the final solution is quite workable.

The first difficulties were: 1) quickly and accurately determining the procedure transaction traceback; and 2) designing a format for quickly and concisely logging the per-transaction information. The first attempt at logging information for X server startup (i.e. no clients running) took roughly 30 minutes to log the approximately 17 megabytes of information. The first attempt used a generic HP-UX traceback utility which produced full ASCII strings for the entire traceback, accounting for most of the time and space.

Producing an accurate traceback on an HP-UX, PA-RISC system is difficult (because of shared libraries), which is why the generic utility was initially used. The final solution involved writing a custom utility (with the help of HP's compiler engineers) which returned an array of addresses. Correlating these addresses with procedure names from the program's symbol table was deferred till post-processing (which proved more efficient and less obtrusive during benchmark runs). The final logging format was a very tight, binary format. The final solution was 2-orders of magnitude more space efficient, and 3-orders of magnitude more time efficient than the first attempt.

Next, it was important to modify the *libc* shared library, which contained the version of *malloc()* most programs use. Again, the first attempt was humorous--we unintentionally introduced an endless loop where *malloc()* called *fprintf()* in order to log the information, and *fprintf()* called *malloc()* in order to allocate some buffers, which called *fprintf()*, etc. This was easily solved with a flag inside the *malloc()* procedure, which didn't allow reentrant logging.

Time stamping the heap transaction information was time consuming until we enlisted the help of HP's kernel engineers. The heap data is now passed to the kernel. The kernel time-stamps the data and merges it with the page fault data in its special measurement interface buffer (described above). This allows one data logging tool to log all information.

Correlating Heap Transactions to C Data Structure Types

In the previous section, a general approach was presented for correlating allocated blocks of heap memory to *C* data structure types. The idea is to create one or more *rules*, which describe what an allocating or freeing transaction looks like, and compare the rules with each transaction. The MemSpy tool implements this approach in an interactive fashion.

MemSpy rules aren't guidelines *for users to live by*; they are the selection criteria that MemSpy uses to determine which transactions correspond to which *C* data structures. In other words, users give rules *for MemSpy to select by*.

For programs with large numbers of structure types, rule creation can be time consuming. MemSpy provides several features that make rule creation easier:

- A *rule manager* allows users to interactively manage sets of rules.

- A *rule editor* dialogue allows users to interactively create and edit rules.

- Each portion of a rule can be *wild-carded*. This increases the power of each rule, which decreases rule creation time.

- When viewing any heap transaction, users can start the rule editor with the initial values being set to those of the viewed transaction (Note: transactions can be viewed in a number of ways--see below).

- *Rule files* can be read and written to preserve rules between MemSpy sessions.

MemSpy's *wild-card* features require further explanation. Using the *Window* structure example from the previous section, you will recall that the traceback for each allocating transaction contained the *AllocateWindow()* procedure. Further, the *AllocateWindow()* procedure only made one call to *Xalloc()* (to create a *Window*). Thus, an obvious rule identifying the *Window* structures is any transaction for which the traceback contains the word *AllocateWindow*. Notice that no other portion of a transaction is specified in this rule--all values are considered to match all *wild-carded* portions of a rule.

Often, when taking a first look at benchmark results for a given piece of code, it is reasonable to not specify any rules up-front. If some unidentified structure is causing a lot of page faults (a "high roller"), a menu selection pops-up the rule editor dialogue with initial values set to that of the structure's allocating transaction. The initial rule values can be edited (e.g. to make it more general) and given a name (typically the actual *C* data structure type name). When the rule is saved, it is compared with all transactions to identify all matching memory blocks. The user can now examine information for every data structure of that type.

Even with all of MemSpy's rule creation features, rule creation can still be time consuming. Additional tools can help (e.g. build rules by scanning source code). This hasn't been implemented, but would be beneficial.

Information Processing

Before the logged information can be explored, it first must be processed. ADM benchmarks can produce large amounts of data. MemSpy was conceived as an interactive tool, which made the implementation of this portion challenging. This section describes MemSpy's general processing algorithm with some attention given to performance concerns.

Transaction Processing

First, the targeted process's symbol table must be read into a convenient data structure (e.g. a hash table). Then the heap transaction data can be read and processed.

Each heap transaction must be identified as an allocating or freeing transaction. The allocated address of each allocating transaction is hashed. This simplifies the code that matches allocating and freeing transactions. When a matching set of transactions is found, they are cross-linked.

Each line of a traceback must be converted into a procedure name (recall that each line of a traceback is logged simply as an address), file name, and offset within the procedure (i.e. how many bytes from the start of the procedure). Since each line of a traceback can be seen multiple times, each line is put into a hash table. This hash table generates a unique, 32-bit *key* value for each unique traceback line. This reduces the amount of data MemSpy keeps, and the time it takes to do further processing.

Each traceback is stored as an array of traceback line keys. As with traceback lines, each traceback is also put into a hash table, and a unique key value is generated for each unique traceback. Each transaction stores the unique key for its traceback. Note: the number of unique tracebacks is displayed in MemSpy's main window.

Page Fault Processing

Next, the page fault data can be read in and correlated with the heap transaction data. Links are setup between corresponding data structures and page faults.

User Analysis

At this point, the data can be analyzed in many different ways. For example, data structure identification can be done (interactively or by reading rule files). The data can be sorted (e.g. by number of page faults, by structure sizes) with MemSpy displaying histograms. Each histogram line can be selected, and additional information can be requested. For example, if an interesting data structure or set of page faults is found, its allocating transactions can be displayed, a rule editor can be popped up, etc. "Memory map" graphs can be displayed, which graphically show the size and placement of selected data structures. Even memory leaks can be found.

Rule Matching

Rules are matched with transactions whenever they are created or read from a *rule file*. The structure of the transaction database makes rule matching straight-forward.

First, each line of a rule is compared with each traceback line in the transaction database. If matches are found the unique key(s) are recorded (note: because of wild-cards, a rule line may match more than one traceback line). If any rule lines don't find a match, the entire rule won't match any transactions and processing for stops this rule.

After rule lines have been matched, the traceback rule is compared with each unique traceback from the transaction database. The unique key is recorded for each matching traceback. Then, the transactions themselves are compared with the full rule (matching tracebacks is a simple integer compare of the 32-bit keys). Cross-links are set up between rules and matching transactions, which improves interactive performance of MemSpy's Motif interface

Memory Tuning HP's X Server Using MemSpy

This section relates some of the experiences the USF team had while memory tuning HP's X server using MemSpy. Prior to joining the USF effort, the author had spent considerable time working in HP's X server. This made the server a natural choice for trying out MemSpy. An additional reason was the fact that the X server was significantly contributing to the total page faults for the USF team's first ADM benchmark.

Before discussing this tuning effort, it is important to mention some things about the sample X server provided by the X Consortium. The Consortium staff did considerable memory tuning work for the 4th Release of X11. The sample server's design reflects this attention. Most of the server's memory usage is for protocol-visible data structures (e.g. windows, pixmaps, GCs), and these structures are very tight--there's no wasted memory. Also, care was given so that *private* structures are allocated next to their corresponding DIX data structure (i.e. good locality). Despite all of these good practices, there was still room for improvement. Also, HP's DDX code was memory-inefficient in some cases.

Unfortunately, only a few examples can be shared in a paper of this size.

Windows

Three types of improvements were made for window structures. First, the locality of the window tree was improved with the use of a general-purpose library called *ChunkAlloc*. Second, the size of the window private structures was reduced. Finally, the locality of the WindowOptRec data structures was also improved using ChunkAlloc.

Window Locality

As illustrated in previous sections, each window structure is individually allocated. Windows are linked together according to their hierarchical (i.e. tree) relationships. The window tree is walked relatively frequently. Intuition suggests that window structures will have poor locality with each other, which will increase the X server's VWS, and cause unnecessary page faults.

MemSpy confirmed this intuition. ADM benchmark runs showed that window structures are frequently accessed (i.e. in the AWS) and have poor locality (i.e. increasing the VWS). When running the same benchmark during light paging (as opposed to normal ADM runs), the window structures caused many of the X server's page faults.

Around a year before this memory tuning effort, the author had developed a window-specific ChunkAlloc library in the hopes of increasing x11perf performance (calls to malloc() can be time consuming). This *ChunkAlloc* library allocated *chunks* of memory, large enough for many Window structures. Instead of the *AllocateWindow()* calling *Xalloc()*, it now calls the ChunkAlloc library, which returns a pointer to a portion of a chunk. Not much x11perf performance was gained during that effort, but ChunkAlloc improved window structure locality greatly. However, window structure page faults didn't decrease as much as desired. This was partially due to hiding data structures (discussed previously), and partially due to the improvement discussed in the next subsection.

Size Reductions

In addition to newly improved locality, MemSpy showed that the window structures were rather large. This meant that relatively few windows fit into each page. Thus, each window tree traversal would still access a large number of pages.

HP had recently made major improvements in its X server performance. An entirely new generation of DDX code had been developed. Unfortunately, the new DDX code still used private structures from a previous generation. Only a few fields were used from those old privates, leaving considerable memory wasted for each window.

After private structure restructuring, the newer DDX code used approximately 200 fewer bytes per window. When combined with ChunkAlloc, windows were now local and small, which resulted in many fewer page faults.

WindowOpt Locality

The core X11 protocol specifies a number of attributes for each window. During the R4 effort, the Consortium staff noticed that most windows didn't use several of the attributes. This led them to split the window structure. They created a new, WindowOpt, structure, which is allocated if a window uses the less-used attributes.

MemSpy analysis showed that a sizable percentage of the windows (at least for the particular benchmark) used WindowOpt structures. MemSpy also showed locality problems, similar to those seen with the main window structure.

The initial approach was to clone the window-specific ChunkAlloc code. However, a theme was developing. The ChunkAlloc approach would probably prove useful again. Therefore, a general-purpose ChunkAlloc library was created that replaced the structure-specific versions.

Resource Locality

Given the client-server nature of X11, clients don't directly reference server-internal data structures. Instead, clients use *resource identifiers* to operate on these structures (a.k.a. resources). The server maintains a *resource database*, which contains a mapping between resource identifiers and server-internal data structures.

For each resource in the database, a small, 16-byte data structure is allocated. MemSpy showed that these small structures were causing many page faults. Looking at the memory map of these structures showed a definite locality problem. Once again, ChunkAlloc was used. Locality was increased and page faults were reduced.

Fonts

Using MemSpy, we discovered that the code which opens bitmap fonts was very wasteful. Each time a bitmap font was opened, one large structure (approximately 80 KBytes) and many small structures were allocated, used, and then freed. Because other operations occurred between the time each bitmap font was opened, these transient structures fragmented the heap, decreasing the locality of other AWS structures.

Investigating what the bitmap font code was trying to do revealed that the large data structure was large by accident--it only needed to be a few KBytes, not 80.

A small utility library was created, allowing the smaller transient structures to be allocated from larger, less-transient chunks of memory. This further reduced fragmentation. Using this same library for non-transient font structures improved locality further.

Future

In its current form, MemSpy is more of a prototype than a production quality tool ready for commercial use. Many implementation shortcuts were taken because the focus of the USF effort was memory tuning, not the creation of a "cool tool" (though one was produced anyway). In other words, MemSpy was a means to an end, not the end itself.

While MemSpy currently provides a lot of analysis functionality, more possibilities exist. Also, MemSpy could benefit from some memory tuning and performance enhancements. A lot of attention was given to MemSpy's size and performance characteristics (improvements generally came in orders of magnitude), but to allow for interactive analysis of much larger data sets, additional improvements will need to be made.

Summary

Memory tuning seems to be an art, resulting from a lack of tools and best practices. A set of memory tuning tasks (i.e best practices) was presented for shrinking a process's VWS. These tasks required knowledge of the process's heap AWS. A method and set of tools was presented that gave knowledge of the heap AWS. Examples were given from an actual memory tuning effort. The method and tools allowed HP's X server VWS to be reduced.

References

[1] P.J.Denning, "The Working Set Model for Program Behavior," Communications of the ACM, Vol. 11, No. 5, May 1968, pp. 323-333.

[2] P.J.Denning, "Working Sets Past and Present," IEEE Transactions on Software Engineering, Vol. SE-6, No. 1, January 1980, pp. 64-84.

[3] R.K.Gupta, and M.A.Franklin, "Working Set and Page Fault Frequency Replacement Algorithms: A Performance Comparison," IEEE Transactions on Computers, Vol. C-27, August 1978, pp. 706-712.

[4] H.M.Levy, and P.H.Lipman, "Virtual Memory Management in the VAX/VMS Operating System," Computer, Vol.15, No. 3, March 1982, pp. 35-41.

[5] H.Loren, and H.Deitel, Operating Systems, Reading, MA: Addison-Wesley, 1981.

Acknowledgments

Thanks to Jim Stearns, Alan Ward, and Dave Lechtenberg who helped develop parts of MemSpy and/or the corresponding data logging tools. Thanks to Jeff Wood for developing the USF ADM benchmarks. Thanks to Todd Spencer who did most of the X server tuning work. Thanks to Nathan Meyers who memory tuned the font code. Thanks to Mike Jones and his team for supporting the X server tuning effort. Thanks to Larry Rupp for greatly improving the general-purpose ChunkAlloc library. Thanks to Brad Sherwood, my manager during the USF effort, who offered great strength and encouragement. Thanks to Dave Sweetser, my current manager, who supported the X server tuning effort and supported me in doing this paper. Thanks to Dan Garfinkel, Jeff Walls, Cal Selig, Todd Spencer, Jeff Wood, Tim Frye, Tom Yip, Charline Polifka, and Mary Jones who reviewed this paper.

Great thanks to my wife, Julie, who not only reviewed drafts of this paper, but took on an extra load at home while I wrote this paper! She's my wonderful wife, the love of my life, and of all eternity too!

Author Information

Ian Elliott is a Technical Contributor for Hewlett-Packard Company in Fort Collins, Colorado. He is the technical lead for HP's DDX Group, and is co-architect of the loadable working group. When he's not writing X Server code and working within the X Consortium, he spends time with his family and volunteers in his church.

Embedding of X Applications

Jan Newmarch[†]

Abstract

This paper investigates the problem of embedding the windows of one application within another using an extension of the Session Management protocol of X11R6. It tackles the problems of geometry management and focus and shows that these can be handled by a simple protocol for both the implicit and explicit focus models of Motif. The sharing of menus between embedded applications is also discussed. Issues of window and session management are discussed, and the paper concludes with a look at Style Guide issues.

Introduction

The Unix Operating System has a large number of tools which share a philosophy that each one is dedicated to doing one thing only, and doing that as well as it can. Currently available software, particularly from other environments, has not followed this and tends to be large and complex, performing many tasks often in a rather poor manner. A typical example is the spell-checking component which can be found replicated among word-processors, spread-sheets and many other applications.

It is becoming accepted that small communicating components are preferable, and much work is being done in setting infrastructure mechanisms in place to support this.

In the X Window system [Scheifler92], where the components may be graphical applications, there is a need to produce a visual coherence between the applications. Currently, there is little of this. For example, the Mosaic system which acts as a graphical interface to the World Wide Web will use other applications such as JPEG viewers to display images. These are run as separate applications and share no window space with Mosaic.

To produce a visual coherence, it is neccessary to "embed" the windows of one application into the windows of another. The embedding application will then act as a manager for the embedded

---

[†]*Jan Newmarch is a Senior Lecturer at the University of Canberra.*

client, and be responsible for the geometry of the embedded client among other things. An application may have many embedded clients, and an embedded client may in turn embed further clients of its own. This is at a much coarser level of granularity than the Fresco system [Linton93]

This paper reports on a project done as a sabbatical project at the OSF to investigate the issues involved in embedding applications, in particular, Motif [OSF94] applications.

In this paper all applications will be assumed to be Xt-based [Asente90] unless otherwise stated.

Reparenting

Typically an application will have a principal toplevel window which is parented from the root window. A window manager such as mwm may reparent this window. The window manager is responsible for various aspects of this toplevel window, including its geometry and location. If we wish to embed one application within another then we do not want it to be under the control of the window manager but under the control of the embedding application.

A simple way to achieve this is to create the toplevel of the embedded application with parent window being a window of the embedding application, or after creation to reparent the toplevel to a window of the embedding application. Either way should be equally valid.

This system works using Xt widgets [Asente90]. To give minimal disturbance to Xt, the reparenting approach was adopted. This way the normal window creation functions of Xt can be used unaltered.

The CORBA-based system of [Price93] reused the window of the embedding application, whereas the inset library of Leon [Leon93] did not reparent at all.

Geometry management

Widgets within an Xt application have a complex mechanism for setting geometry. A widget that wishes to resize itself may issue an *XtMakeGeometryRequest* to its parent. This will filter up through the widget hierarchy and then the responses will make their way back down. A request may be accepted, denied or modified.

The interaction between a toplevel window and a window manager is controlled by the ICCCM [Rosenthal93]. A toplevel window will attempt to set a new geometry. This geometry request is intercepted by the window manager. It will decide what to do with this, and may generate a *ConfigureWindow* event to resize the toplevel.

When an application is embedded into another, both types of interaction may be needed. One single window tree will have been created by the reparenting, but this will be made of two widget trees. The interaction within each tree is controlled by Xt, the interaction between the two trees is controlled by ICCCM. So when a widget in the embedded application wishes to resize, it informs its parent and the request makes its way to the top of its widget tree. The toplevel widget will attempt to resize its window. The parent window in the embedding application traps this request and starts a geometry request within its own widget tree. When a response is obtained to this, it may resize the toplevel of the embedded application. The embedded application will then respond to this resizing by propagating a geometry change down through its widget tree.

A widget may be requested for its preferred size. In general it calculates this from knowledge of what its own contents are, or in the case of a composite widget, using the preferred size of its children. Such a degree of knowledge may not be available about the preferred size of an embedded application. A simple solution of recording the last requested size of the embedded application as its preferred size was adopted. An alternative method of looking at the window manager hints on the toplevel window could have been used.

No additional mechanisms are required above those of Xlib and Xt for this.

Two widgets

On the embedding side, a window must be prepared to act as geometry manager for the embedded application. On the embedded side, the toplevel window must be reparented. The cleanest way to do this is to define an extra pair of widgets, one for each side.

On the embedding side an embedding container widget was defined (*EmbeddingContainer*). The principal task of this widget is to manage the geometry of its embedded toplevel window. This widget does not have any widget children, so in Motif it was implemented as a subclass of *Primitive*. This has as one resource the window ID of the toplevel of the embedded application so that it can issue *ConfigureNotify* events to it. The way it gets this ID is to watch for a *ReparentNotify* event.

In addition, the embedding container contains a command string to start the embedded application in some way. This is discussed in more detail later.

On the embedded side, most applications have a principal toplevel shell which is an *ApplicationShell*. Applications are advised to have more than one *ApplicationShell* only under unusual circumstances such as running on multiple displays. Thus this shell is the best candidate for reparenting. In X11R6 a subclass of this is defined - *SessionShell* - and because we would probably want to partake in session management, an embedding shell widget (*EmbeddedShell*) was defined as a subclass of *SessionShell*. Due to a problem in inheritance depth, this widget could not be defined in Motif 1.2, but only in Motif 2.0.

This widget has a resource of parent window. If this is not a *None* window, then the resource is used to reparent the toplevel window. This allows an application to run either as a standalone or embedded application without recompilation: if the resource has the value *None* then the aplication runs standalone, and if it is not *None* then it attempts to embed itself.

The manner in which this resource is set is left unspecified. It could be set by X resource files, by application resources or by the application setting resource values. This is to allow alternative methods of starting the embedded application.

Session management

X11R6 introduced a session management protocol, a session management library and a sample session manager [Wexler94]. A *SessionShell* widget was created as a subclass of *ApplicationShell* to manage the client side for Xt applications. This session management protocol allows the session manager to tell clients to save themselves and to die, allows the client to request saves, and allows the session manager to restart clients.

An embedding application should act as a session manager for its embedded clients. For example, when an embedding application wishes to exit, it should send a *Die* message to each of its clients so that they can exit gracefully. Similarly, when *Save* is selected on an embedding application it should be able to send a *SaveYourself* message to each of its clients.

Thus an application should be able to act as a session client for its own session manager, and at the same time be a session manager for its own embedded clients.

The most logical place to put such a nested session manager is in the *EmbeddingContainer* widget. Then there will be a one-to-one correspondence between the session manager, its embedding side and its embedded side. If multiple applications are embedded then this will result in multiple session managers running within the embedding application, one per *EmbeddingContainer*.

Unfortunately, the implementation of the session manager side of the library does not allow this to take place (global variables are used to maintain state) so there can only be one session manager running within an application. This means that the session management must be run from the *EmbeddedShell*. A further consequence of this is that an application cannot embed other applications and act as session manager for them unless it has changed its *ApplicationShell* (or *SessionShell*) to an *EmbeddedShell*. This is unfortunate, but not serious.

Embedding management

There are a number of issues to do with focus, menus, etc that are not part of session management. However, they need to dealt with by embedding and embedded applications. Rather tha"n modify session management, this was dealt with by a separate "embedding management" layer. However, it has been done in a way to preserve maximum compatability and flexibility with session management.

The X11R6 session management library is built using the ICE communications library [Mor94]. This library allows multiple protocols to exist on a single connection. The embed protocol shares the session protocol connection already established between an application and each of its embedded clients. In addition, the embed code was simply adapted from the session code by global substitutions and defining embed message identifiers to be disjoint from the session message indentifiers. This will allow easy movement of code from one to the other if it is judged that a given message more appropriately belongs in the other library.

For the same reasons as in session management, embed management is not done as a function of the *EmbeddingContainer*, but of the *EmbeddedShell* for the embedding application.

When a client connects to the embed mangement side of the *EmbeddedShell*, an "embed connection" object is created and managed by the *EmbeddedShell*. X events and general interaction occur not between the *EmbeddedShell* and the embedded application, but between the *EmbeddingContainer* and the embedded application, either through the toplevel window of the embedded application or the window of the *EmbeddingContainer*. Messages must be sent using the embed connection object, though. It is neccessary to link this embed connection object with the right *EmbeddingContainer/EmbeddedShell*. An early message from the embedded client to the embedding manager is the window ID of the client's toplevel window so that the *EmbeddingContainer* can make the correct link.

Starting embedded applications

The *EmbeddingContainer* has a resource which is a command line to execute. At some suitable stage it runs this command with an added command line option of the window ID of its own window. In most cases the command line will just start up the application which is to be embedded.

An application which is not designed to be embedded will need some changes to make it embeddable. First, it must use an *EmbeddingShell* instead of the *ApplicationShell* or *SessionShell*. Secondly, it must set the parent window resource of the *EmbeddingShell*. For the case where the command line starts up the application, it can treat the window ID as an application resource and set the *EmbeddingShell* resource from that.

This arrangement allows more complex systems to be built, such as "embedding servers". For example, an application (say an encyclopedia) which wishes to show many images would not want to fire up an independant application for each image. Instead, it would send a message in some unspecified way to an image server that would create another *EmbeddingShell* as a separate logical application.

There are some timing issues involved in this. The *EmbeddingContainer* does not have a window ID till after it has been realized. It would appear that this window ID is not valid till the window has been created so the command line cannot be executed until after it is certain that the window of the *EmbeddingContainer* has been created. On the embedded side things are not so bad, and the *EmbeddedShell* can perform the reparenting in its *Realize* procedure.

Focus

Focus models

There are currently two focus models in use by toolkits such as Motif. The first is the *explicit* or *click to focus* policy. In this the keyboard focus remains on a widget no matter how the pointer is moved inside an application, until an explicit action is taken to move the focus. This can be either a *BSelect* action or one of the keyboard traversal mechanisms. The other policy is the *implicit* or *pointer* policy, in which the focus follows the pointer. There is no keyboard traversal mechanism in pointer mode, though menus can still be activated by use of menu accelerators.

The window manager also has a choice of these two policies. In the explicit policy the focus is set to the toplevel window of an application and is not moved until an explicit action is taken by the user to move it (of course, when an application is given the focus, it may move it internally acccording to its own focus policy). In the pointer model, the window manager moves the focus between applications according to the position of the pointer.

Focus behaviour

In a non-embedded situation there are thus four cases to distinguish, two for the window manager times two for an application. In the embedded case there may be more, as each application may have its own policy. It is tempting to make every application in an embedded situation adopt the same policy, say that of the toplevel application. This may not be feasible in practice, because different aplications may have been designed to function best under a particular policy and only work with difficulty under a different one. Even worse, some toolkits only support one policy (Tk with explicit [Ousterhout94], Athena with implicit) so mixing these will require mixed focus policies.

The relation between the window manager and the topmost application should not change. In addition (and this is a statement of policy), the relation between an embedding manager and its embedded client should mirror that of the window manager to application. Thus we should have these cases:

Manager: explicit, client: explicit

> If the focus is on the manager, it will stay there until explicitly moved away. If the focus is on the client, it will stay there until explicitly moved away. The focus within the client will also be explicit.

Manager: explicit, client: implicit

> If the focus is on the manager, it will stay there until explicitly moved away. If the focus is on the client, it will stay there until explicitly moved away. However, the focus within the client will follow the pointer, so that if the pointer is moved out of the application events will be discarded.

Manager: implicit, client: explicit

> If the focus is on the manager, then it will move to the client if the pointer is moved over the client. Within the client it will be explicit. If the focus is on the client, it will move to the manager when the pointer moves out of the client into the manager (note that it cannot move out of the client to anywhere else without first moving back into the manager).

Manager: implicit, client: implicit

> The focus follows the pointer.

Reparenting problems

The embedding mechanism takes two widget trees and joins them into a single X Window tree. Within each widget tree there is an event dispatching mechanism which sends events to the widget that has the focus. In addition, Motif keeps track of when the focus enters or leaves this widget tree. Motif has an additional mechanism of keyboard traversal. It maintains a *Traversal* data structure and additional information about how the focus is changing. It uses this information to move the Xt focus around, and also to generate *FocusIn* and *FocusOut* events on internal widgets.

This gives rise to a number of problems. The first of these concerns pointer motion between the two hierarchies. As the pointer moves from embedding manager to embedded client, an *EnterWindow* event will be generated on the toplevel of the embedded client. If the focus is currently set to the embedding manager, then because the two are in the same X Window tree, the focus detail of this *EnterWindow* event will be set to *True*. Now in standard Xt this situation is interpreted as one of the two window manager possibilities of implicit focus, with the pointer being moved into the application. In this case the embedded client will assume that it has been given the focus and act accordingly, by e.g. showing the focus on its own focus widget. This will be incorrect if the embedding manager is under the explicit model as it will not in fact have given the focus away. Thus without modifications to the standard Xt event processing, errors in behaviour will occur.

The second problem arises in the same situation when a keyboard event actually occurs. Because the pointer may be in a window belonging to the embedded client which has an ancestor (in the embedding manager) with the focus, the keyboard event is sent to the embedded client. This enters the Xt and Motif key despatching mechanisms for the embedded client and will end up somewhere in the embedded client even though they should have gone to the embedding manager. Again, the Xt event processing mechanism is in error here.

These problems can be handled in many cases by looking at the detail field of events, setting the Xt keyboard focus and the X input focus, etc. It becomes quite complicated very rapidly, and it is not clear that any solution is either completely valid or portable to other toolkits.

Event dispatching

Due to this mix of Xt widget and X Window trees, an application may believe that it has the focus when in fact it should not. The default Xt *EventDispatcher* will dispatch any event that it understands. When the application should not have the focus but gets the event anyway we need to interpose into the dispatch mechanism to direct the event elsewhere, say to the embedding manager for this client. Similarly, when a *BSelect* occurs we may need to take additional actions to set the focus to this application before processing the event in the usual way.

X11R6 supplies a mechanism to replace the event dispatcher for selected event types. This was originally intended to allow for processing of extension events that the default dispatcher was not coded to handle. Here, we put in our own key and button dispatcher which will examine the focus state for the application before deciding whether to call the default event dispatcher or take other action such as forwarding the event to an embedding manager.

Focus protocol

The simplest way of moving the focus between applications is to use the Xlib call *XSetInputFocus()* , as the window manager does. There are two ways that this can be done: one application can set the focus to another, and the other can react to it (i.e. the container sets the focus to the embedded application), or an application can set focus to itself (i.e. the embedded application sets the focus to itself).

In the first case the application receiving the focus must interpret the set of *FocusChange* and *WindowCrossing* events to determine whether or not to take the focus. As mentioned earlier, this approach seemed to become very messy and although initially explored was then discarded.

In the second case the application must decide on the basis of other information because no explicit *FocusIn* occurs. Since an embedding protocol was already in place using ICE, a protocol was explored in which applications would send messages conveying focus change requests. Then an application could decide on the basis of its own state what should happen, send a message to another one to take/lose the focus and the other application would respond based on its own state and the message.

Three primary messages seem to be needed

TakeFocus

An embedding container may have the focus and decide to set it to an embedded client. This may occur when the focus moves to an *EmbeddingContainer* through keyboard traversal, because it is a "default focus" widget, or because the focus moves to it by pointer motion under an implicit model.

In this case, the embedding manager sends a *TakeFocus* message to the embedded client. On receipt of this message, the client may in turn forward it on to one of its own embedded clients, or set the X input focus to itself. To avoid a potential race condition (discussed below), this message should block in the manager till an acknowledgement of completed action is received from the client.

RequestFocus

When a *BSelect* occurs in an application under the explicit model, it should have the focus set to it. Two events may be generated by a window manager: a *FocusIn* may be sent to the toplevel window of the topmost application, and the *ButtonPress* may be sent to the window the event occurred in. In the non-embedded case, these events will both be sent to the same application and so be in the same event queue. Thus they will be processed sequentially.

In the embedded case, they will be sent to different applications, the *FocusIn* to the containing application, the *ButtonPress* to the embedded application. The *FocusIn* sent to the toplevel window will possibly generate a set of *TakeFocus* messages down to what is the default or last focus application/widget, which will set the X input focus to itself. This most likely will not be the window in which the *ButtonPress* occurred. We cannot set focus to the application with the *ButtonPress* till this is all over or a race will occur.

To avoid a race to set input focus caused by the two events, the *TakeFocus* blocks until an acknowledgement is received. Meanwhile, the application with the *ButtonPress* sends a *RequestFocus* message up which eventually reaches an application which either has the focus or has set it to a client. This will have blocked until any *TakeFocus* message has completed, by which time the X input setting will also have completed. So at this stage it is okay to send another *TakeFocus* event back down to the client which had the *ButtonPress*. This has the potential for a visual "hiccup": if an application had lost the focus and then a click occurs in one of the embedded applications, the focus may initially be set to the application that previously had the focus and then be moved to the one in which the button was pressed.

LoseFocus

While it is sending a *TakeFocus* down to the client which should have the focus, it should also inform the client which currently has the focus that it is to lose it (and maybe remove any visual efects). This is the purpose of a *LoseFocus* message.

These messages provide enough information to an application to decide what it should do. This may involve a non-trivial set of actions to occur, though. For example, when a *TakeFocus* message is received, the application should set state to signify that it is prepared to take focus, and then set the X focus to itself. This state variable is needed to ensure that spurious *FocusIn* events (which can come from a number of places) do not cause the application to believe it has the focus. When it receives a *FocusIn* and is prepared to take focus, the application will then set a flag so that the installed key event handler will call the default event handler.

A problem that arises here is that a *FocusIn* has to be generated when the focus is set. Motif traversal code does not necessarily generate a *FocusIn* if it believes that the focus widget has not changed. So it is also necessary to fool this code into believing that the focus is moving into this widget hierarchy by setting the *old_focus_widget* to *NULL*. This is still quite, quite messy.

Problems

The interaction between the window manager and the topmost application is not controlled by this embedding protocol. So this has to be subject to special-case treatment. This case is not hard to spot, though, as the *EmbeddingShell* here has parent window resource set to *None*.

When applications are using the pointer policy, motion of the pointer out of a client into a manager should cause the manager to set focus to itself. In a nested case it may be possible to move through several managers very quickly, all of which will attempt to set focus to themselves. In this case the X server will have to decide which X set focus requests to honour based on the timestamp from the *EnterWindow* events. However, with a resolution of milliseconds the possibility exists that two events may have the same timestamp. In this case the X server will have no basis for decision.

Menus

A commonly accepted style issue is that an application should have a menubar with pulldown menus. In the Macintosh world there is a single menu bar for the root window that changes as focus moves between applications, whereas Microsoft Windows and Motif applications have one menubar per application (in the non-embedded case).

In the embedded case, Microsoft Windows adds additional entries to the menus when an embedded application has the focus [BrockScmidt94]. The question is what to do in Motif? Whatever is decided, there clearly must be a way of communicating window information between an application with the focus and the topmost application.

The situation is made more complex in X by the existence of multiple toolkits, each with their own system of menu creation and manipulation.

A simple approach was dealt with here, for proof of concept. A menu is specified using a format to represent the menubar, its component buttons, the pulldown menu panes and their component buttons. This was encoded as a String (in fact, as a list of lists using *tcl* syntax [Ousterhout94]) so that it could be easily parsed by an application using any toolkit. It may be necessary at some time to determine a more formal syntax which may contain semantic clues as well (for example, an X atom representing the *File* button may be quite specific in meaning). Another possibility - but very toolkit specific - would be to use a UIL specification of the menu [OSF94].

When an application gains the focus, it sends its menu specification up to the topmost application using the embedding protocol. Here we have to make some assumptions about the widget structure of an application in order to proceed. A Motif application will generally have a *MainWindow* with a menubar. We assume this is the case. The *EmbeddedShell* at the toplevel checks for the existence of this *MainWindow* , and if its exists it creates the menu from its specification and puts it in place, destroying the old one. At present this is done anew each time a menu specification is received, but this could be cached if neccessary. The main reason for doing this in the *EmbeddedShell* was to leave the Motif *MainWindow* code alone and place all this experimental code in a single place.

When a menu button is pressed, its activate callbacks should be executed. However, the menu is in one address space (that of the topmost application) but the callback functions may be in another (that of the embedded client). This is resolved by using general callback handlers in each application. When a menu is sent up, each button carries information specific to itself. Presently this is the address of the callback function that should be invoked in the embedded client's address space. When it reaches the top, the *EmbeddedShell* places this information in the client data of a callback to a generic callback function. When this is invoked it sends the client data back down to the embedded client which then invokes the callback function in the correct address space.

Window manager problems

The next two sections consider some of the problems that may arise in the ICCCM protocol when embedding takes place. They attempt to point out the problems but are not prescriptive about solutions. Solutions tend to involve policy, so one must be careful about adoption of any one.

Under ICCCM, the window manager may send a WM_DELETE_WINDOW message to a client. The client may choose to respond to this, or to ignore it. In Motif, behaviour to this message may be controlled by the Motif *VendorShell* resource *XmNdeleteResponse* .

In an embedded system, here is the problem of how to handle this for all the embedded children. One possibility is for the topmost application to handle the message itself without informing the embedded applications. So if it chooses to ignore the message it just carries on, but if it were to terminate, then it should first terminate the embedded applications.

The alternative is to pass the WM_DELETE_WINDOW message on to each contained application, regardless of the response of the container.

Messy situations occur when the container consults the embedded children. It cannot be done by just passing on the WM_DELETE_WINDOW message without ending up with situations where the container terminates but an embedded application does not, or vice versa.

It would appear to be simpler for the topmost container to make a unilateral decision for all embedded applications. If the container decides to terminate then it will have to terminate its embedded applications. This should be done in a way that allows them to preserve state if needed, so essentially involves session manager mechanisms.

In the embedded case, *window manager protocols will have to interact with session manager protocols.*

Session management problems

There are a variety of messages that may be sent from a session manager to a client. A simple one is the *Die* message. This is pretty straightforward: it should be forwarded to each child. This system was implemented using the sample session manager from X11R6, and this particular message was forwarded.

Less straightforward is the *SaveYourself* message. This may be sent from a session manager to the client in a form that allows the application to request user interaction, or to deny user interaction. Clearly, this message must be forwarded to all embedded clients. The *shutdown* and *fast* fields should be passed on unchanged. However, there are a variety of different interaction styles that can be specified, and these can lead to a number of different possibilities. If the interact-style is set to *None* then the application is denied any chance of interacting with the user, and any embedded applications should similarly have interaction denied. The other two values of interact-style are *Errors* and *Any*. One extreme is for the topmost application to be the only one allowed to interact. In such a case it would forward the *SaveYourself* with interact-style set to *None*. The other extreme is to pass on the same interaction-style. Allowing the embedded applications to interact in any way leads to a number of cases.

An embedded application may request interaction by *InteractRequest* to its container. The container should not grant this directly, but only by negotiation with its own session manager. If the container has not yet sent an *InteractRequest* to its session manager, then it should do so. If the container has already sent such a request but not yet received an *Interact* reply, then it should not send another, as this is not allowed by the state transitions of the session manager protocol. Instead, it should store the identity of the embeddee and continue to wait for an *Interact* message. If it has already received the *Interact* and not yet sent an *InteractDone*, then it should schedule an interaction with the embeddee according to an application-specific algorithm.

When a container receives an *Interact* message, it should send *Interact* to all embedded clients that have outstanding requests, according to an application-specific algorithm. Once all of these have responded with *InteractDone* then the container can send an *InteractDone* to its own session manager.

Similarly, when all embedded clients have sent a *SaveYourselfDone*, the container can send *SaveYourselfDone* back to its session manager. The *success* flag should be the Boolean 'and' of those of the embedded clients.

Style guide issues

A primary style guide issue is the visibility of the focus mechanism. While developing this system, it proved invaluable to highlight the border of any application when it had the focus, so that it could be seen what was happening. On the other hand, this is supposed to be a mechanism that is transparent to the user, so such highlighting should not occur in general. This issue can be dealt with by the usual resource mechanism, by setting the default border thickness to zero.

In Microsoft OLE, when focus is placed on an embedded application, additions are made to the menu system in an essentially invisible mechanism - it is not until the menubar pulldowns are activated that the additions become visible. In the mechanism implemented here, each time the focus changes a new menu is put in place. This is highly visible.

The means by which the Microsoft mechanism works is because there is already a strong policy system in place - one can always add to an "Edit" menu, because such a menu should always be there.

This has many implications on implementation. At one extreme is the system done here, in which there is no semantic content associated with a menu outside of its address space. A pointer to a function call in an a particular address space is the total of semantic content.

The opposite extreme is to have all elements of a menu with semantic content. A simple example is a "Save" element (in whatever locales are used in each embeddee). Selection of this should cause a save operation to take place not only on all applications that form the chain of focus, but on all of the embedded aplications. This would require a large degree of policy.

A curiosity arose in the interaction of dynamic menus and focus policies. In the pointer focus model, if the menu follows the focus then moving the pointer into an application will set the menu for that application. Regrettably, when any attempt is made to select from that menu, the pointer will have to pass through intermediate applications which will promptly reset the menu to themselves!

Clearly, a "menu follows pointer" policy cannot work. Possibilities include a "click to set menu" or time delays.

Conclusion

A working prototype of this has been built using X11R6 and Motif 2.0. This consists of a container application with two embedded clients, each of which has two further embedded clients. This has shown that it is feasible to perform nested embedding using the tools available in X11R6 without having to use additional mechanisms. This prototype is in the X11R6 *contrib* software.

However, it does raise a number of issues related to window management, session management and style guides. In particular, the "obvious" way of dealing with floating menus breaks down under the pointer focus model.

The system has been designed so that it is possible that an embedding container may contact "embedded servers". The exact means by which this is done is left unspecified, as it is beyond the scope of this project - it could involve directory services, for example.

References

[Asente90]   Paul J Asente and Ralph R. Swick. *XWindow System Toolkit: The Complete Programmer's Guide*. Digital Press, 1990.

[Brockschmidt94] Kraig Brockschmidt. *Inside OLE2*. Microsoft Press, 1994.

[Leon93]   Jean Michael Leon.   anonymous ftp to ftp.x.org /R5contrib/insetlib-0.2.tar.gz.

[Linton93]   Mark Linton and Chuck Price. *Building Distributed User Interfaces with Fresco*. Proc. Seventh X Technical Conference, Boston, Massachusetts, 1993.

[Mor94]   Ralph Mor. *Inter-Client Exchange (ICE) Library*. X Consortium, Inc, X11 Release 6, 1994.

[OSF94]   Open Software Foundation. *OSF/Motif 2.0 Programmer's Reference*. Prentice-Hall, 1994.

[Ousterhout93]   John Ousterhout. *Tcl and the Tk Toolkit*. Addison-Wesley, 1993.

[Price94]   Charles A. Price. *Extending Xt to Support CORBA-Based Embedding*. 8th Annual Tecnical Conference, X Resource issue 9, pp. 47-61, 1994.

[Rosenthal94]   David Rosenthal. *Inter-Client Communication Conventions Manual*. X Consortium, Inc, X11 Release 6, 1994.

[Scheifler92]   Robert W. Scheifler and James Gettys. *X Window System*. Digital Press, 1992.

[Wexler94]   Mike Wexler. *X Session Management Protocol*. X Consortium, Inc, X11 Release 6, 1994.

Acknowledgements

This work was performed as part of a Sabbatical program at the Open Software Foundation from February to June, 1994.

Author Information

Jan Newmarch is Director of the Research Center for Information Technology and Associate Dean of the Faculty of information Science and Engineering at the University of Canberra, Australia. His email is jan@ise.canberra.edu.au.

OpenDoc and Its Architecture

Chris Nelson - IBM

Abstract

OpenDoc and its related technologies is an important standard for compound documents and component integration. IBM is a both a member and a contributor of technology to the CI Labs consortium, holder of the OpenDoc technolgy. IBM is also producing the Unix referance implementation of OpenDoc. This paper is an overview of the architecture of OpenDoc and its related technologies; OSA, Bento, ComponetGlue Technolog, and SOM. It also discusses the programing model for developing software based on OpenDoc.

A Short History of Compound Documents

The 70's - Documents by Hand

In the late 70's and early 80's, tools were available to handle a wide variety of user needs. There were text tools, charting tools, accounting tools etc. But each tool knew how to work with its own particular data, and output that data in a limited fashion. If a document was to be created that included output from all of these tools, it was a literal cut-and-paste operation. If a change needed to be made to the document. it often meant starting from scratch, running each tool in-succession and hand pasting the results together again.

Figure 1: - The 70's - Documents by Hand

The 80's - Tool Level Integration

In the middle-late 80's, platforms were developed which allowed output from tools to be captured and placed in documents (much as this document). There was one application or editor which owned the document. Document layout-space was set aside for "pictures" of the embedded data.

Although much easier to use then the manual cut-paste operations, there were several problems with this approach:

- The output data was static or "dead". If changes needed to be made, the user had to go back to the original tool to make the changes and then go through the electronic cut-paste operation

- For the most part, only pictures of the document could be traded across computers, since the document was tied to the local data and the tool

- The model for building a document was to run a series of tools and to merge the output through electronic cut-and-paste operations. This was still a "tool" oriented model of computing.

- Things that could be put into a document were limited to a small set; text and graphics, and these were "pictures" of the data. There was no link back to the original data

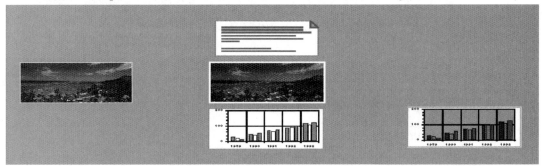

Figure 2: The 80's - Tool Level Integration

There is an additional problem with the tool integrated approach. As applications extended functionality by supporting more and different kinds of data, the complexity of those applications increased significantly. Release cycles become stretched, requiring more programmers, increased test time, smaller increases in functionality between releases and significantly higher development cost. They became complex and fragile.

The 90's - Document Centric Computing

With the advent of OpenDoc and other compound document architectures such as OLE and the document framework in Taligent, the model to the user switched from a "tool centric" to "document centric"

In a document centric model of computing, the user can focus on the document that they want to create rather than the output of some specific tool. To the user, a document is now composed of several parts that are all embedded and integrated into a document. The types of parts that now could be part

Figure 3: The 90's - Document Centric Computing

of this document is only dependent on the availability of a part handler (editors and viewers). Some of the parts and features that we might expect to see early in these documents are:

- Formatted Text

- 2 and 3d graphics

- images

- audio

- video

- structured data such as appointments and calender

- UI control structures

- inter and intra document links

- document draft control

Because the focus is on the parts of the document - the data, exchange of documents across platforms is greatly simplified. All that is required is to have an available part handler for the data contained in the document, not a specific application.

This approach can also have a significant impact on the cost and method of software development. OpenDoc provides the structure for integration. Applications are now developed as small components - part handlers. These part handlers can be developed independently from other part handlers. In general, complexity is significantly decreased allowing faster and less costly development cycles.

It also broadens the functionality to the end user. The user can now acquire part handlers which automatically integrate and do not have to be dependent on one vendor for an integrated solution.

Compound Document Architectures - What's Out There

Currently there are three available compound document architectures:

- Microsoft's OLE - Object Linking and Embedding
- CI Lab's OpenDoc and associated technology
- Taligent's document framework

OpenDoc is designed to sit in the middle for ISVs. It is a bridging strategy for application vendors that want to work in an OLE, OpenDoc, or Taligent environment with existing applications. It will allow developers to extend the life of existing software products with a quick port to OpenDoc, and a migration path to providing Taligent based products by incremental introduction of Taligent technology into their software base.

Component Integration Laboratory - CI Labs

OpenDoc is not an IBM solution or an Apple solution, it is an industry solution. All of the technology that makes up the integrated components of OpenDoc has been placed in an independent consortium; Component Integration Laboratory or CI Labs. This technology, including the source code, is then made available to all members of CI Labs.

The initial technology base which will be contained in CI Labs consists of the five integrated Open-Doc components:

- OpenDoc - Compound Documents
- Bento - Object Container System
- Open Scripting Architecture - Policies, Protocols, and Software for Scripting
- ComponentGlue Technology - the OpenDoc-OLE interoperability technology
- SOM - System Object Model, Single Machine Version of CORBA (includes multi-process object invocation)

CI Labs Provides

The form and function of CI Labs looks very similar to that of the X Consortium. Members of the consortium work and contribute towards the technical direction of the products. There will be source code reference implementations of the technology components. Members are allowed to modify and add value to those reference implementations, and to base products on this code.

CI Labs will also play two other roles which have not been strongly part of the X Consortium. CI Labs will provide a certification service for developers. And they will provide a marketing role for CI Labs, its services, and for its technology base along with other standards based technology which becomes important to the goals of content integration (such as the technology from OMG)

Cross Platform Coverage

Reference implementations for the CI Labs technology will be available on all of the major platforms. These platforms, and the companies providing the reference implementation are:

- Macintosh   Apple
- OS/2   IBM
- Windows   Word Perfect - Novell
- Unix   IBM

Compound Document Architecture In General

Before looking at the specifics of the OpenDoc architecture, we'll first take a look at the generic problem of putting together a system for supporting the embedding of objects into a document and the building of component software. Most of this can be translated to both the technology of OLE and Taligent's document framework.

Fundamental to the concept of a compound document is that it can hold different kinds of data - document parts. And that each kind of part is handled by an independent application or part handler. Each part handler understands its own intrinsic content, and even though other kinds of parts may be embedded into it, it need not know anything about the intrinsic content of that embedded part.

The integration and cooperation of those parts is accomplished by the architecture, policies, and protocols of the compound document system

There are other differences which separate a document consisting of parts and a document created by a conventional application

- Content is not limited. Users are not limited to the kind of content that can be put into a document. The only practical limitation is the availability of a part handler - editor or viewer. As new part editors are acquired, they can be used immediately.

- Content is built differently. The user will rely on the clipboard and drag-drop mechanisms more.

- Part handlers can be changed. Users can replace part handlers to fit their needs. This can be done independent of existing documents (which don't depend on a specific part editor)

- Pervasive use of links both internal to the document such as hyper-text type links and external to the document for data transfer and navigation.

Generic Compound Document Architecture

This section refers to figure 4 below. It uses a simple compound document to describe the problems faced in a compound document system, and the interfaces for solving those problems. It takes the perspective of "If you where going to architect a compound document support library, what are the problems you would have to solve, and the interfaces you would need to supply to the application developer. There are several other problems associated with a compound document system that are not described here, but these are the principal ones

Data exchange - how do I build this document. Many compound documents will be built-up by the movement of data from one document (or the desktop) to another either through a cut-paste or drag-drop operation by the user. These interfaces deal with how data is moved from one document to another. These interfaces need to define how data is put on and taken off of the clip-board, along with passing type and attribute information so that the correct part handler can be accessed from the part handler data base. Since the clipboard will be passing complex data - objects, there needs to be an in-memory object container. The storage format for clipboard data will be a Bento container in the reference implementation of OpenDoc.

Part Registration - Finding the right part handler for the data. When a container receives data on the clip-board of a particular type, it needs an interface to help it find the correct part handler for this type. Also, when a part handler is installed into the system, it needs an interface where it can register itself and the type of data (part types) that it supports. Often, a part handler will register itself claiming to handle several types of parts (say different image formats), or you might find several part handlers which claim to handle the same part type. The user, for convenience, may set up a preferences file which defines which specific part handler they want to use for a particular type of part. An example of this would be if the user has two word processors on their workstation - MegaWrite and MuchoText. They both have their own proprietary binary format, but also support the import of other formats, including the binary format of the other. The user might set up a part handler preference such that MegaWrite is used for MegaWrite binary and MuchoText for MuchoText binary thinking that each will handle its own data best. This preference could of course be overridden if the user wanted to do a conversion.

Document Part - Part-to-part communication. With a bunch of embedded parts in a document, there needs to be an interface between parts and between the containing part and its embedded parts. The sorts of things that this interface provides is:

- access to internal part data

- commands to the part such as "save your data", "externalize yourself", etc.

- requests to receive or give up control of some global resource such as the menu bar or input focus.

Windows/Frames - geometry of part windows and frames. With all of these parts sharing space on the screen and in the printed document, there needs to be central coordination over layout. This set of interfaces deals with the geometry of the document window and the geometry of the embedded parts,

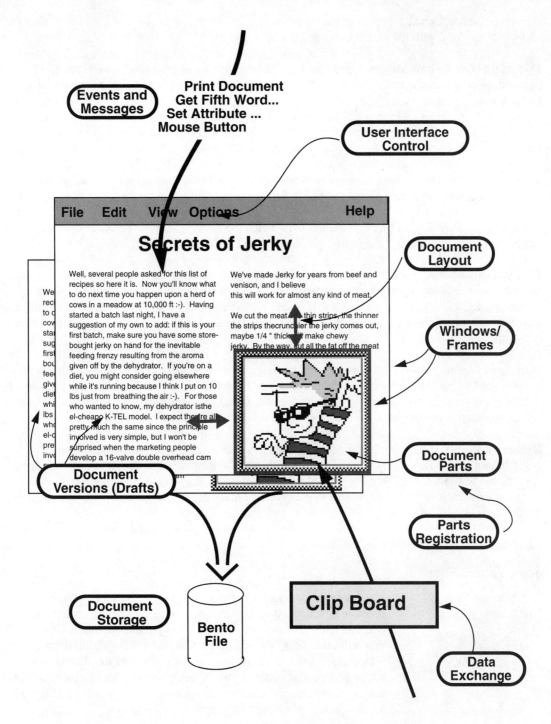

Figure 4: Generic Compound Document Interfaces

It contains information about the size, shape, position, clip extents, and transformations of the frames and windows along with the means to set and manipulate them

Document layout - how big can I get. This interface handles the negotiation between the part handler and the container for space resources. It is used when the part needs to grow or shrink in size because of user interaction such as editing the picture, or the data changes because of a link update of the data. The container sets the policy for document layout and has the final say. The result of this negotiation may be that the part is placed on a new page, the part is split into more then one piece, or the document is rearranged to accommodate the new size, or even that the part is not allowed to grow.

User interface control - whose menus are active?. This set of interfaces is for negotiation for access to the user interface and other global resources. When a user selects a part with the mouse, the part handler needs to put its user interface and menus up replacing the previous ones. Additionally there needs to be some policy set by the container over which menus are global to the entire document rather then the selected part - under the "file" menu, what does "print" mean?

Events and messages. There needs to be several interfaces for distribution, sending, receiving, and interpreting events and messages. These interfaces cover low level events such as mouse moves or button pushes, middle level events such as window manager events, along with high-level events or semantic messages. These interfaces are also the foundation for scripting since scripts can be collections of semantic messages.

Document version (drafts) - document collaboration and versioning These interfaces deal with having multiple drafts or versions of a document. They have to deal with the selection and creation of a draft, along with the management and reconciliation of multiple drafts. These interfaces are closely related to the storage interfaces.

Document storage. These interfaces deal with the storage and retrieval of the document and it's parts. It needs to be abstracted from the underlying storage system so that a multiplicity of storage systems can be used. In the OpenDoc reference implementation, the storage system will be built using Bento containers. It is likely that storage systems using OLE storage, Taligent storage, and object data bases will be available.

OpenDoc Programmer Model

Some Terminology

Part	A part of the document, the thing that gets embedded into the document. In OpenDoc, the embedded data is referred to as the **part**, and the editor or viewer of that part is referred as the **part handler**. However, you will often hear the two combined with both the data and the editor/ viewer referred to as a part. Conceptually, the **part handler** is an application program in today's sense. Many of today's applications such as image editors, graphics editors, audio players etc., will be modified to act also as OpenDoc **part handlers**.

Container Part	This is a part that is capable of containing other parts. It has all of the properties of a normal part, but also needs to keep track of and respond to its embedded parts.

The outermost or **root** container part is a somewhat special case. It is a part which takes up the entire document window and is the container of all other parts. An example of a root part would be a word processor type application. It has text as its native content, but can contain other parts to produce compound documents. These root parts will often set the tone for document capabilities.

There is s default root part which is just a container of other parts with no native content of its own. It would just provide a background. |
| **Shell** | The document shell and the root part are closely linked. However, it is useful to separate them functionally. The shell worries about access to global information and the distribution of that information (by providing object references). It is also the receiver of low and high-level events for the document. |
| **Link** | A link is a reference or pathway to an object. In compound documents links are used in two manners; inter document links such as hypertext links, and intra document links providing automatic update of embedded information. |
| **Event** | There are two levels of events that need to be worried about, low level events such as mouse moves and key clicks, and high level or semantic events which are requests on an object to perform a function.

The definition of the semantic events provide the basis for scripting. |
| **Frame** | A Frame is the area or border of a part. It encompasses the data in the part which is to be viewed. It can be of non-rectangular shape. The Frame is displayed in one or more Facets.

In OpenDoc, parts can have multiple frames. Each frame represents a different view of the data.

Frames are persistent and are stored with the document. |
| **Facet** | The facet is there area on the canvas where the frame is to be displayed.

Facets are not persistent. they are created and destroyed as frames are displayed and erased. As an example, consider a multi-page document with many embedded parts. Parts which are not on the current displayed page do not have a facet. Parts which are displayed would have facets. |

Canvas	A display surface. The place to display frames in their facets. A canvas can be the display surface, a piece of paper, off screen display etc.
Window	In OpenDoc, Window refers to the outermost window of the document, the window for the root container. Other regions are referred as frames or menus (even though they may be implemented as windows in the native windowing system).
	This limitation of the use of the term "window" is to provide a cross platform way of talking about OpenDoc regions.
In-place Editing	This refers to the document-centric metaphor. When a user selects a part for editing or viewing, the edit can be done in-place. A new window with the data need not be opened (although it can if that's the policy of the part handler).
Document Draft	This refers to carrying along multiple versions or drafts of a document in a single document structure. These drafts might be simple snapshots of the document as it is modified, or they may be drafts targeted for an audience such as each draft localized to a language.

Class Library of Objects

In the previous section, the basic interfaces for a compound document architecture were generalized. In OpenDoc, all of the interfaces are realized as a class library of objects, SOM or CORBA objects to be specific. Figure 5 shows the inheritance relationship of the OpenDoc class library.

More meaningful to the developer is the runtime relationship of the objects. Figure 6 shows the runtime relationship of the major OpenDoc objects.

Part Developer Major Interfaces

Your major programming task in creating an OpenDoc part editor is to subclass the class ODPart and override its methods. ODPart has 62 methods as part of its interface, however for simple parts, and for quick prototypes, only a dozen of these interfaces need to be changed. At a minimum, your editor needs to:

- draw its part
- retrieve its part's data
- activate its part
- handle events sent to its part

It will likely need some sort of command or user interface. Thus it will need to

- provide menus for the menu bar
- along with optional windows, dialogs, and palettes

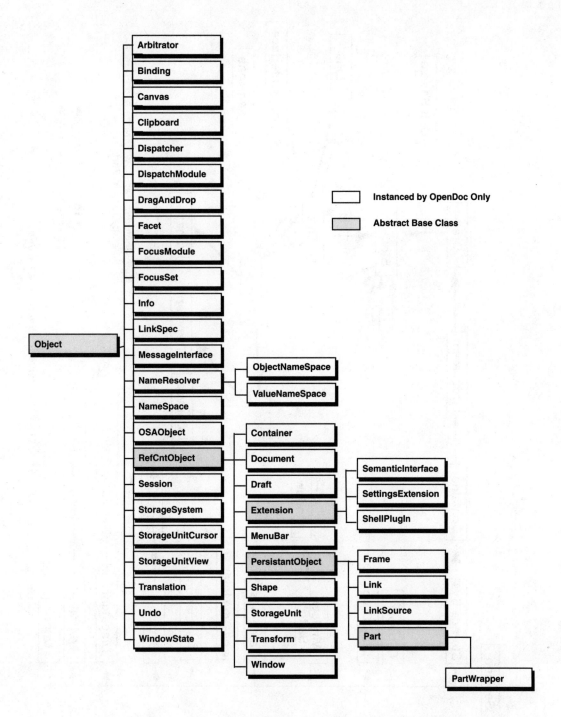

Figure 5: The OpenDoc Class Hierarchy (principal classes)

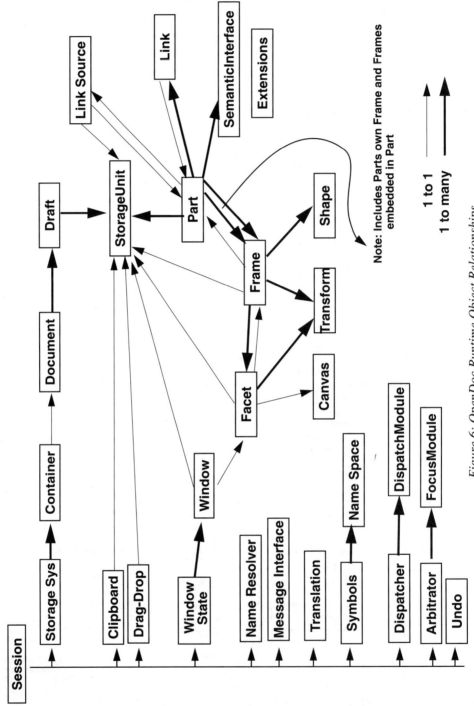

Figure 6: OpenDoc Runtime Object Relationships

If the part editor is to contain other parts, then your part editor must

- embed frames

- create facets for visible frames

- store frames

Beyond these capabilities, you may want to extend the functionality of your part editor by supporting

- asynchronous drawing

- drag-drop and cut-paste

- scripting

- and links

For converting an existing application, the simplest technique is to start with one of the provided sample parts and to subclass it. This insures correct default behavior for content independent actions, but allows for rapidly adding application functionality. Past OpenDoc developer labs (Parts Kitchens) have seen the majority of prototype applications converted in less then a week during lab times. Note: most of the platform vendors continue to offer Parts Kitchens. See section - Where to Get More Information - at the end of this paper for how to participate.

Bento - An Object Container System

Bento is a nice simple piece of technology for containing objects (note: the word container is being used differently here then in the OpenDoc sense). You can think of it as a "Federal Express" envelope for objects. You can put anything into it, and there are established procedures for moving it around, looking at the inventory list, taking things out, and adding new things to the envelope, all independent of what is put into it.

In OpenDoc, Bento will serve three functions:

- It will be the reference file storage system

- it will be the object container for things placed on the clip-board

- It will be the container of choice for transporting documents across platforms.

You could think of Bento as a file system within a file, but rather then being a tree structure reflecting the embedding relationship, it is a flat structure. Figure 7 shows the structure of the Bento container. It has a series of objects. Each object has one or more properties associated with the object, and each property has a set of values or data. In the Example in Figure 7, property q might be formatted text stored in several different formats, say RTF, SGML, and flat ASCII. Another valid value might be a reference to another Bento container.

Normally, the OpenDoc programer does not deal directly with the Bento structure, but deals rather with the OpenDoc StorageUnit interface.

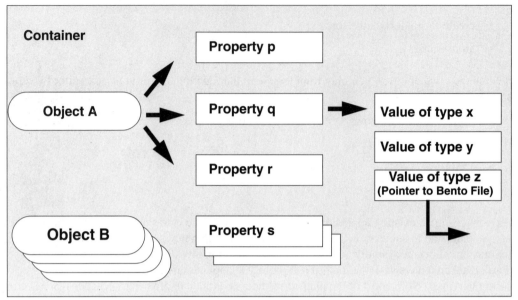

Figure 7: Bento Data model

The structure of the StorageUnit object is similar to that of Bento, but can be the front end for other types of storage such as an OODBMS, or other object storage system such as the OLE Doc File Format. Figure 8 shows the structure of the OpenDoc StorageUnit.

OSA - The Open Scripting Architecture

OSA or the Open Scripting Architecture provides an open architecture for scripting languages such as

- OREXX
- Apple Script
- ScriptX
- OLE Automation

The architecture is composed of two major components. The first is the typing of script types which allows for the inclusion of the correct scripting engine for script processing, and the second is the standardization of script semantic messages in the form of Open Events which all OSA compliant scripting languages will emit.

Scripts become part of the document, attached or embedded as needed. They can be the foundation for control structures, as front or back ends to operations, or instructions for use embedded into document that is mailed out.

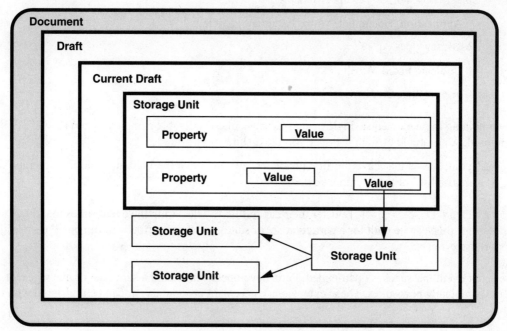

Figure 8: OpenDoc StorageUnit Structure.

Open Events

Open Events are based on standard registry of verbs and object classes. The basis of this technology comes from Apple Events.

Open Events are arranged in "Application" suites. Some examples of these suites are:

- Required
- Core
- Text
- Table
- Database
- Compound document
- etc.
- New suites defined by user community

Each event is composed of three elements. These elements are the:

- Events (the verbs) e.g.
  - Open, Close, Select, Get, Put, etc.

- Object classes or Object Specifiers e.g.

  - Application, Document, Word, Paragraph, Circle,

- Descriptor types e.g.

  - Boolean, Fixed, Attribute

  - greater then, 3rd, bold

By combining these elements, single event messages of considerable complexity and richness can be composed. An example of such message for a text suite application is:

- Get all words that have the first character "w" and have the bold attribute in paragraph 5 to paragraph 12 of the document called "foo"

Parts which are OSA scriptable register their capabilities by declaring the event suites that they support. Scripts then can be built for a particular set of suites and those scripts will run on all parts which support those suites.

The set of event messages is open-ended. Parts developers can extend a suites set of messages, or define completely new suites. These extensions can remain proprietary, or can be registered with CI Labs.

The set of events for the suites beyond Required and Core is small. In most cases, the verbs from the Core suite are used with some of the semantics redefined. It is the Object specifiers for each suite which provide the real richness. Each suite has a hierarchy of objects on which it can act. The characteristics and attributes for each of the object specifiers is spelled out in the suite documentation. Making a Part Scriptable.

It is beyond the scope of this paper to give any kind of detailed discussion on how to script your application or part. There are some excellent documents and white papers on this subject available via anonymous ftp directly from CI Labs. The last section of this papers gives details for doing this. However, this section will try to give you a feel for what is involved and how your product can benefit from scripting

Figure 9 below shows the steps taken for a script to be generated, transmitted, acted upon, and information returned. A couple of key points can be made from this figure:.

- There are utility functions which are part of OpenDoc that help in:

  - building event records,

  - delivering event records,

  - and decomposing event records for action

- For each of the event messages that a part supports, it has registered a function that should be invoked - essentially a callback. This is also the mechanism by which it extends the set of event messages it understands. This is part of the Semantic Interface of OpenDoc.

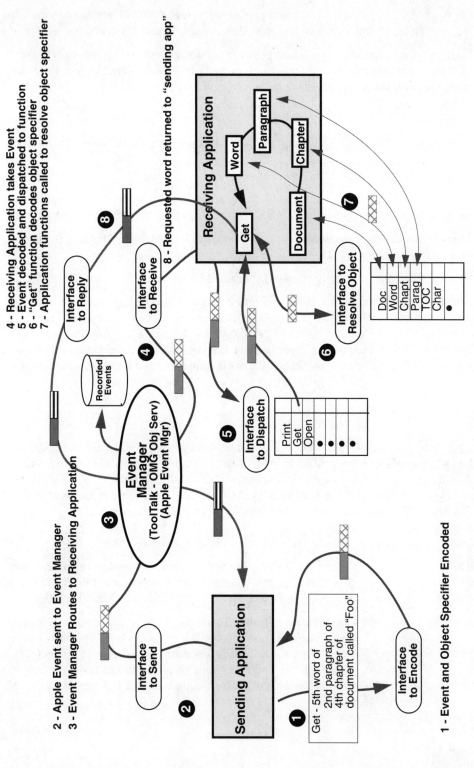

Figure 9: How Apple Events Work - Sorta

4 - Receiving Application takes Event
5 - Event decoded and dispatched to function
6 - "Get" function decodes object specifier
7 - Application functions called to resolve object specifier

8 - Requested word returned to "sending app"

2 - Apple Event sent to Event Manager
3 - Event Manager Routes to Receiving Application

1 - Event and Object Specifier Encoded

Get - 5th word of 2nd paragraph of 4th chapter of document called "Foo"

- For each of the object specifiers that a part supports, along with object descriptors, it has registered a set of functions which support them. Again, essentially callbacks.

- Complex object specifiers are decomposed in a outside-in or top-to-bottom fashion. At each step a reference to the acquired data is passed - first we find the file, then the chapter in the file, then the paragraph in the chapter in the file ...

The example used;

- get the 5th word of the second paragraph of the 4th chapter of the document called "foo"

perhaps looks somewhat contrived. But now consider this:

- That the sending application and the receiving application might be the same application, the application has been factored into a UI component and a data engine component.

- That the description of the example is a word selected by a user - highlighted, and is about to be put on the clipboard. Or perhaps is a hypertext reference.

- That the event message can be captured and stored (along with others) for future use.

- And that these stored events can be fed into a scripting interface, generalized as needed, and turned into usable scripts.

The main job for the developer then is to provide functions that support the event messages and object specifiers and to factor their application into a UI component and a Data Engine component.

SOM

SOM, or the system Object Model, is an object-oriented technology for building, packaging and manipulating binary class libraries. SOM is IBM's implementation of the OMG CORBA standard. All interfaces for OpenDoc objects are written as CORBA IDL interfaces. SOM is one of the technology components that is part of the CI Labs OpenDoc technology, and all four of the current OpenDoc reference implementations use SOM as their object request broker.

The following are some of the features and characteristics of SOM and CORBA:

OMG	Object Management Group. A consortium set up to standardize an object architecture. The three main components of that architecture are; an ORB, Object Services, and Common Object Facilities.
ORB	Object Request Broker. This is the entity which brokers all request one object makes on another. It is expected to transparently handle issues of location. It is also responsible for supporting object services such as creation/deletion, security etc. The OMG defined ORB is called CORBA for Common Object Request Broker Architecture.

IDL	Interface Definition Language - defined by OMG. This is how CORBA compliant objects are specified. It has a similar look-and-feel to C++. All OpenDoc interfaces are defined in IDL. IDL specified interfaces are converted to a target language via compilers for the implementation of CORBA. SOM has IDL compilers for both C++ and c with other languages such as Smalltalk in the works.
Object Services	These are the services needed to effectively work with objects. OMG is defining the interface and functionality of a set of services. Examples of objects services are; lifecycle - create, delete, security, object naming, notification, and persistence. SOM has a framework for adding object service functions. Customers can select the capabilities they need and plug them in.
Language Neutral	Because SOM sits in the middle of object transactions, objects written in one language can transparently make request on objects written in another language.
Binary Compatibility	SOM maintains binary compatibility between versions of class libraries. A binary class library such as OpenDoc shipped as a DLL can be upgraded and changed without requiring a recompile or link of applications using it.

ComponentGlue Technology - OpenDoc and OLE

Technology being developed by Word Perfect Corporation for CI Labs will allow OpenDoc parts and OLE parts to be seamlessly used in each others documents. This is accomplished by wrapping the parts with the appropriate object interfaces. This parts wrapper is called the ComponentGlue Technology or Component GT. This technology also supports the exposure of OSA enabled part handlers as an OLE automation interface. Figure 10 depicts the ComponentGlue technology. A similar approach is being produced by IBM and Taligent for the Talignet document framework.

This ability to interoperate with both OLE and Taligent makes OpenDoc an ideal development platform for providing parts for all three architectures. It will allow developers to extend the life of existing software products with quick port to OpenDoc, and a migration path to providing Taligent based products by incremental introduction of Taligent technology into their software base.

Where to Get More Information

The best source of information is directly from CI Labs. Documents; white papers, reference documents, and programmer guides, which cover all of the technologies are available via anonymous ftp from

- cilabs.org

Also, information along with subscribing to various CI Labs interest groups can be gotten directly from the CI Labs mail server. To find out how to get access, send a message to

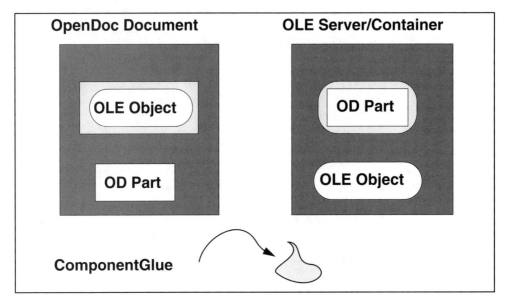

Figure 10: OpenDoc-OLE Interoperability - ComponentGlue Technology

- listsproc@cillabs.org.

In the body of the note, on a line by itself put the word "help". You will receive back a set of instructions. You must be able to receive internet mail to do this.

Developer CDs, Parts Kitchens and Beta Programs

Developer CDs, Parts Kitchens and beta programs are available by writing to:

- Macintosh - opendoc@applelink.apple.com
- Windows - opendoc@wordperfect.com
- OS/2 - 1-800-6DEVCON
- Unix (AIX) - opendoc@austin.ibm.com

Finally, if none of this works, drop me a line. I'm at:

- cnelson@austin.ibm.com

Author Information

Chris Nelson is an architect in IBM's AIX desktop group.

A Pseudo-Root Extension

X Window System Nesting on a Budget

Keith Packard[†]

Abstract

The notion of encapsulating a screen inside a sub-window has been around for a long time. Rob Pike's 'layers' went as far as possible; the only way to create nested windows was to run a new copy of the window system from within a window. Release 6 provided an X server which could do the same (Xnest). However, both of these suffer from performance problems as each client request must be delivered over two network connections and be interpreted by two window system servers. The X Window System provides for nested windows already, and has only a few references in the protocol to which window is the magic "root" of the window hierarchy on each screen. By changing which window appears to be the root in the context of a particular client, a full-speed window-system encapsulation has been achieved. Functionality to encapsulate additional global resources is also included.

Introduction

What is a Pseudo-Root?

In the most simplistic view, pseudo-roots attempt to provide the effect of a nested *window system* using nested *window* semantics. This is only possible where the underlying window system provides for nested windows; window systems like Pike's "layers" which don't provide for nested windows cannot provide pseudo-roots. Because a window system often manages resources other than the display (e.g. the keyboard and mouse), additional semantics may be required of the pseudo-root system to make the effective nesting workable.

[†]*Keith Packard (**keithp@ncd.com**) has been a member of the Network Computing Devices engineering staff since June 1992. Prior to that, he was the senior staff member at the X Consortium. He has worked with and participated in the design of much of the X Window System since early days of the X Consortium.*

What is a Pseudo-Root Good For?

Historically, one of the original goals in designing an X pseudo-root system was to allow for the debugging of window managers with a single display. However, window managers have a habit of grabbing devices or the server itself during execution. If such a grab was in place when the window manager hit a debugger breakpoint, the debugger might not be able to receive input from the user. This makes it impossible to continue the window manager to release the resource. Catch 22. The correct solution in this environment is the true window system encapsulation provided by Xnest.

Today, with X servers running in a wide variety of environments, including in cooperation with other window systems, there are new reasons to consider pseudo roots. The most basic is for applications which fail to work properly when presented with an extremely small screen. Typically these have been developed on X terminals or workstations and are being used on Mac or PC systems where the screen can be as small as 640x480. While it is easy to blame the application in this case, simply making the application believe it has a larger screen solves the problem easily.

Another case is in sophisticated user environments like HP Vue which "take over" the entire screen. Running these in a mixed window system environment can cause significant problems. E.g. HP Vue places a window at the bottom of the screen which can't be moved or resized. Both the Macintosh and MS Windows environments use the same area; the Mac places the trash can in the lower right corner while MS Windows 3.1 places application icons along the bottom of the screen. This real estate conflict can easily be solved by placing the entire Vue environment within a pseudo root, allowing it to be moved or even iconified en masse.

In debugging applications which perform complex color manipulations, it can be useful to provide a different set of Visuals to verify correct execution; most X servers provide the ability to change the root Visual class, but simply running the application inside a pseudo-root enables the developer to test many combinations in a much shorter time.

Pseudo roots have a place in some environments; that place has changed as the X window system has grown.

Origins of an X Pseudo Root System

The ICCCM DRAFT version of February 25th, 1988 [Rosenthal88] contains a description of a pseudo root mechanism which identified a window which was to be treated as the root window by clients. This mechanism used an addition to the DISPLAY environment variable to indicate a property on the real root of each screen which contained the information about the pseudo root. The extent of this convention was to change which window was returned by the RootWindow et al, and to change the results of the DisplayWidth/DisplayHeight to match the pseudo root.

Xlib was modified in August of 1988 to support this definition and this code was shipped in Release 3 of the X Window System from MIT in October of that year. Significant problems were discovered with this mechanism, the most obvious of which was that X events with encoded root-relative positions were being interpreted incorrectly by clients with the result that menus and dialog boxes would appear in strange places on the screen. In addition, the real-root window manager and pseudo-root window manager conflicted on some global resources (input focus and colormaps among others).

Discussions at the X Consortium resulted in the removal of the pseudo root conventions from the ICCCM and the removal of the pseudo root code from Xlib in March of 1989 with the realization that an X extension would be required to correctly implement a pseudo root system. Over five years have passed and the original language which introduced the pseudo-root ICCCM conventions remains behind; the conventions themselves having been replaced with a single phrase:

> Doing so properly requires an extension, the design of which is under study. [Scheifler92]

As the limitations of pseudo-roots, even in the presence of an extension to support them, became more evident, progress on a replacement for the ICCCM conventions ground to a halt. With the growing prevalence of window managers providing "virtual root" and "rooms" [Henderson86] functionality, the usefulness of pseudo-roots was further eroded making them seem like a quaint but out-moded idea.

Requirements for an X Pseudo Root System

To make a pseudo-root system work in the X window system, several problems must be solved.

- Identify and modify protocol references to the core root window.
- Manage conflicting demands between clients inside the pseudo root and outside.
- Provide a mechanism for selecting which pseudo root a particular client connects to.

The ICCCM conventions solved the last and part of the first of these problems. Selecting a pseudo root was done by augmenting the display name used to connect to the server. At connection setup time the information received by the server was edited to replace real root window information with pseudo root information.

A Pseudo Root Extension

Each of the requirements placed on the pseudo root extension were solved in different ways. In general, the changes were extremely minor and have no effect on rendering performance with minimal effect on overall performance. One significant advantage over the ICCCM based solution is that to operate correctly, the Pseudo Root Extension requires a cooperating Pseudo Root Manager client. This client is in charge of filling in parts of the illusion which can't be handled directly by the X server.

Disguising the Pseudo Root Window as the Root Window

References to the root window occur in only a few places in the protocol. Each case is handled by modifying the protocol data as seen by the pseudo root client.

Connection Setup Information

For each screen, the root window id, geometry and visual information must be replaced with the pseudo root information.

Replies which contain root-related information.

GetGeometry and QueryTree both return the root window id for the screen containing the specified window which can simply be replaced with the pseudo root window id. Additionally, QueryTree returns the parent window which, in the case of a pseudo root, must be replaced with None.

QueryPointer returns both the root window id and the current pointer position relative to that window. Replace the root window id with the pseudo root window id and adjust the position to be relative to the pseudo root window.

Requests which act differently for root windows

ChangeWindowAttributes modifies its behavior based on whether the window specified is a root window. Changing the Background to None or ParentRelative restores the default background. Changing the border to ParentRelative restores the default border. Changing the Cursor to None restores the default cursor. This request should has the same behavior for pseudo-root windows.

DestroyWindow, ConfigureWindow, and UnmapWindow are all ignored for the root window. Right now, the extension doesn't do this for pseudo root windows, but it would be easy to add.

GrabPointer returns NotViewable for windows beyond the edge of the root window; the extension doesn't currently augment these semantics to use the pseudo-root instead.

Events which contain root-related information

Keyboard and pointer events all contain root window ids which are replaced with the pseudo root id and root-relative position information which is modified to be relative to the pseudo root.

More obscure is that FocusIn/FocusOut events delivered to children of a pseudo-root must not receive detail Ancestor or Virtual when the focus is moving to or from an ancestor of the pseudo-root window. These details are rewritten as Nonlinear and NonlinearVirtual respectively so that it appears that the focus moved to or from a different screen.

Global Resource Contention

X contains many global shared resources, from grabs on devices or the server, to input focus and the list of installed colormaps. Device and server grabs are usually transient, so the extension ignores them. The keyboard focus window and installed colormaps are not transient and must be handled by the system.

Keyboard Focus Contention

Managing the focus between pseudo-root clients and other clients is handled completely within the pseudo root manager. Problems arise only when the window manager within the pseudo root uses explicit focus while the core window manager is using PointerRoot. In this case, the pseudo root window manager will not release focus to other core clients. In other cases, the core and pseudo root window manager cooperate without intervention from the pseudo root manager.

When the pseudo root window receives input focus, it records whether it received focus from the core window manager or whether it was taken by a pseudo root client. If the focus was taken by a pseudo root client, and not given by the core window manager, the pseudo root manager assumes that the focus was originally PointerRoot. In this case, when the pointer leaves the pseudo root window, the pseudo root manager resets the focus to PointerRoot.

Colormap Contention

Unlike keyboard focus, colormaps must be managed by every window manager. This means that the pseudo root manager can make strong assumptions about the capabilities of the enclosing core window manager, in particular, it can assume that the core window manager will install whatever colormap it wants as long as it uses ICCCM conventions to specify that colormap.

When a pseudo root client makes an InstallColormap request, the extension redirects that request to the pseudo root manager and takes no other action. The pseudo root manager then simply configures its colormap conventions to indicate which colormap is desired for the pseudo root window itself, and lets the enclosing window manager handle the rest.

A small complexity is added when the colormap doesn't match the visual for the pseudo root itself. In this case, the pseudo root manager uses one of its own windows with the appropriate visual type and indicates that window to the enclosing window manager.

Starting a Pseudo Root Client

This extension wouldn't be nearly as useful if it required client-side cooperation in selecting a pseudo root window to attach to. Therefore, selecting a pseudo root must only use information already presented by the client to the X server.

One piece of information presented to the X server is which display number the client used when connecting to the display. For each screen, one pseudo or real root window is dynamically associated with each display number. When a client connects to the server, the display number is used to select the set of real/pseudo root windows for each screen. The server was modified to accept client connections using multiple display numbers so that multiple pseudo or real roots could accept clients at the same time. Here's some example code which uses this functionality:

```
/* Create a pseudo root associated with a window */
XPRootCreate (display, pseudoRootWindow);
/* Create a new listening address and get a new display number */
pseudoRootDisplay = XPRootListen (dpy);
/* Attach the pseudo root window to the returned display */
XPRootAttachDisplay (dpy, pseudoRootWindow, pseudoRootDisplay);
```

Clients connecting to <hostname>:<pseudoRootDisplay> will have pseudoRootWindow as their root on that screen. Other screens may use either the core root window, or some other pseudo root. To use the core listening address, use PseudoRootListenCore instead of creating a new listening address. When a pseudo root attaches to a listening address, an event is sent to whatever pseudo root is currently attached to that address for that screen.

Conclusions

This extension grew out of the combination of customers demanding support for intransigent applications and a desire to create something more generally useful than simply encapsulating the entire X window system within a window of the enclosing window system. By implementing pseudo-roots, the system needn't be reconfigured when operating such applications. Better behaved applications can be run at the same time using the real root window.

Providing server side support for pseudo roots has allowed a much more complete illusion of window system encapsulation than was possible with a client side approach; the technique of redirecting some requests (colormap installation) made it possible to get full performance for most operations, and only inflict a speed penalty occasionally.

The pseudo root extension is not a replacement for Xnest. Xnest provides a complete encapsulation, including device and server grabs. Moreover, Xnest is the easiest environment in which to develop extensions (like this one) and other server code.

However, for the class of problems presented by our customers, a pseudo root system is clearly the better alternative, providing full-performance encapsulation along with cut & paste between all applications on the screen.

References

[Henderson86]   D. Austin Henderson, Jr. and Stuart K. Card, *Rooms: The Use of Multiple Virtual Workspaces to Reduce Space Contention in a Window-Based Graphical User Interface*, ACM Transactions on Graphics, July 1986, Vol. 5, Number 3 page 211-243.

[Rosenthal88]   David S. H. Rosenthal, *Inter-Client Communication Conventions Manual DRAFT 25th February 1988*, Included in the X Window System Release 3, 1988.

[Scheifler92]   Robert W. Scheifler and James Gettys, *X Window System*, Digital Press, 1992.

Teleporting

Mobile X Sessions

Tristan Richardson[†]

Abstract

This paper examines issues involved in making an X session mobile. A *mobile X session* is one which is not fixed to a particular X display, but can be materialised on demand at any suitable display. The *Teleporting System* developed at Olivetti Research Laboratory (ORL) is a tool for experiencing mobile X sessions. It provides a familiar, personalised way of making temporary use of X displays as the user moves from place to place. When linked to location facilities such as those provided by the Olivetti Active Badge[‡] System the traditional log-in process can be almost entirely eliminated, allowing the nomadic user to easily make use of computing resources which are to hand.

Introduction

Traditional interaction with character-based terminals has taken the form of a session where the user "logs in" by entering a user-id and password, interacts with applications one at a time from the command line, and eventually "logs out" to end the session. Workstations using a windowing system such as X have extended this traditional session to allow the user to interact with multiple applications at the same time, each being displayed in a different window. However, the process of logging in and out has remained largely the same.

When the user runs a number of applications there is a considerable amount of state involved in a session. It is unrealistic to expect a user to log out every time the workstation is left temporarily. Users tend to stay logged in to a workstation for long periods of time, often for a whole day and sometimes for several days or weeks.

[†]*Tristan Richardson (trichardson@cam-orl.co.uk) is a Research Engineer at Olivetti Research Laboratory, Cambridge, England.*

[‡]*Active Badge is a registered trademark of Ing. C. Olivetti & C., S.p.A.*

Making temporary use of a workstation where someone else is logged in can be a problem. It can be considered antisocial to interfere with another user's session, and interacting with another's session is likely to be frustrating since the applications will be running as the wrong user-id and will be configured in a way which is unfamiliar. Logging the original user out before logging oneself in is likely to be considered antisocial as well, because it loses the state inherent in the original user's session.

In an environment where people are mobile, portable computers are one way of accessing computing resources, but they will always be restricted due to size, weight and power considerations. A relatively unexplored alternative is to facilitate the temporary use of workstations and other equipment which is to hand. In X, one obvious way of making this possible is via a mobile X session, which is not fixed to a particular X display, but can be materialised on demand at any suitable display.

Related work

One way of appearing to move an X session from one display to another is to shut down the session on the original display, and start up a session with the same clients in the same state on a new display. This could be achieved in X with the help of a special client known as a "session manager".

The purpose of the session manager is to record the state inherent in a session in such a way that the clients can be restarted in the same state. Using a special protocol it tells clients when the session is about to be shut down so that they can save their state. Previously this has been attempted using the ""WM_SAVE_YOURSELF" protocol of the ICCCM. Release 6 of X has introduced a new "Session Management Protocol" as an attempt to rectify the deficiencies in the old protocol. However, the vast majority of existing clients use neither of these protocols. Furthermore, even if clients are written which participate in the session management protocol, there may be aspects of a client's state which are difficult or impossible to save. For example there is no way of "saving" the state of a unix process which has pipes or sockets connected to other processes.

In general, the only way to avoid losing the state of a client when moving an X session is not to shut down the client at all. Instead the client must be able to close its connection with one server, connect to the new server, create all its windows and other server resources as before, and so continue where it left off on the original server.

There have been attempts to develop such "mobile applications" in X. Trestle [Manasse93] and XTk [Jacobi92] are both toolkits designed for the development of applications whose windows are redirectable between displays. Interesting new applications can be developed using such a toolkit, but clearly this approach cannot be used to add mobility to existing, unaltered applications.

In order to make existing applications mobile without alteration, a different approach is required. This is to put a level of indirection between the client and the real server, called a *proxy server* (also called a pseudoserver).

Proxy servers are not a new idea. Many have been written in order to duplicate an application's output on to multiple displays [Abdel-Wahab91] [Altenhofen90]. However, these are not directly applicable to client mobility. They all use one X server as a "master" server to which the clients must remain connected throughout their lifetime. There is no way in which this connection for a client can be closed without shutting down the client.

More recently, new proxy servers have been developed specifically for the purpose of application mobility. These include our "teleporting" proxy X server, *tpproxy* [Richardson94], and *xmove* [Solomita94]. These two proxy servers are in many ways very similar, but there are some important design goals in xmove which make it unsuitable as a basis for making X sessions mobile.

Xmove is designed specifically for moving clients on an individual basis. Although one instance of xmove can cope with several clients, it deals with each client separately, not as a coherent session with a root window and a window manager.

Much effort has gone into making a client running through xmove appear on the real X server just as it would without xmove. Private protocols for communication between clients running through xmove and clients running directly on the real X server (needed for features like drag-and-drop) must be understood and translated by xmove. This means that each time new inter-client protocols are developed, an extension to xmove must be written which understands the protocol. This is unnecessary when one considers a mobile X session as a whole.

The Olivetti Teleporting System

The teleporting system's main component is *tpproxy*, a proxy X server for making X sessions mobile. A mobile X session running through tpproxy is called a *teleport session*. Tpproxy acts more like a real X server than other proxy servers. It has its own root window, on which the windows of its clients can be placed under the control of a window manager.

Normally, tpproxy behaves as a filter, much like other proxy servers. It takes requests from its clients, translates them and sends them on to the real server, and in the reverse direction takes replies, events, and error packets from the server and sends them on to the appropriate client. While doing this, tpproxy also records all changes to the state inside the server relevant to its clients. When told to materialise the teleport session on a new server, tpproxy can generate requests to the new server to bring up to date the state of each of its clients as seen by the new server. Most of the issues involved in this have been covered elsewhere [Chung91] [Richardson94] [Solomita94].

When told to dematerialise, tpproxy disconnects from the real server. It continues to process requests from its clients, and for most requests, simply records any state changes before discarding the request. For some requests, however, the client needs a response from the real server. A client which issues such a request while the teleport session is dematerialised will be suspended, and no more requests from that client will be processed until the session is rematerialised on a real X server.

Security

Authorisation for connection by a client to tpproxy is just the same as for any X server, using the normal authorisation mechanisms, the "host list", and the "magic cookie" scheme. Clients which are in tpproxy's host list, or which provide the correct value of the magic cookie are allowed to connect to tpproxy, while any others are rejected.

A separate and more difficult problem is how tpproxy is given authorisation to access real X servers. Within ORL this is achieved by running tpproxy as a special privileged user-id which has access to the magic cookies for all real X displays at ORL. This scheme clearly does not scale outside a single administrative domain. For teleporting to displays at other sites a different scheme is needed whereby the cookie for the real display is passed to tpproxy just before it connects to the display. Further research is needed to find a secure way in which permission to connect to an X display can be given temporarily to visitors from other sites.

Integration with the underlying X session

The teleport session's root window appears as a normal client window on the real X server, decorated in the usual way by the window manager in the underlying X session. Each of tpproxy's clients' windows appear as subwindows of this "pseudo-root window", controlled by the window manager running in the teleport session. This is much like the Virtual Screen program [Lin92].

If no window manager is running on the real X server, the teleport session's root window simply covers the whole screen. This most commonly occurs when no-one is logged in and the XDM login window is showing. In this case tpproxy must also unmap the XDM login window to release XDM's keyboard grab.

Another aspect of integration with the underlying X session is how inter-client communication is affected. Because tpproxy deals with an X session as a whole, it is usually only necessary to consider inter-client communication between clients of the same proxy X server. Any private protocols between these clients need not be understood by the proxy server in the same way that they need not be understood by a real X server.

In general, inter-client communication will not work between a client in the underlying session and a client in the teleport session. One reason for this is that the space of identifiers for server resources as seen by a client of the proxy server is different from that seen by a direct client of the real server. Any private protocol in which these clients exchange resource identifiers is likely to fail. One important exception to this rule is the normal selection mechanism, which is part of the X protocol. Thus cutting and pasting of text between a client in a teleport session and a client in the underlying session works in the normal way.

Keyboard personalisation

In a normal X session, users can personalise the keyboard according to their preference by altering the keyboard (and modifier) mapping[†]. This facility should also be provided in a mobile X session. Tpproxy achieves this by keeping two different keyboard mappings, one for the teleport session, and one for the underlying session running on the real server. When the input focus enters the teleport session's root window, tpproxy saves the mapping for the underlying session and installs the mapping for the teleport session. Similarly, the teleport session's mapping is saved and the underlying session's mapping installed when the input focus leaves the teleport session's root window.

[†]*Users can also customise the pointer mapping, key-click, auto-repeat, etc, but no users of the teleporting system have found these to be important.*

Because a keyboard mapping is specific to a physical X display, it makes no sense to copy the keyboard mapping when the teleport session is moved to a new real X server. What tpproxy does upon materialisation is to copy the default keyboard mapping for the real X server to be the starting point for the teleport session's mapping. The user can then modify the teleport session's mapping as desired, completely isolated from the mapping in the underlying session. A mechanism is provided by which these modifications to the keyboard mapping can be automatically applied upon materialisation, so that for a given display, the keyboard is always personalised to the user's preference.

Display heterogeneity

X servers have a wide variety of characteristics such as screen size, depth and framebuffer format, which are exposed to the client. Tpproxy has to present a view to all its clients of the kind of X server it is, and maintain this consistently, even when the underlying real X server has substantially different characteristics. We review some of the problems this causes and the solutions which tpproxy adopts, some of which are only partial solutions.

Screen size

Screen width and height vary greatly between different X servers. When the teleport session is moved from a large display to a smaller one, obviously not all of the root window can be visible at once[†]. The teleporting system provides two solutions to this, both of which treat the window on the real X server as a "viewport" on to tpproxy's root window. This viewport is similar to the facilities offered by "virtual desktop" window managers such as *tvtwm* (available in the contributed software section of R5 and R6).

The first solution involves running a special window manager called *tpwm* which is a version of tvtwm, modified to be aware of the possible resizing of the viewport. The disadvantage of this solution is that it forces the user to adopt a particular window manager. Since most users at ORL use a twm-like window manager (tvtwm is based on twm), this has been found to be the best solution.

The second solution allows the use of any window manager, and effectively adds virtual desktop functionality by the use of a special client called *tpviewport*. The disadvantage of this approach is that there is a potential conflict between the window manager and tpviewport, especially if the window manager already has a virtual desktop feature.

Colour handling

Colour handling is one area where the X protocol exposes a lot of detail about the server to the client. There is a wide variety of possible combinations of framebuffer depth and mapping of pixel values to colours on the screen. Tpproxy's solution to these problems is a compromise which we have found to cope satisfactorily with nearly all clients. However there will always be clients which cause problems when teleporting to monochrome servers and servers which do not allow writable colormaps.

[†]*The same problem occurs when tpproxy's root window is managed by the underlying window manager and the window is resized.*

The current version of tpproxy normally tells its clients it is an 8-bit "StaticColor" server, meaning that it has a read-only colormap. If the real server also has a read-only colormap, then all pixel values must be translated between the client and the server. This means that functions such as exclusive-or on pixel values may not work as the client expects. In addition, image data has to be translated a pixel at a time, which can be somewhat time-consuming.

If the real server allows writable colormaps then tpproxy will normally install its own colormap so that functions such as exclusive-or on pixel values may be freely performed. If the server happens to also be an 8-bit server then image data can be passed through untranslated, virtually removing any performance problem.

Controlling The Teleporting System

There are two issues in controlling where a mobile X session is displayed. Only the correct user must be able to control the teleport session, so some sort of authentication is needed. Secondly, the user must somehow specify which X display the teleport session should appear on. The proxy server offers a textual command-line interface which meets these requirements. In addition, its integration with the location facilities developed at ORL provides a simpler and richer interface.

The command-line interface

The command-line interface to the proxy server offers one single command, `teleport`. This command is used to initialize a teleport session, as well as control its materialisation to, and de-materialisation from, any X display within the building. The `teleport` command can be executed from within another user's session by quoting a user name and password. However, finding a suitable terminal window in the other user's session may not always be trivial. A preferable approach to controlling the teleport session is not to have to interfere with the underlying session at all.

The automated control interface

Integration with the Active Badge Location System [Want92] [Harter94] has introduced a level of automation to the teleporting procedure, making it much easier to make temporary use of X displays.

The Active Badge System provides a means of locating individuals and equipment within a building. Personnel and equipment wear a small infra-red transmitting *Active Badge*, which has a unique identity. With a networked infra-red receiver in each room, the Active Badge System creates a dynamic database describing the location of individuals and equipment within the building. The teleporting system uses this database to determine which X displays are co-located with a particular individual.

In addition, the Active Badge can be used as a control mechanism. One of two small buttons on the badge is used to select an appropriate X server within the room, and the other is used to confirm the selection and materialise the user's teleport session.

The badge acts as the required authentication mechanism, since it has a unique identity, and is generally worn by its owner at all times. An additional security feature is that when a user leaves a room in which they have teleported, the teleporting system can automatically dematerialise their teleport session without any action by the user.

Conclusion

The original goal of the teleporting system, to add mobility to X sessions based on existing X applications, has been achieved. The system is in everyday use and for many users has completely replaced the standard log-in session.

The main feature of the teleporting system is that by using a proxy server it makes existing applications mobile, without the application being aware of any redirection. However, it has also provided a framework for experimenting with new applications which are aware of their own mobility. The first of these to be developed were tpwm and tpviewport, described earlier, which adapt to the screen size of the real display. Further ways of adapting to a smaller screen have been devised, including the ability to automatically iconify particular windows, and to reduce the font size for text windows.

Using the Active Badge database, mobile applications can be aware not only of the properties of the X display they are materialised on, but also of the surrounding environment. For example, applications can send documents to a "virtual" printer, which will automatically print the document on the user's nearest printer. Another simple example is a "display selector" tool which shows a menu of all the X displays in the same room and can be used to redirect the teleport session between them.

Teleporting is an important example of a nomadic style of working using an infrastructure of static resources. In a suitably-equipped environment, a mobile user need not be constrained by the limitations of equipment that can be carried. Instead, more powerful, networked computing devices can be used in a way that is familiar and personalised for the needs of each user.

References

[Abdel-Wahab91]   Hussein M Abdel-Wahab and Mark A Feit. *XTV: A Framework for Sharing X Window Clients in Remote Synchronous Collaboration.* Proceedings of IEEE TriComm 91: Communications for Distributed Applications & Systems, Chapel Hill, North Carolina, April 1991.

[Altenhofen90]   Michael P Altenhofen. *Erweiterung eines Fenstersystems für Tutoring-Funktionen.* Diploma Thesis, Universität Karlsruhe, Karlsruhe, Germany, 1990.

[Chung91]   Goopeel Chung, Kevin Jeffay and Hussein M Abdel-Wahab. *Accommodating late-comers in a distributed system for synchronous collaboration.* Technical report TR91-038, Department of Computer Science, University of North Carolina at Chapel Hill, October 1991.

[Harter94]   Andy Harter and Andy Hopper. *A Distributed Location System for the Active Office.* IEEE Network, Special Issue on Distributed Systems for Telecommunications, January 1994.

[Jacobi92]   Christian P Jacobi. *Migrating Widgets*. Proceedings of the 6th Annual X Technical Conference, January 1992.

[Lin92]   Jin-Kun Lin. *Virtual Screen: A Framework for Task Management*. Proceedings of the 6th Annual X Technical Conference, January 1992.

[Manasse93]   Mark S Manasse. *The Trestle Toolkit*. Proceedings of the 7th Annual X Technical Conference, January 1993.

[Richardson94]   Tristan Richardson, Frazer Bennett, Glenford Mapp and Andy Hopper. *Teleporting in an X Window System Environment*. IEEE Personal Communications Magazine, Third Quarter 1994.

[Solomita94]   Ethan Solomita, James Kempf and Dan Duchamp. *XMOVE: A Pseudoserver For X Window Movement*. The X Resource, Issue 11, O'Reilly & Associates Inc, July 1994.

[Want92]   Roy Want, Andy Hopper, Veronica Falcao and Jonathan Gibbons. *The Active Badge Location System*. ACM Transactions on Information Systems, January 1992.

k-Edit: a communication library built on ICE

Anselm Baird-Smith

Philippe Kaplan [†]

Abstract

A common misuse of the X environment consists in private inter-client communication via the X server [Marks94]. The distribution of X11R6 comes with ICE, an inter client exchange library. ICE offers a low-level communication package, but lacks the power and the simplicity of an X property-like mechanism.

We present here an all-purpose communication package built on top of ICE, named k-Edit. It enables point-to-point communication between two X clients without the help of the X server. In particular, we present a solution for the rendez-vous problem, i.e. how to initialize the communication.

Introduction

The X server has been intensively used to provide private communications between X clients, because of its central place in UNIX workstation software architecture.

The 6th release of X11 comes with the Inter Client Exchange library (ICE), which provides a low-level application programming interface to the transport level of protocols. Nevertheless one still needs to define an exchange protocol and some encoding rules in order to offer the same communication facilities as X.

In the following we present *k-Edit*, an all-purpose protocol implemented on top of ICE. *k-Edit* allows any process to export information and provide notification through client events. We describe first the *k-Edit* package, then how to achieve inter-client communications with high-level interfaces.

[†]*Philippe Kaplan (Philippe.Kaplan@sophia.inria.fr) is a research engineer and Anselm Baird-Smith (Anselm.BairdSmith@inria.fr) is a PhD student; at Koala project, Groupe Bull, France. They are hosted at the French national research institute in computer science (INRIA).*

Presentation of k-Edit

The *k-Edit* package consists of a *small* communication library implementing a fixed protocol, and is based on a client/server architecture. Application programmers can export their application states through *k-Edit* for remote access or monitoring purposes. The underlying protocol itself is not dedicated to a specific domain, but we have already developed several applications on top of it in order to validate our concept. Figure 1 describes how *k-Edit* is embedded in an application.

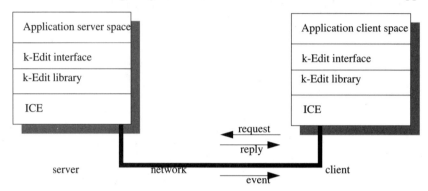

Figure 1: k-edit architecture

There is a balance to strike here, between the *genericity* of the protocol and the *interoperability* between clients and servers. One of our major guidelines while designing the protocol was the ability to write generic clients (i.e., clients that are able to dialog with any *k-Edit* server). This implies that servers must provide a description — at some level — of how clients access them. We have developed applications, like an *Xt interface* allowing graphical applications to export their widget states (an enhanced Editres); a *mpeg* film server, etc. Although all those servers are supposed to work with specific clients matching their semantics, we created one "universal" client compatible with any k-Edit servers at a low level.

k-Edit is composed of the following three parts:

- *The protocol specification* defines the list of requests, replies, and events the protocol understands. This component is language independent, like the X protocol.

- *The client side library* for the C language provides a C application programming interface to the protocol.

- *The server side library* for the C language provides a C application programming interface to answer to protocol requests, and to send notification events.

The protocol

The protocol is designed around the concept of **node**. We introduce it here, and present the protocol requests, replies, and events.

Nodes

A node encapsulates an information entity exported through *k-Edit*. On the server side, nodes represent any kind of information: data, callbacks, etc. On the client side, nodes provide the needed handles pointing toward the information exported by the server.

The protocol itself only deals with *node identifiers*. An identifier represents the same node for all the clients.

All nodes are described through the following set of attributes:

- A *name* (any 8bit ASCII string) which provides a user-friendly description of the node,
- A *mode* which indicates the type of request it supports (i.e., read, write, exec.),
- A *mask* which indicates what kind of notification the server supports for it,
- A *size* representing the size of the node value (if any),
- An optional *info* node, which typically gives the type of the node (see below).

Nodes are arranged in graphs inside a server: a node can have a list of child nodes (such a node is named *directory*). For example, servers exporting complex data might have one *directory* containing all the attributes describing the complex data, e.g. [Cohen93].

Protocol synopsis: requests

The protocol defines a small number of "primitive" requests, that can be divided into three classes: inspecting the server, accessing exported data, and monitoring data changes. Requests are summarized in Table 1. All of them may trigger appropriate error events when they can not be satisfied.

Request type	signature	function
Ls	node -> node list	fetch the children of a node
Stat	node -> attributes	fetch the attributes of a node
Get	node -> value	fetch the content of the node
Set	node, value -> ()	store a new content into a node
Exec	node -> ()	execute the action related to the node
Notify	node -> ()	change the mask of notification for the client that issues this request

Table 1: k-Edit client request description

1. Inspecting the server

A client that wants to communicate with a k-Edit server needs to know the nodes it can reach, and to be able to retrieve the node attributes described above.

An *Ls request* on a node identifier retreives the list of node identifiers representing the child nodes. All *k-Edit* servers export a *root-node* whose identifier is given at connection time. The *Stat request* allows a client to fetch the node attributes.

Ls and *Stat* are dissociated to save network traffic: nodes are shareable and the structure of the graph might change, even if node attributes remain constant.

At first glance, this inspection scheme seems inefficient by incurring a large number of round trips with the target server. However requests are bufferized. The number of network round trips needed for inspection of a tree structure is proportional to the depth of the tree (depending on buffer sizes).

2. Accessing exported data

The *Get request* retrieves the content of a node. This content is, at the protocol level, a stream of bytes. The *Set request* sets a node content with the provided value.

The protocol supports a last access means: it defines the *Exec request* to execute a given node.

The semantics associated with these three requests are only suggested. A server can associate some actions with a *Set request*. However *Get*, *Set*, and *Exec* have different signatures. Actually a single request (i.e. *Access*: node, value -> value) is enough to fulfil the same functionalities, but tests revealed it was less pleasant to use.

3. Monitoring node changes

The last request, *Notify*, allows a client to express interest in node state changes. A mask argument describes the operations the client is interested in (each client has its own mask for a given node). Masks are defined for the following set of events:

- node creation and destruction,
- node set, get, or exec access,
- node notification request from other clients.

To help synchronizing clients, events may carry the new content of the node.

Implementation architecture
Layers

The general architecture of *k-Edit* servers is depicted in Figure 1. Starting at the bottom, the *transport* layer (ICE) deals with low level network communication. Above, the raw *k-Edit* server library has two purposes:

- maintaining the database of created nodes, and registering client notification masks,
- decoding requests, dispatching them to upper layers, and encoding the replies.

Interfaces represent the upper *k-Edit* layer. They usually map objects to nodes using some conventions and present to the programmer a higher level interface than the raw node hierarchy.

On the client side the layers offer a programming interface to the protocol requests.

Node implementation

Nodes are defined in the server by an unique identifier and a callback set (corresponding to the requests allowed on the node). A node actually does not contain a value by itself. When a client requires a node value, the *k-Edit* server side invokes the callback that returns the value of the node, and sends it back to the client. This principle applies to the other requests, too. This is why *k-Edit* does not memorize the node graph structure: indeed the server controls the node hierarchy via the "ls" callbacks, which returns the children of a given node. Nodes are usually created "by need" (in response to *Ls requests*), so *k-Edit* saves memory and does not slow down the application at start-up time.

Managing typed content

General interoperability between clients and servers requires a way to describe node content encoding. As we wanted to keep the API simple, and still provide a pragmatic solution, we have implemented the following scheme:

Servers can convey in the *info* attribute of nodes any arbitrary node to clients. The info attribute advertises how the server encodes the node. For example, if a server exports an integer as a *CARD32*, the corresponding node will have the info attribute referencing an encoder node named "CARD32". Servers may define new encoders. For the sake of simplicity, clients can not negociate the encoding rules (i.e., the info attribute) with the server at the protocol level.

However, a server can implement a conversion mechanism with a separate hierarchy of nodes. An example is shown in Figure 2. The letters d,r,w,x respectively means the node has children, is

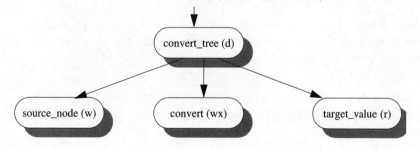

Figure 2: An exemple of type conversion

readable, is writable, is executable. If a client needs to turn the content of node "color" (an X Pixel) into a value of type "RGB_name", it issues the following (symbolic) requests once it has retrieved the node list via "ls" requests:

```
set (source_node, color)
set (convert, RGB_name)
exec (convert)
get (target_value)
```

The `exec` request invokes a server callback that reads the "source_node" and "convert" values, does the conversion and puts the result to the node "target_value". The last request returns the converted value.

This example shows off the genericity of the node approach. The protocol allows only basic operations, but *ad-hoc* node hierarchies can solve very complex problems (like type conversion, atomicity, concurrent access, etc.).

The Xt interface

As an example of *k-Edit* usage, we describe our proposed package for an enhanced Editres (this subject has been discussed actively for a year on the `x-agent@x.org` mailing list).

The *Xt interface* provides the glue between the Xt Object Model and the *k-Edit* server library. It allows graphical applications built on top of this toolkit (e.g. Motif or Athena) to export their graphical states. *Editres* [Peterson91] opened the door of remote edition allowing *external agents* to inspect application graphical states and to set widget resources. People interested in providing blind people with access to graphical UI have also worked on this topic[†] [Mercator93]. The Xt interface to *k-Edit* allows more operations than *Editres* to be performed on the edited application, these include:

- to *get* and *monitor* the value of widget resources[‡].
- to *trigger* widget actions and callbacks execution.
- to be *notified* when a widget action is executed.

The Xt interface maps the concept of *widget hierarchy* and *widget resources* into the *k-Edit* concept of *nodes*. This is very easily achieved by having one *directory* node per widget which contains one node per child widget, plus two nodes:

resources
is a directory containing one node per widget resource. Depending on the resource type, the node is readable, writable and/or executable (i.e., callbacks).

actions
is a directory containing one node per widget action. To trigger an action, just set the corresponding node to the argument list provided to the real action.

This mapping is just an example of what can be done. There are still a lot of open issues here, such as how the value of resource should be encoded. Actually this is not a *k-Edit* matter, but rather a question of how to deal with Xt resource values: should they all be strings, for example.

Nodes are cheap enough to make this mapping possible: the total memory cost of exporting one widget is approximately 40 bytes. This cost is paid only when a client inspects the application.

[†]*This thread is currently discussed in the mailing-list* `x-agent@x.org`.

[‡]*Unfortunately, the Xt interface does not benefit yet from the new hook facilities available in the X11R6 Xt.*

Existing applications just need to call a single function in order to be able to export their state (like *Editres*). There is an enhanced *Editres* (the X client) in the *k-Edit* distribution.

The Struct interface

The *Struct* interface builds a node hierarchy from a C *struct* value. The application provides *accessors*, which are functions to get and set the different fields of the structure. The Struct interface knows some default accessors for the basic types. This set of accessors is extensible, though.

Using this interface, the application only needs to define a *StructClass* which specifies the field names and the accessors corresponding to the C structure. Then the application declares to the *k-Edit* server layer the *StructClass* instances it exports. Clients are then able to consult the different fields of the exported structure.

The Rendez-vous problem

Goals & motivations

A well-known problem of communication is how to initiate it (the rendez-vous problem). One must be aware that the rendez-vous problem is inherent to all communication schemes. Lots of solutions exist, like a simple file containing host and port references, the portmapper (for RPC protocols) and, more recently, the message bus approach. In the X world, various *ad-hoc* solutions rely on X properties (e.g. the Tcl/Tk clients register their interpreter on a property located on the root window), or on X client messages (e.g., *Editres*).

We discuss here a more general mechanism which holds also outside the X world.

Description

It is fairly easy to build on top of *k-Edit* a simple rendez-vous server, whose role is to register server descriptions and to manage client connections. This server is bound at some fixed network address, making any clients capable of contacting it easily with the help of an environment variable.

The description of registered servers benefits from *k-Edit* structuring facilities. A new server sends its description, i.e. the services it provides and the protocols it understands, to the rendez-vous server. A client willing to use a specific service contacts the rendez-vous server, acquires the list of registered servers, examines their descriptions to select the one that proposes the best match with its needs.

There are two main advantages to this approach. First, it clearly separates the mechanism to be used (i.e., nodes representing server descriptions), from the conventions (i.e., syntax and semantics of these descriptions). The second point is that the client looking for the service does the matching, not the rendez-vous server. The system is clearly open to new extensions.

Now, the difficult part is to define the conventions to be used on top of this mechanism.

Conventions

Defining conventions on top of properties to solve the rendez-vous problem in its generality is quite difficult. Our proposition here should be considered only as a starting point.

A minimal server description consists of:

- The list of services it provides. The node name gives the service type, the node value completes the service description.

- The list of the protocols the server understands for each service. In term of nodes, protocols appear as children of services. The name gives the protocol type, and the value holds the access reference for the protocol.

For example, an X application understanding *Editres* and linked with *k-Edit* declares itself to the rendez-vous server. Its description contains an "Editable" service, with protocols "Editres" and "k-Edit". The values of the two protocol nodes are respectively the window ID of the toplevel window, and *k-Edit* network identifier of the application. An editres-like client may then contact the rendez-vous server to convert the window identifier (obtained through a mouse click) to the k-Edit network identifier. Then editres can establish the communication with the application without consuming X server resources.

We already have implemented a prototype of such a rendez-vous server, with a client library defining an API to directly get the list of available servers and their descriptions.

An example

As a concrete example, let us consider how *TkSend* could be replaced with *k-Edit*, and the advantages and disadvantages of such an approach. This example reflects typically the use of the X server to achieve private communication between two X clients. *TkSend* enables remote evaluation of Tcl scripts between Tcl/Tk applications. The *TkSend* mechanism has two parts:

interpreter registration
    At creation time, interpreter registration solves the rendez-vous problem by using an X property on the root window to hold the list of currently running Tcl/Tk interpreters.

the *send* command itself
    It sends an expression to be evaluated by another Tcl/Tk application via an X property on the target application window.

This mechanism works well and is simple but has several drawbacks:

- Registration requires to grab the X server while updating this property, to protect it against concurrent access.

- Interpreters might exit without the opportunity to remove themselves from the list.

- TkSend consumes X server resources.

- TkSend uses the same data stream as the X protocol, hence the need for some synchronization code to manage the send-related part extracted from the normal X protocol.

All these drawbacks vanish when redesigning *TkSend* with *k-Edit*. *K-Edit* benefits also from a more precise description of the services offered by interpreters. The cost remains:

- a rendez-vous server running all the time,

- another opened socket toward the rendez-vous server for each client. Today we are currently looking for a connectionless mechanism.

We do not advocate the use of *k-Edit* to reimplement *TkSend*. We just want to point out that there exists a different communication means to achieve the same functionalities more cleanly.

Conclusion

The X Consortium has always marked its will to dissuade programmers from using the X environment as the transport layer for private communications (see [Scheifler93]). The ICE library represents a step in this direction. Our work completes the gap opened by ICE to reach a level that offers at least an equivalent ease of use than the X communication facilities. Staying outside the X world, *k-Edit* enables also communication for processes that are not X clients.

We proposed in this paper a solution to the rendez-vous problem, inherent to all communication systems. The rendez-vous server seems expensive, but unavoidable.

K-Edit is still under development. The protocol, after two revisions, is now stable. We are now working on the ability to transfer node content incrementally, to read large values.

The current implementation of k-Edit is available via anonymous ftp on:

```
avahi.inria.fr:/pub/K-Edit/k-Edit-1.0.2.tar.gz.
```

The packages contain:

- Client and Server libraries,
- Xt and Struct interfaces,
- sample clients and servers.

References

[Cohen93]   Ellis S. Cohen, "Describing Formats For X-based Data Interchange", The X Resource, Issue 5, Winter 93.

[Marks94]   Stuart W. Marks "Inter-Client Communication In X11R6 and Beyond", The X Resource, Issue 9, Jan 94.

[Mercator93]   W. Keith Edwards et al. "The Mercator Project, A Non Visual Interface To The X Window System", The X Resource, Issue 7, Summer 93.

[Peterson91]   Chris D. Peterson "editres protocol", The X Resource, Issue 0, Fall 91.

[Scheifler93]   Robert Scheifler "Buddy, Can You Spare an RPC?", The X Resource, Issue 7, Summer 93.

Re-engineering the CDE/Motif Graphical User Interface for Pens

James Kempf
Sue Booker
Ethan Solomita
Jackson Wong

Abstract

Software platform providers for pen based systems have taken two approaches to supporting the pen in the graphical user interface (GUI). One approach has been to add pen features to an existing desktop GUI but maintain the same application program interface (API). The other is to completely reinvent both the GUI and the API. Advantages of the first approach are that the users are faced with a familiar GUI and application programmers don't need to port their applications; on the other hand, the disadvantages are that interactivity with the pen is often difficult in a GUI designed for the mouse. While the second approach is easier to use with the pen, applications need to be rewritten to the new API, a difficult and time-consuming process. In this paper, we report on a different approach. We revisit some of the fundamental design decisions that went into designing the mouse-based CDE GUI, changing those which affected interactivity with the pen and avoiding gratuitous changes. The resulting GUI design is implemented by using existing resources in the CDE window manager and Motif or by adding new resources, so that no changes in application source code are required. We conclude that the optimal approach to supporting the pen in a GUI would be to make deep changes to interactivity in those areas where using the pen is different, but maintaining the API except where programmatic access to new pen features is needed.

James Kempf (james.kempf@sun.com), Sun Microsystems, Inc., 2550 Garcia Ave. UMPK14-207, Mountain View, CA, 94043

Sue Booker (booker.sue@applelink.apple.com) Booker Design, 147 Highland Ave., San Carlos, CA, 94070

Ethan Solomita (ethan@cs.columbia.edu) Dept. of Computer Science, Columbia University, 500 W. 120th St., New York, NY, 10027

Jackson Wong (jackson.wong@sun.com), Sun Microsystems, Inc., 2550 Garcia Ave., UMPK14-305, Mountain View, CA, 94043.

Introduction

Software platform providers for mobile pen-based computers, PDA's, and desktop tablets have taken either one of two approaches to supporting the pen in the GUI:

- Add a few enhancements to a desktop GUI, and modify the API to allow programmatic access to special pen features such as digital ink and handwriting recognition. Microsoft Windows for Pen Computing [MSWPC92] is an example of such a platform.

- Provide an entirely new GUI specifically tailored for the pen, with a new API as well. The Newton operating system and Go's PenPoint [CARR91] are examples of this approach.

The advantage of the first approach is that users don't have to learn a new GUI and application developers don't have to rewrite their applications to a completely new API. The disadvantage is that desktop GUI's were not designed for use with the pen, so some operations (such as dragging) may be very difficult. The advantage of the second approach is that the GUI can be optimized for the pen, making it easier for users. The disadvantage is that users must learn a new GUI and, perhaps more importantly from the point of view of software availability, developers must port their applications to the new API.

In this paper we report on the results of applying a different approach to modifying the Common Desktop Environment (CDE). Taking the CDE/Motif GUI as a starting point, we examine how it might be changed based on consideration of what substituting a pen for a mouse in a GUI makes easier or more difficult. Rather than simply adding a few enhancements, we revisit the basic graphical design and human factors decisions that went into designing the mouse-based GUI in the first place. We then modify the design decisions to reflect the human factors properties of the pen. The result is a GUI design that allows users to leverage the skills learned from the mouse-based CDE, but simplifies interaction when using the pen. The paper continues with a description of how the changes are implemented using existing Motif and CDE window manager resources or by adding resources that would allow configuration of CDE for pen hardware without requiring source code changes to applications. We conclude that the ideal approach to providing a GUI for pen systems is a combination of the two: deep GUI changes to better support the pen where needed but no changes in the API except to add function calls allowing access to pen-specific features for those applications that need to take advantage of them.

How Does a Pen Change the GUI?

The way people use pens is very different from the inherently more remote method of using a mouse or keyboard. A mouse and keyboard need to be set on a flat surface, with the display orthogonally located in front. For a display consisting of an integrated pen and flat panel, the display can be set in the user's lap, on a desk, or wherever is convenient. Cursor positioning and text entry are done directly on the display. For a desktop tablet, the relative location of the tablet and the display are similar to a keyboard and a mouse, but interaction with the pen differs considerably. A mouse remains in a fixed position where the user left it when a hand is removed; whereas, the pen cannot stay in the same position, it must either be held there or set down. Dragging a mouse across the desktop is relatively easy; in fact, it is the only way to move the mouse from one place to another. With a pen, dragging is a difficult action, because the user must work to keep the pen tip in contact with the tablet. It is easier to lift the pen off the tablet, move it through the air to the new position, and set it down again. A pen may not have buttons, but might have pressure sensitivity; a mouse always has buttons and never has pressure sensitivity. Pens can make sweeping marks and taps, but not easily in the same place, whereas a mouse stays always stays in the same place while buttoning. As a consequence of these physical differences, a GUI designed for use with the keyboard and mouse is not always easy or even possible to use with a pen.

In the following subsections, we revisit some of the design considerations that are affected when a pen becomes the primary pointing device. In the next section, we describe what changes were made in the CDE/Motif GUI to implement these changes.

Larger Target Sizes

Many factors affect the accuracy of aiming for a target with a pen. Anchoring the palm of the hand allows for greater precision, but may not always be possible, depending on the location of the tablet. The viewing angle, subsequent location of the target, and the amount of friction (or lack there of) between the pen tip and the tablet can also influence the accuracy of positioning. Accuracy is improved by pen hardware which senses the pen location above the tablet, so the cursor can "hover". This allows the cursor to change shape when the pen moves over a sensitive area, increasing user feedback. Cursor hovering may not be available on all pen hardware, however. Larger target sizes are recommended in some areas to provide the user with a larger area on which to set the pen.

Improved Feedback

The logical mapping of a mouse button click into a GUI for the pen is a pen-down/pen-up event. Since it is difficult to pen-down and pen-up in the same location (the pen is usually lifted off at an angle), it is easy to unintentionally escape from a button boundary, change a selection, or add more ink to a mark when using software originally designed for a mouse. More feedback helps people anticipate what they are about to do, as well as figure out if what they just did is what they intended. Enhanced graphics, careful (and subtle) use of sound and animation can enrich the interface considerably.

Compensation in Target Accuracy

This issue is related to the need for feedback. Double-clicking and exact control of pen location can be difficult and compensation for possible inaccuracies should be made. Whenever possible these actions should not be required in the interface. Also, accidental taps on the screen should not cause the user grief since they are much more frequent than unintended mouse clicks.

Alternatives to 2- and 3-button Mice and Keyboards

There are often no buttons on a pen, and no keyboard for short cuts. If the pen does not support hover, contact of the pen tip is considered a button 1 mouse click, and there are no other events. In order for existing mouse/keyboard-based applications to work, alternative methods are required for accessing menus and modifying actions currently expressed by pressing mouse buttons 2 and 3, or by using a keyboard.

Simplified Interface

If the pen is the only input device, the number of different ways for a user to perform a particular action should be limited to those easy to perform with the pen. There is no need for a button, a menu item, and an icon for the same functionality. Excessive redundancy creates visual clutter and is confusing, besides presenting a pen user with difficult interactivity.

Dragging Minimized and Sticky Menus

Dragging an object a long distance without accidentally lifting the pen tip off the screen is very difficult. If the hand is anchored and dragging is less than a few inches, it is easier, though dragging in a slight arc is most natural. The user interface design should compensate. For example, when using a menu, multiple taps are easier than maintaining constant contact with the screen, as is currently required for pull down menus. In CDE, only menus selected from menu bars are sticky.

Menu and Menu Bar Locations

Current menus open down and to the right, which is directly under a pen user's hand if the user is right handed. This makes single menus difficult to read, and cascading menus very awkward to use. In general, menus should pop up and to the left for right handed users and up and to the right for left handed users. If menus pop up instead of down, the location of the menu bar also needs to be changed; otherwise, the menu bar is obscured by the menu. Moving the menu bar to the bottom of the window improves visibility and reduces visual clutter surrounding the window.

Having the menu bar at the bottom improves user interactivity in another way. After writing on the screen, the hand naturally returns to the bottom or side bezel, especially if the tablet is held rather than being on a desk. Since the bottom of the window is also frequently near the bottom of the screen, and since this is an awkward location to write, due to the lack of palm rest and poorer tablet quality at edges, it is a good place to put real-estate consuming items such as menu bars.

Modifying the CDE/Motif GUI for Pens

Based on the underlying design considerations discussed in the previous section, modifications to the CDE/Motif GUI are appropriate in a number of areas. The modifications proposed in the following subsections are in keeping with the current CDE design guidelines [OSF91]. To fully support the pen, deeper modifications would be needed, a topic discussed later in the paper.

Window Border Width

The window border width as specified in the CDE design (5-7 pixels) is too narrow to accommodate the lack of accuracy often found with a pen. The border width should default to 10 pixels for pen hardware and be adjustable by the user in an easy way, such as a choice in the style manager. Advanced users and those with highly accurate hardware might prefer to keep the borders at the mouse default width. These changes are illustrated in Figure 1.

When using a mouse, a cursor change occurs when the pointer is dragged over a window border. Such feedback is helpful, but is only possible if the pen hardware supports hover. Instead, the designated section of the window border can recess upon pen-down, and the cursor can be eliminated entirely. A button down and drag action is currently interpreted as a command to move the window. A dashed line showing the proposed new window border location appears. Some improvements to increase feedback for pen users are necessary. Increasing the boldness of the dashed line in order to make it more visible is a simple step, but even better would be to move a copy of the window border. The border would appear recessed and would be located directly under the pen tip. As the pen is dragged away from the existing window border, a "copy" would peel off and move with the pen. Upon pen up, the original window would grow to meet the copy, wherever it was placed. If the window is being reduced in size, transparent artwork would look best.

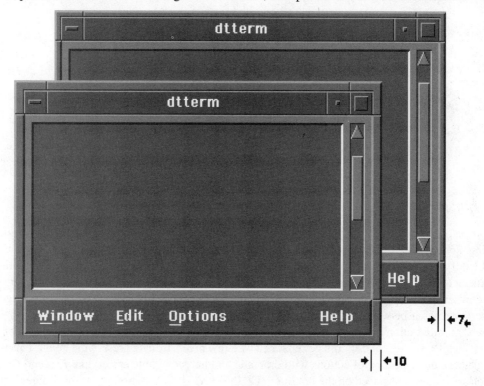

Figure 1: Window Border Width Changes

Resize Corners

The resize corners suffer from the same target size and feedback problems as the window borders. The lower resize corners should be enlarged in both width and height. The lower corners are used most, especially the lower right, and therefore should be easy targets to hit. In addition, the visual proportion of leaving the upper corners alone and modifying the lower corners is more pleasing when the menu bar is moved to the bottom of the window. When the resize corner gets a pen-down event, the behavior of the corner needs to be modified to provide better feedback. One possibility is to invert and recess the border. This graphic effect would be consistent with the CDE/Motif guidelines for target areas, though it is not currently used on window borders. Another possibility is a color change, though this would be a departure from the CDE/Motif guidelines. See Figure 2 for an example of the corner changes.

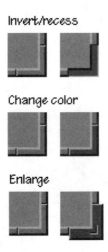

Figure 2: Resize Corner Changes

Menu Behavior and Menu Bar

Menus should popup vertically, and should be flush left or right depending on the handedness setting, i.e. up and left for right handed, up and right for left handed. Cascading menus should be avoided if at all possible. If cascade menus are necessary, they should cascade in the direction of the menu (ex. left for right handed people) to improve visibility. Menu item order should remain top-down, since people still read from top-to-bottom and a change of order would be confusing for those that switch between pen-based and mouse-based machines. The bottom item in a menu (closest to title button and pen tip when the change in display direction is made) should *not* be automatically selected, and should be separated by a few pixels from the rest of the items. This will avoid accidental selection of actions with dramatic and unrecoverable effect, like *Exit* and *Close*, which are commonly placed on the bottom in CDE/Motif. The separation should be implemented as a wider border at the bottom of the menu, and should be transparent until the item is selected. Dragging out of the active menu area to escape selection should remain possible. The menu bar should be moved to the bottom of the window to accommodate the change in menu display direction.

Button Behavior

As mentioned previously, it is easy to unintentionally escape from a button press due to the movement of the pen upon pen-up. Currently no feedback is available when this occurs, since the button highlights or recesses upon pen-down. A solution could be some graphical or sound feedback if the button was not activated, for example, a flash if the pen escapes, a quick button-down animation if the button really was pressed, or a soft tone when the button returns to its original state.

Scrolling

Although there are other, more convenient methods of navigating through a document with a pen, the scroll bar is such an integral part of the CDE GUI design that it would be difficult to replace without a major change in the CDE user's expectation of how to navigate through a document. As with window borders, more feedback is needed under the pen to show the user that the intended target has been touched. This is especially true if the target size remains the same. To be consistent, the scroll box should recess when tapped. It is difficult to draw a perfectly vertical line with a pen if any part of the hand is resting on the screen. A vertical swipe with a slight arch to it is much more natural. As a result, the pen might stray from the graphical borders of the scroll bar and enter into the main portion of the window. This is currently allowed with a mouse, and should be allowed with a pen, but a graphic tie back to the scroll bar is required. A graphic addition would help avoid the feeling of drawing on the contents of the window and being disconnected from the scrolling mechanism, problems which simply don't occur with the mouse. The location of the scroll bar also needs to be adjustable, and it currently can be set as a resource. Most left-handed users need the scroll bar moved to the left side of the window in order to be able to see what is being scrolling. Figure 3 illustrates an example design.

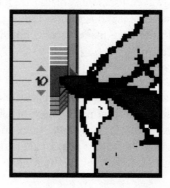

Figure 3: Scroll Bar Modifications

Alternative designs that take advantage of pen attributes, such as pressure sensitivity and superior fine motor control, may be more appropriate if less familiar to the desktop CDE user. Joy stick type mechanisms have been used successfully in the past, as well as page viewing navigation methods and direct "flick" scrolling, where the pen is flicked on the page and text scrolls in that direction until stopped with a quick tap. Pressure sensitivity can allow the user to accelerate, decelerate, and choose the depth within a Y plane in which to navigate, if the appropriate hardware is available. There are also scroll "modes", where the pen tip mimics a suction cup and grabs the page to move in any direction.

Replacing a 2 or 3 Button Mouse

The right mouse button in CDE currently brings up a context-related menu, which won't work with a zero or one button pen. If every CDE/Motif application is required to have a menu bar, and thus access to application-specific menus, the context-related menu can be eliminated in most cases. For non-CDE/Motif applications and in rare cases where the menu is so context-sensitive that it doesn't make sense to have it on the menu bar, a gesture or an alternate graphic representation is needed to substitute for the lack of a mouse button.

Currently, the background menu on the desktop is brought up by clicking and holding the right mouse button. Double clicking to bring up the background menu on the desktop is better for a pen, because there may only be one pen button. Although double clicking is usually difficult with a pen, it works here since there is no designated target area and the two pen clicks can be far apart and still work. Double clicking does not work within a window since the application is looking for pen clicks and will associate them with other actions. Similarly, the window manager will associate any clicks on the window frame with particular actions. In order to be consistent, the same gesture used for other context-related menus should also be used for the background menu. A check mark gesture (✔), drawn over the intended context, should be recognized by the Motif library and the window manager as the indicator for a context-related menu.

Gestures

Gestures are often used in pen-based GUI's to allow for shortcuts and to take advantage of the fluid nature of marks made with a pen. Gestures avoid the problem with double click and the lack of buttons on some pen hardware; however, users must memorize them and thus they should be used sparingly. Some existing point-and-click actions in the current mouse-based interface will work with a pen if some minor modifications are made, others should be replaced with gestures. The following subsections outline the changes.

Opening icons

Currently double clicking on an icon is used in most areas of the interface to mean "open", and single click is reserved for selection. The front panel does not follow this rule (see Figure 4 for a picture of the front panel); however, and uses a single click to open since selection serves no purpose. Since double clicking is difficult with a pen, an alternate means for designating open is required. A simple check mark on an icon is a better way for opening an icon.

Selection of text

The current method for selecting text is mouse button-down, drag, mouse button-up. This selection method is difficult with a pen due to a number of factors. When the pen is lifted off the screen it is often lifted off at an angle, or jiggled slightly. When this happens, the selection often changes by a character or two. Although very careful and deliberate vertical pen-up motions can help, often the inherent jitter in the pen hardware causes inaccuracies. If handwriting recognition software is in operation, it may be difficult to distinguish a selection from a line. Introducing a time-out to the selection gesture can make it usable with the pen, while still keeping it close to the same motion used with a mouse.

Selection with a time-out works in the following way. When the pen is clicked in an area, the location is recorded based on the location of the button press (pen-down), not the button release (pen-up). If the pen is kept pressed longer than a specified time, a bold vertical bar cursor appears under the pen tip, indicating that a selection will occur if the pen is moved. If the user lifts the pen up without dragging, the selection is canceled. Once the pen is dragged over text, the text highlights just as it does in the mouse-based system. Once the user has highlighted the desired text, they pause again to "set" the selection. After a specified time-out, the highlighted text changes color (from gray to inverted, for example) and the pen can be lifted off the screen without changing the region which is part of the selection. To extend the selection in either direction, a vertical bar gesture (|) can be drawn between any characters.

Drag and Drop

Currently the drag and drop cursor appears on button- or pen-down after movement of 5 pixels. This feels fine with a mouse, but might not be enough with a pen. If the number is too small, accidental dragging might occur. The default pixel movement number should be increased slightly for pen hardware, but should also be an editable resource, rather than being hard coded as currently, so users can set the drag distance to whatever feels comfortable.

When using the pen, the drag and drop cursor appears under the pen tip and is partially obscured by the user's hand if the user is right handed. The existing artwork should be flipped horizontally for right handed users; however, the cursor triangle should remain under the pen tip. On pen-up, the cursor animation must change to happen in the direction of the pointer (i.e. where the text is appearing), rather than centered over the entire artwork as is currently the case. Changing the animation directs the eye to where the text appears, aiding the user in finding what was dropped. An additional help in finding the text is to keep the entire dropped text highlighted (although not selected). These changes in cursor animation are particularly important for systems in which the tablet is integrated into the display, since users tend to focus their attention more on the area of the pen action as they would with a book or paper, rather than scanning the entire display.

Absence of a Cursor

The current CDE/Motif interface always has a cursor of some type present, and cursor changes occur when the pen moves over target areas. During normal text entry and window management activity, there is no need for a cursor if the tablet and display are integrated, because the pen tip acts as the cursor. For many users, having the cursor adds visual clutter and obscures text where the user is looking. During special actions and in certain modes, like drag & drop, a cursor informs the user of the mode. A cursor can also be displayed when the pen moves over target areas if the pen hardware supports hover. If the tablet and display are not integrated, then a cursor is required just as with a mouse.

Front Panel

The front panel in the CDE/Motif environment provides access to commonly used applications and files. It is displayed as a long, narrow window at the bottom of the screen, containing icons, buttons and graphical state indicators. The front panel example of an application that is very well designed for pen input. The icons are all single click to open, the panel is displayed at the bottom of the screen by default, the menus pop up, and the graphics are rich and easily readable. The front panel also provides easy access to multiple desktops, by simply clicking on a button. Multiple desktops are particularly useful on machines with smaller displays, as is typically the case for portable, pen-based hardware, since they allow users to minimize the amount of tedious window manipulation and increase the size of the desktop without requiring panning or a larger display.

Figure 4: Comparison of Front Panel Designs

The current CDE/Motif front panel, at 1017 by 81 pixels, is too large horizontally for machines with narrow displays. The recommended redesign reduces it to 660 by 81 through eliminating the number of icons possible, reducing the icon grid and menu grid size, limiting the number of desktops to four (and limiting their names to numbers), and altering the layout of the indicator graphics (lock, network and exit). The new design allows standard icons to still be used, and introduces changes only to the graphics and layout. See Figure 4 for a comparison of the mouse and recommended pen designs.

Setting Pen Preferences

Users require easy access to pen preferences. Window border widths, right/left handed, pressure calibrations (if available), double tap distances and time delay thresholds are a few items that need to be set. An addition to the style manager is the preferred way of providing this capability, since most users expect preferences to be settable there. Preferences should also be grouped, so a choice like "right-handed" causes the default settings for widgets to be appropriate for a right handed user.

Partial Implementation

The changes discussed in the previous section were partially implemented in the Developer's Release of CDE/Motif. For the most part, the changes were primarily a matter of setting a few resources and adding resources to Motif to allow control of certain aspects of the GUI that CDE/Motif currently hard wires. The following subsections detail how the changes mentioned in the previous section were implemented.

Window Border Width

Changes to the window border to facilitate movement with the pen were made by changing resources in the CDE window manager (*dtwm*) resource file. The resources changes were:

```
Mwm*clientDecoration:-maximize

Mwm*resizeBorderWidth:10

Mwm*moveThreshold:5
```

The change to `Mwm*clientDecoration` causes top level windows to be displayed without the maximize button. The maximize button causes the window to fill the entire screen, but it is positioned so closely with the minimize button that it is easy to miss when hitting the minimize button. The maximize behavior is available through the window menu. The change to `Mwm*resizeBorderWidth` causes the resize borders to be increased in width to 10 pixels, while the change to `Mwm*moveThreshold` allows the pen to slip by half a border width, which is easy to do with the pen, without causing the window to move.

Menu Behavior and Menu Bar

A resource was added to allow the direction of menu pop up and cascade to be modified and to modify menu display to avoid accidental activation of menu commands with drastic effect:

```
*XmRowColumn.menuPullDirection:
```

```
[ menupull_upleft / menupull_upright /
    menupull_downleft / menupull_downright ]
```

```
*XmRowColumn.marginHeight: 3
```

The `XmRowColumn.menuPullDirection` indicates in which direction the menu should pop. The `XmRowColumn.marginHeight` resource indicates the number of pixels that should be inserted in the border around menu to avoid accidental activation of commands.

The following resource was added to change the display position of the menu bar:

```
*XmMainWindow.menuBarLocation:
    [ menubar_bottom_mainwindow / menubar_top_mainwindow ]
```

Scrolling

A standard resource is set to allow scrollbar location to be changed:

```
XmScrolledWindow.scrollBarPlacement:
    [ XmTOP_RIGHT / XmTOP_RIGHT ] [ XmBOTTOM_LEFT / XmBOTTOM_RIGHT ]
```

This resource indicates on which side the top and bottom scrollbars should be placed.

Replacing a 2 or 3 Button Mouse

The `DtButtonBindings` table in *.dtwrc* was replaced with the following:

```
Buttons DtButtonBindings {
    <Btn1Click2>      root          f.menu DtRootMenu
    <Btn3Down>        root          f.menu DtRootMenu
    <Btn1Down>        frame|icon    f.raise
    <Btn3Down>        frame|icon    f.post_wmenu
    Alt<Btn1Down>     icon|window   f.move
    Alt<Btn3Down>     window        f.minimize
}
```

With the exception of the first binding, these are the same as the default. *dtwrc*. The first binding causes double click on the desktop background to bring up the desktop menu.

Gestures

We implemented two prototypes for gesture/handwriting recognition in Motif. The first prototype intertwines handwriting recognition deeply into the Motif/Xt widget architecture. The second is based on a design for an API that abstracts many of the details for handling handwriting recognition into a programmatic layer called Arabesque [SOLO94]. Both implementations used the handwriting recognition application programming interface (HRE API) for X/Unix [KEM93], now available on the Internet.

The intent of changing to a more abstract interface for gesture recognition is to allow portability for many of the details involved in handling handwriting recognition and position identification behind an interface that can be ported to other toolkits (e.g. Athena widgets, Tcl/Tk, etc.). The Arabesque handles these details by allowing the toolkit to register callbacks that provide information about text and its layout and inform the toolkit of recognition events. Arabesque does not handle digital ink rendering, since that will depend on exactly how the toolkit does rendering in general (e.g. Xlib, DPS, etc.). The Arabesque interface can be configured to handle full text recognition or can restrict recognition to gestures (thereby improving the recognition rate).

The resources:

```
*XmText.gestures: True
*Recognizer.recognizerName: filename
```

control whether gesture recognition is enabled. The `Recognizer` widget encapsulates handling of handwriting recognition.

Drag and Drop

The resource:

```
*XmDragContext.dropGrace: <n>
```

allows a grace period of *n* milliseconds between releasing the button over a drop target and actually causing the drop to occur. The user can abort the drop by pressing the button again, avoiding an accidental drop if the pressure on the nib of the pen is relaxed during movement. The default for this resource is 0.

Front Panel

The CDE front panel was reimplemented along the lines shown in Figure 4, reducing the length and width for smaller screens.

Keyboardless Text Entry

A major difference between pen and mouse platforms is that text entry is sometimes desirable directly with the pen rather than through the keyboard. For portable pen systems, the reasons why pen input of text might be desirable are fairly obvious: it allows the computer to be used in situations where a keyboard is cumbersome or unnecessary, such as while standing or where there is no free horizontal space for a keyboard. For desktop pen systems, having the tablet in a fixed position on the desktop might suggest that keyboardless text entry is less useful; however, in some cases, being able to enter a few characters or words while holding the pen can avoid the motor and cognitive switch required to move from pointing device to keyboard. For long stretches of text entry, the keyboard is clearly preferable, even when in a portable setting, but the need for a keyboard can be reduced by a properly engineered keyboardless text entry interface.

Existing pen platforms take three approaches to providing keyboardless text entry:

- Text widgets that normally take keyboard entry respond to written input by converting the user's writing to text using handwriting recognition. Correction procedures with varying degrees of sophistication are supported in the event the translation provided by the handwriting recognition algorithm is not what the user intended.

- A handwriting recognition widget available as a desktop application translates the user's handwriting, so the user can compose a piece of text and send it to the active application rather than write directly on the application's window.

- A "virtual keyboard" application projects a model of a standard keyboard on which a user can type in the text by pressing buttons corresponding to characters. The text is sent to the active application.

Current handwriting recognition algorithms attain an accuracy of about 96.8% [HACC94], the same as for human observers, but an accuracy threshold of around 97% exists, below which users deem recognition accuracy to be unacceptable. Note that this implies that people demand an accuracy level from automated handwriting recognition at or beyond what they themselves are able to achieve. Because entry with a keyboard always gets the correct character (unless the user makes a typo), the failure of the handwriting recognition algorithm to translate written text into what the user expected (even if the handwriting is barely legible to a human) results in a perception that handwriting recognition is inferior. Furthermore, unlike typos on a keyboard, where correction of an error requires only muscle memory, correction of an unexpected handwritten translation often requires interacting with a GUI, or use of unfamiliar gestures. While handwriting recognition algorithms and their supporting GUI are improving, these drawbacks, together with the inherently slower speed of handwritten text entry, suggest that users not be given the perception that handwriting recognition is, in any way, a replacement for keyboard input.

As a consequence, the decision was made to avoid doing handwriting recognition within the Motif text widget (although a text widget with handwriting recognition was prototyped). Rather, a combined application for handwriting and virtual keyboard text entry was designed. The following subsections describe the design and system architecture of the keyboardless text entry application.

Graphic Design

The keyboardless text entry application consists of two displays, the virtual keyboard and the digital ink pad, one of which will be active. The user chooses which display is active by pressing one of two iconic buttons in the lower right corner.

Virtual keyboard

The virtual keyboard, as shown in Figure 5, has the standard QWERTY key layout, with the option to add function keys and numerical keypad if desired. A text display area above the keys shows a record of the text that has been entered with the keyboard put not yet placed in a document. Simple editing can be done here by using the keyboard or gestures. Selected portions can be dragged and dropped, or cut and pasted into other windows using the X selection service. The *Send* button pastes the entire contents of the text display, or a portion that has been selected, into the document in the window with keyboard focus. If no insertion point is marked in the document, drag and drop must be used to place the text. The *Clear* button clears the entire text display or any text that is selected.

Key size can be enlarged or reduced by resizing the window. The *Options* button brings up a dialog box with choices relating to the virtual keyboard. These include: keyboard size, key layout, key graphics, language, use of sound for feedback, size of the text window, etc.

Figure 5: Virtual Keyboard

Digital ink pad

The digital ink pad, shown in Figure 6, allows handwritten, recognized text to be inserted into documents. Graphical character boxes segregate letters for block handwriting recognizers, but can be eliminated if cursive recognition is available by a setting in the *Options* box. The number of character boxes can be increased or decreased by resizing the window. If text has been entered prior to reducing the window size, character/word wrap occurs. The size of the character boxes can be changed by a setting in the *Options* box. As with the virtual keyboard, the text display area can be resized to more than one line.

Recognized text is displayed in both the character boxes and text display. The text display works like the text display in the virtual keyboard. Editing commands are accessible either directly, through gestures, or indirectly, through the menu on the *Gestures* button. The *Cut* command cuts out the selection or the item under the gesture and deletes it. Similarly with *Copy* and *Paste*. The *Add Line* gesture begins a new line, while the *Add Space* gesture adds a blank space. These gestures are not menu commands because of the difficulty in marking the insertion point prior to selecting the menu item, but are shown on the menu for reference. The *Clear* button clears the entire text window and handwriting window, since, unlike the virtual keyboard, the *Cut* gesture is available to delete individual selections. As with the virtual keyboard, the *Send* button sends all or the selected part of the text to the window with keyboard focus.

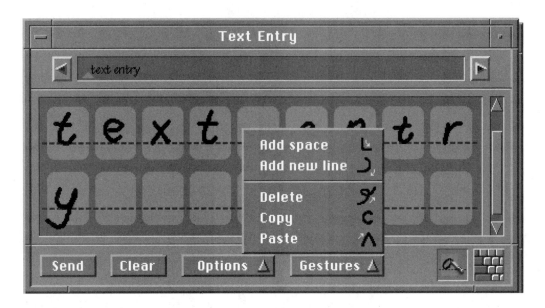

Figure 6: Digital Ink Pad

System Architecture

Figure 7 illustrates the system architecture for keyboardless text entry. Unlike virtual keyboard applications in other X GUI's, keyboardless text entry for CDE/Motif does not use X window system mechanisms as the primary channel for delivering text to the window with keyboard focus. A virtual keyboard pseudodevice driver in the operating system allows applications to insert ASCII text into the keyboard entry stream. This text is delivered to the X server via a multiplexor stream module that mixes input from the hardware keyboard (if present) and the virtual keyboard. The X server then delivers the input to the window with keyboard focus. Of course, the user can also use the X selection service and drag and drop to move text from the virtual keyboard application to another application, just like any other X window.

The most important reason for using a pseudodevice driver rather than an X mechanism is to allow operating system security mechanisms already in place for the hardware keyboard to be used with the virtual keyboard as well. Since some pen machines will be employed without a keyboard, the virtual keyboard will become the primary channel for text entry including (potentially) logging into the machine. Virtual keyboard entry must therefore be secure from access by unauthorized users over the network. If an X mechanism is used, then the security permissions established by that mechanism apply to the entire X session, not just to the keyboard stream. A pseudodevice driver allows restrictive security to be put in place for the virtual keyboard alone without constraining security on user-level applications. Of course, like any X application, the virtual keyboard application can be run on one machine and display on another, but, in the standard case where the virtual keyboard runs on the same machine it displays, operating system mechanisms for securing access to the virtual keyboard and hardware keyboard devices are the same.

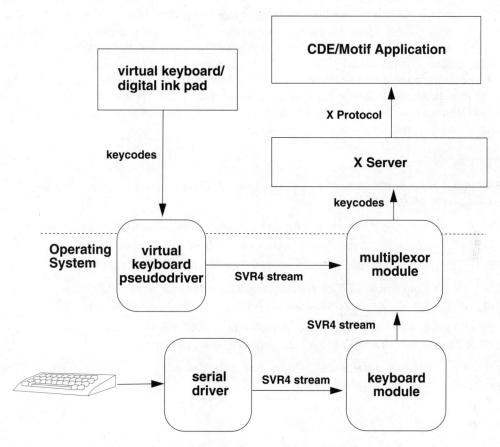

Figure 7: Keyboardless Text Entry System Architecture

Conclusions and Suggestions for Further Research

Many, in fact most, of the deeper GUI modifications recommended above were not implemented in the first round of changes made to CDE/Motif. Work on pushing these changes into the GUI is ongoing. We are also assessing the whether having a programmatic layer to handle the details of positioning and event notification for portability is justified, or whether most of the code for handling these details ends up in the callbacks and therefore would be better to include directly in the toolkits.

The value of maintaining compatibility between the mouse and pen for CDE lies in intuition that the user will enjoy instant familiarity when switching between a mouse and a pen based machine. The theory is that this familiarity will overcome any residual difficulty surrounding mouse-oriented features in the GUI. It is an open question whether this theory is correct. User testing, comparing a number of pen and mouse usage scenarios, may be able to help determine whether this is so. If it is the case that users derive little benefit from maintaining GUI compatibility, a complete redesign of the GUI for pens may be a better solution.

On the other hand, there is no question that maintaining API compatibility between the mouse and pen versions of Motif is a plus for application developers. Porting applications between different, incompatible API's is a major job, and most application developers would rather avoid it. If pen features such as digital ink and gesture/handwriting recognition can be made available in some form to existing applications on CDE/Motif without requiring source code modifications, users benefit from being able to run their current applications unchanged. Toolkit API additions for pen-specific features can enable the development of new applications that use the pen in new and different ways, i.e. not simply as a pointing device.

References

[MSWPC92] *Microsoft Windows for Pen Computing: Programmer's Reference,* Microsoft Corp., Redmond, WA, 1992.

[CARR91] *The Power of Penpoint*, Robert Carr and Dan Shafer, Addison-Wesley, Reading, MA, 342 pp., 1991.

[OSF91] *OSF/Motif Style Guide*, Open Software Foundation, Prentice Hall, 1991.

[HACC94] "A Comparison of Two Handwriting Recognizers for Pen-based Computers," Larry Chang and I. Scott McKenzie, presented at CANSON'94, Toronto, Canada, 1994.

[KEM93] "Integrating Handwriting Recognition into UNIX," James Kempf, *Proceedings of the USENIX Summer 1993 Technical Conference*, pp. 187-204, 1993,

[SOLO94] "The Arabesque API," Ethan Solomita, Internal Memo, SMCC Technology Development, Sun Microsystems, 1994.

xbb: A Blackboard for X Applications

Mark S. Ackerman[†]

Eric Mandel[‡]

Abstract

User agents require some method of coordination among themselves and other processes. A blackboard architecture provides a readily available mechanism for inter-process coordination and communication. Such an architecture is relatively simple to implement above the property mechanism within X.

This paper describes an easy-to-use library that provides an interface to a blackboard using the X server. The library, xbb, provides a small set of routines to write data tuples to a common blackboard using Linda coordination mechanisms. Because of the X server's volatility, routines are also provided within xbb for clients to copy the blackboard contents to a ndbm file for static store.

Introduction

User agents and critics require some method of coordination among themselves and other processes. For example, a critic might watch how the user interacts with some application and make suggestions. Or an agent might start processes on other machines in anticipation of user requests. There are many examples, but they all require coordination among the applications. We would like to make it easy and straight-forward to create families of cooperating agents that monitor the user's actions.

A blackboard architecture provides a readily available mechanism for inter-process coordination and communication. Such an architecture is relatively simple to implement using the property mechanism within X.

[†]*Department of Information and Computer Science, University of California, Irvine, ackerman@ics.uci.edu, http://www.ics.uci.edu/CORPS/ackerman.html.*

[‡]*Harvard-Smithsonian Center for Astrophysics, eric@cfa.harvard.edu.*

This paper describes an easy-to-use library that provides an interface to a blackboard using the X server. The library, xbb, provides a small set of routines to write data tuples to a common blackboard using Linda coordination mechanisms. Because of the X server's volatility, routines are also provided within xbb for clients to copy the blackboard contents to a ndbm file for static store.

The paper provides a brief overview of blackboard systems and the Linda coordination language. The paper then discusses the implementation of the xbb library and concludes with an example of use.

Coordination and the Blackboard Mechanism

For particular types of applications, the coordination mechanism required is essentially some type of broadcast. All of the agents, or secondary applications, may wish to watch for changes, and in turn, they may need to post changes or results for others (including the primary application) to see.

There are two standard coordination mechanisms of value here: the blackboard mechanism, used largely in Artificial Intelligence (AI), and the message bus mechanism, used extensively in software engineering. The message bus mechanism (Cagan 1990; Taylor, Selby, and Forester 1992; Gorlick 1992; Oliver 1991) has the advantage of narrow-casting, sending appropriate messages to only those processes requesting them. It, however, has the disadvantage of requiring an additional mechanism over that of X. Libraries for message passing are available (e.g., ToolTalk), but these are not readily available across platforms. Implementing such a mechanism within X is possible, but it would require an additional message server to track and route messages. While X's ClientMessage event can be used to send an arbitrary message, it suffers from two deficiencies for this purpose. It does not allow for the transfer of large amounts of data. Additionally, it requires each process to route the client message to any other, interested processes, or again to have a central message server.

We have, instead, concentrated on the second type of coordination mechanism for broadcast, the blackboard (Nii 1986, Engelmore and Morgan 1988). We chose to use a blackboard architecture for our applications because of its relative simplicity, especially in an X environment.

For user interface programming, the blackboard is a simple method of narrow-casting with limited notification. Processes post data on a global blackboard, and other interested processes can retrieve and modify that data.

One can see the blackboard model as an extension of classic expert-system processing. As Engelmore and Moore (1988) note:

> ...the blackboard model is a very simple yet powerful idea for coping with problems characterized by the need to deal with uncertain data, make use of uncertain knowledge, and apply a non-deterministic solution strategy. (p. ix)

Blackboards have been used in AI systems since the early 1980s starting with the HEARSAY-II speech recognition and the HASP sonar signal recognition systems (Nii 1986). Both of these systems were marked by an opportunistic inferencing strategy, multiple knowledge sources, and multiple levels of inferencing. In these systems, a shared memory structure was devised to coordinate and communicate among multiple program units (which were logically separate but not necessarily in separate operating-system processes). The idea of the blackboard, then, was a place where these multiple program units could post their complete or partial findings and could determine what next to do. This required global access to the data.

As researchers became interested in the problems of distributed artificial intelligence, blackboard architectures allowed for an easy extension of this type of inferencing (Bond and Gasser 1988). Blackboards have been used in a wide variety of applications, including signal and image recognition, planning, scene analysis, crisis management, process control, and distributed problem solving (Nii 1986, Engelmore and Morgan, 1988). There are also blackboard-oriented shells and generic blackboard systems (e.g., Corkill, Gallagher, and Johnson 1988)

The model of a blackboard system is not precisely defined. Generally agreed-upon components include separate and logically independent knowledge sources interacting with a globally accessible blackboard. Supplemental features in blackboard architectures include the hierarchical ordering of the blackboard data, associative retrieval, linking by name, and various control mechanisms. In general, some type of control mechanism needs to exist, largely to determine what knowledge sources are next triggered as well as to order the access to the blackboard itself. However, no particular control mechanism has been agreed upon; often the access is serial.

In summary, the blackboard serves as a general-purpose posting mechanism. It provides broad-casting and narrow-casting capabilities that are of particular interest in user interface programming, especially where sets of agents and critics may wish to examine the user's actions. In such a case, the current application can merely post relevant information about its state, and the auxiliary agents can make their evaluations. It is obvious that the blackboard architecture can be extended for use by many types of processes that need to see aspects of one another's internal states.

Linda

The Linda language (Gelernter 1988, Carriero and Gelernter 1989, Carriero and Gelernter 1988) is the coordination language upon which xbb is based; it is well-suited to blackboard systems. While Linda was defined largely for parallel processing, it has been used in a variety of language settings and environments. (The claim is that, being a coordination language, it is orthogonal in capability to normal functional or processing languages.) In Linda, all data transfer among processes is through data tuples, arbitrary vectors of data. These tuples can be read by any process with access to the tuple space (or in our parlance, blackboard). The language consists of only six primitives, all of which read or write data tuples, as shown in Table 1.

This deceptively simple language (or language add-in) provides all of the basic capabilities required by a blackboard architecture. However, as one might expect, several Linda mechanisms were problematic. First, performing associative retrieval using X properties is extremely time-consuming. Therefore, we found it useful to add the capability to retrieve by property name, essentially making the first element of the data tuple the most critical. Second, we provide the eval mechanism, but it merely spins off a child process.

Command	Description
in	Blocking read for a tuple. Non-destructive read. Indexing is associative.
rd	Blocking read for a tuple. Read deletes the tuple from the tuple space.
out	Write.
eval	Write, but starts process to evaluate one of the tuple elements. Write occurs at end of spun-off process.
inp	Predicate form of in. Returns a boolean.
outp	Predicate form of out. Returns a boolean.

Table 1: Linda commands

xbb Routines

xbb is a small library of procedures that implement a blackboard. The routines sit above the X property mechanism, in much the same way that the Xt selection mechanism does, and allow diverse applications to communicate through this blackboard.

As mentioned, xbb implements the Linda language set. While routines are available both to handle retrieval through associative index and to implement the eval (or process creation) command, they are not recommended. As an efficiency consideration, we recommend retrieving on property name and, in general, avoiding the eval command.

A major issue in implementing Linda or Linda-like features was how to store the data tuples. We decided to optimize for efficiency, removing some of the elegance of Linda in favor of speed. Thus, we store complex tuples as encoded strings in the form (tuple-name, length of first member, ... length of last member, first value, ..., last value). We could have also implemented xbb, for example, as a tree of X properties, but this would require considerably more fetches for each tuple. Encoding is done automatically by the xbb routines, and this can be overridden by the application writer for simple tuples.

In addition to the standard Linda routines, xbb adds routines to watch for changed values (by property name), to lock and unlock properties, and to store and retrieve tuples from a database. These additional routines make using a blackboard considerably easier and robust. One would like the data values to remain across X sessions, or at least have that as a possibility. For example, user-set placement of windows or history values should remain across X server lives. The ability to watch for other processes' changing or setting selected properties (or tuples) provides the capability for triggers within agents and applications. Finally, the ability to lock and unlock properties provides a level of transaction processing that is often quite useful. All of these additional capabilities, except for the database store and fetch, could be implemented using only the basic routines, although more awkwardly. The full set of xbb routines is shown below:

```
void XBB_In(String tuple_name, XtPointer *data_value,
            unsigned int data_length, Boolean delete, Boolean simple_tuple)
void XBB_Read(String tuple_name, XtPointer *data_value,
              unsigned int data_length, Boolean simple_tuple)
void XBB_Out(String tuple_name, XtPointer data_value,
             unsigned int data_length, Boolean simple_tuple)
void XBB_In_Associative(String tuple_name, XtPointer *data_value,
                        unsigned int data_length, String match_tuple)
void XBB_Eval(String tuple_name, String command_string)

void XBB_Lock(String tuple_name)
void XBB_Unlock(String tuple_name)

void XBB_Read_When_Changed(String tuple_name, XtPointer *data_value,
                           unsigned int data_length,
                           Boolean during_waitproc_only,
                           Boolean simple_tuple)
Boolean XBB_Watch_For_Changed_Value(String tuple_name,
                           XtCallbackProc callback,
                           XtPointer client_data,
                           unsigned int watch_duration)

Boolean XBB_Is_Locked(String tuple_name)
Boolean XBB_Exists(String tuple_name)
void XBB_Initialize()

#ifdef XBB_DATABASE
    Boolean XBB_Initialize_Database(String filename)
    Boolean XBB_Store_In_Database(String tuple_name)
    Boolean XBB_Store_All()
    Boolean XBB_Fetch_From_Database(String tuple_name)
    Boolean XBB_Fetch_All()
#endif
```

We implemented xbb using the Xt Intrinsics library. There was no essential reason, but we wanted to use Xt timers, event handlers, wait procs, and data types. One could create a similar blackboard library easily using Tk or other toolkit libraries that provide similar services to Xt.

Examples of Use

Having shown some of the details of xbb, we wish to present two simple examples of its use, GardenSpy and ASSISTmate. GardenSpy is a very simple critic for the Answer Garden application, and ASSISTmate is a set of agents for the ASSIST application.

Answer Garden (Ackerman and Malone 1990, Ackerman 1993) is a hypermedia application that helps people find answers to commonly asked questions. Answer Garden is an example of an iteratively constructed information database and organizational memory, but its exact functionality is not germane to the critic described below. What is important is that one retrieval mechanism for a user is a set of diagnostic questions that hopefully lead him to an answer.

The diagnostic questions that help guide the user within Answer Garden form a directed acyclic graph (DAG) since the user is supposed to be narrowing down on an answer to some question. This is unlike many other hypertext systems (and even contradicts some views within Answer Garden). Since the diagnostic questions form a DAG, a lost user can be detected by observing a repeatedly circular trail as the user backtracks trying to find the correct path through the diagnostic questions.

GardenSpy, then, is a simple critic that watches for this behavior pattern. When it detects the behavior, it pops up a message box reminding the user that he can ask a question of a human expert through the system's messaging facilities and that he can search the answer database using a full-text search facility. That is, if the GardenSpy critic notices that user may be lost, it provides a few constructive suggestions to the user. The user can, of course, tell GardenSpy to go away - either temporarily or permanently.

Such a critic is easy to add to the user's system. Presuming that the Answer Garden hypertext application publishes its state on the user's blackboard, the GardenSpy critic can make its determination. Answer Garden merely writes the user's current node to the blackboard, and GardenSpy reads it.

Obviously, many mechanisms could have been used to organize and coordinate between the Answer Garden application and a simple critic. However, there are several advantages to using xbb. One advantage is that the application and critic can be developed separately as long as they agreed upon information exchange on the blackboard. More importantly, additional critics or agents can be added without difficulty. The Answer Garden application need not know anything about any surrounding processes; it merely publishes its state using xbb's blackboard routines.

The second simple example is ASSISTmate, a set of two agents for the ASSIST, a task-support and community memory application for astrophysicists (Ackerman and Mandel 1995). One of the ASSIST's user interface issues is that it puts up too many windows for its naive users. The inherent complexity of the application leads to many windows, but those without windowing experience cannot handle the number of windows (which, in fact, may not be very numerous).

To ameliorate this problem, one agent determines the complexity of the user's screen and asks the user whether he would like his screen tidied up. (The user can set his preferred complexity and whether window groups should be removed or iconified.) However, the utility of a window, or even an entire group of windows, is dependent on the user's activities. One does not want to remove a window that the user is just about to reference. To avoid popping down important windows, we currently have another agent that attempts to determine which windows are important to the user's current task.

To work, ASSISTmate requires that the ASSIST places its current state upon the blackboard for the use of its agents and critics. The two agents also communicate between themselves through xbb's blackboard, coordinating through a set of asynchronously modified entries. We are currently examining the usefulness of various heuristics for handling window complexity. In fact, the architecture of the agent system allows any number of agents to examine window complexity and importance. Since these agents communicate through only blackboard entries, adding, removing, or modifying agents is straight-forward and easy.

Limitations, Future Research, and Conclusions

xbb has several limitations that restrict its utility. First, retrieval is still relatively costly. Each process using xbb must still determine whether a property or blackboard entry is of interest. To determine interest in any specific xbb entry, either applications must encode areas of interest within the tuple names (i.e., the property names) or the blackboard entry must be retrieved and evaluated. It would be helpful if the blackboard itself could help with this determination. We are examining whether a limited messaging capability would be beneficial. Messages would be posted to each process that self-announced through a tuple or set of tuples that it was interested in a segment of the blackboard (i.e., a subset of the tuple space).

Second, the lack of inexpensive associative indexing also restricts the retrieval possible with the system. Blackboard architectures are clearly useful without associative retrieval. However, if associative retrieval is required, it will not be cost-effective with the current X property mechanism. Either an extension or a secondary process will be required to do true associative retrieval.

Finally, the current xbb architecture does not handle byte order. This limitation could be ameliorated if the type were encoded in the tuple string.

While these limitations exist in the current xbb implementation, we do not find these restrictions overly cumbersome. In general, our uses have been relatively straight-forward, and xbb has sufficed for these uses. Application architectures using agents and critics - or even those architectures using distributed, secondary processes - have substantial power. Using a blackboard in these application architectures provides enormous flexibility when one needs to coordinate and communicate among processes. Because xbb makes using a blackboard relatively easy to implement, we have found xbb to have been extremely useful in our own application suites.

Acknowledgments

This research is supported, in part, by research grants from NASA (NRA-93-OSSA-09) and the UCI Committee on Research. This work was also supported under NASA contracts to the IRAF Technical Working Group (NAGW-1921), the AXAF High Resolution Camera (NAS8-38248), and the AXAF Science Center (NAS8-39073).

Part of this work was done while the first author was at the MIT Center for Coordination Science under research grants from the X Consortium, Digital Equipment Corporation, the National Science Foundation (IRI-8903034), and the MIT International Financial Services Research Center.

The authors would like to thank John Roll, Steve Murray, Roger Brissenden, and Ralph Swick for their support and assistance.

References

Ackerman, Mark S. 1993. Answer Garden: A Tool for Growing Organizational Memory. Massachusetts Institute of Technology, Ph.D. Thesis.

Ackerman, Mark S., and Thomas W. Malone. 1990. Answer Garden: A Tool for Growing Organizational Memory. *Proceedings of the ACM Conference on Office Information Systems* : 31-39.

Ackerman, Mark S., and Eric Mandel. 1995. Memory in the Small: An Application to Provide Task-Based Organizational Memory for a Scientific Community. *Proceedings of the Hawaii International Conference of System Sciences (HICSS 95)* : forthcoming.

Bond, Alan H., and Les Gasser. 1988. *Readings in Distributed Artificial Intelligence.* San Mateo, CA: Morgan Kaufmann.

Cagan, Martin. 1990. The HP SoftBench Environment: An Architecture for a New Generation of Software Tools. *Hewlett-Packard Journal*, 41 (3) : 36-47.

Carriero, N., and D. Gelernter. 1988. Applications Experience with Linda. *Proceedings of the ACM SIGPLAN Symposium on Parallel Programming* : 173-187.

Carriero, Nicholas, and David Gelernter. 1989. Linda in Context. *Communications of the ACM*, 32 (4) : 444-458.

Corkill, Daniel D., Kevin Q Gallagher, and Philip M. Johnson. 1988. Achieving Flexibility, Efficiency, and Generality in Blackboard Architectures. In *Readings in Distributed Artificial Intelligence.* Edited by A. H. Bond and L. Gasser. 541-546. San Mateo: Morgan Kaufmann.

Engelmore, Robert, and Tony Morgan. 1988. *Blackboard Systems.* Reading, MA: Addison-Wesley.

Gelernter, David. 1988. Getting the Job Done: "Linda," a parallel-programming language, is easy, efficient, and portable. *Byte*, November, 1988 : 301-308.

Gorlick, Michael M. 1992. Cricket: A Domain-Based Message Bus for Tool Integration. *Proceedings of the Irvine Software Symposium* : 2-18.

Nii, H. Penny. 1986. Blackboard Systems: The Blackboard Model of Problem Solving and the Evolution of Blackboard Architectures. *AI Magazine*, 7 (2) : 38-53.

Oliver, Huw. 1991. Adding Control Integration to PCTE. Hewlett-Packard Laboratories. Manuscript.

Taylor, Richard N., Richard W. Selby, and Kari Forester. 1992. Experience with a Strongly Typed and a Weakly Typed Event-Based Control Integration Mechanism. University of California, Information and Computer Science. Manuscript.

X Consortium Status Report

Bob Scheifler[†]

Abstract

The presentation will briefly review how the R6 "works in progress" are progressing, what is and isn't likely to be worked on as new functionality for the next release, and how our relationship is progressing with future Common Desktop Environment and Motif development.

[†]*Bob Scheifler is President of X Consortium, Inc.*

Integrating A Color Management System With A Unix and X11 Environment

David T. Berry[†]

Abstract

With X11R5 Xcms was added to Xlib bringing device independent color to the X11 window system. This is a reasonable solution for the window system. Xcms does not provide embedded support for CMYK printing devices and relies on the user to be able to convert their input device data, e.g. a scanner into a known CIE based color space. However, this does not address the desktop publishing market, for example, where a color management system that covers all color devices in a system is required. Taking from work originally developed in the Macintosh arena, SunSoft has been working with Kodak to address the need for a system wide color management system by bringing the Kodak Color Management System (KCMS) to Solaris.

Solaris is used here as an example of a Unix and an X11 based network environment and KCMS as an example of a color management system. It is envisioned that the issues and problems addressed here may be applicable to other implementations of Unix, X11 based systems and their integration with other color management systems.

The paper will describe the architecture of the KCMS framework, highlighting all of the essential elements. These elements provide an interface to allow application developers to access the color management functionality[1], and an interface to allow 3rd party color management vendors to replace the default color management technology.

To make color management work a Device Color Profile (DCP) is needed for every peripheral. The DCP is a characterization of the reproducible colors for a device (i.e an inkjet printer) for a specific viewing environment (fluorescent lighting). In Xcms this is achieved by means of root window properties. Profiles may also represent color spaces, or provide a means to apply some special filter effect to the color data.

[†]*David T. Berry (david.berry@sun.com) is a Member of Technical Staff at SunSoft Inc.*

KCMS will use the ICC format [2] for its profiles. Sun is a founding member of the ICC, and has participated in the development of the ICC specification as a critical step in standardizing color management in the computer industry. Other founding members of the ICC are Adobe, Agfa, Apple FOGRA, Kodak, Microsoft, SGI and Taligent.

Emphasis in the paper will be given to extensions that were added to KCMS to provide support for X11 applications and a distributed environment. This includes support for Xcms, monitor calibration, and integration with imaging and graphics libraries.

[1] KCMS Application Developers Guide, SunSoft September 1994.

[2] ICC Profile Format, Version 3.0, June 1994.

Author Information

David Berry is a Member of Technical Staff at SunSoft Inc. He is the lead engineer for the integration of KCMS with Solaris. He can be contacted by e-mail at david.berry@sun.com.

A Methodology for Multithreaded X Client Development

Murali V. Srinivasan[†]

Abstract

Most of the operating systems such as UNIX, OS/2, and NT, support development of Multithreaded(MT) applications. Multithreading of application decreases the thru-put time and increases the efficiency of the system. The X windowing system provides MT-safe Xlib and Xt in the X11R6 release. Developing a multithreading X client is complicated because of client/server paradigm of X and the asynchronous nature of the X Protocol. There is no methodolgy available for developing MT X client. This paper describes one such methodology and also provides MT definitions, analyzes the conditions when MT X clients are appropriate, compares the methodology with those available for Windows NT and OS/2 applications.

A windowing system application typically has cpu, I/O, network and user-interface operations. These operations have indeterministic completion time in the order listed above. Hence, windowing system applications are more likely to benefit by multithreading than the application which have some of above operations. For example, an application with just cpu operation (cpu-intensive job) will not benefit by multithreading when run on a uniprocessor machine (in fact, tests show that the performance decreases for these applications under certain conditions). Considerable work has been done for multithreading applications with cpu, I/O and network operations. Documents on multithreading applications in Windows and OS/2 environment address some of the issues related to graphics and user-interface operations. In this paper, we attempt to capture all these ideas and present a methodology for MT X client development.

[†]*Murali V. Srinivasan (vsm@eng.sun.com) is an engineer at SunSoft Inc. in Mountain View, CA.*

PhotoKit

An XIE Toolkit

Larry Hare
Bob Shelley[†]

Abstract

The PhotoKit is an extensible, object oriented toolkit designed to harness the power of the X Image Extension (XIE), while providing an environment that is familiar to the X Toolkit (Xt) programmer.

By recasting the innovative XIE element and photoflo concept into a set of Xt objects, the flexibility of low level XIE programming is preserved, while allowing new abstract elements (dynamically constructed from simpler elements) to encapsulate convenience functions, file readers and writers, image processing knowledge, caching of resources, and general policy issues.

Introduction

The XIE protocol provides a very low level, yet powerful, set of primitives that enhance the image display capabilities of the X Window System. XIElib introduces a C binding atop the protocol, providing a one to one mapping between function calls and protocol items. While XIElib exposes all of XIE's power to the application writer, it is also very awkward to use, especially when attempting to employ modular programming techniques.

Over a period of time, XIElib programmers will undoubtedly develop subroutine libraries to support a variety of commonly performed tasks, or for those tasks which are just too complicated to keep re-inventing. The PhotoKit is an attempt to fill this void with an extensible set of tools, patterned after and built upon the X Toolkit, that preserve XIE's efficient data-flow mechanism, the *photoflo*.

[†]*Larry Hare is Chief Software Architect at AGE Logic, Inc. Bob Shelley is Imaging Architect at AGE Logic, Inc. PhotoKit is a trademark of AGE Logic, Inc.*

Although a single image viewing widget might satisfy some needs; it would tend to evolve into a complex mass of switches and options to satisfy a diverse collection of requirements. The goals of the PhotoKit are much more ambitious; to retain the full capabilities of XIE, while recasting it into the more familiar Xt programming environment, and adding a large number of abstractions which comfortably provide convenience and policy.

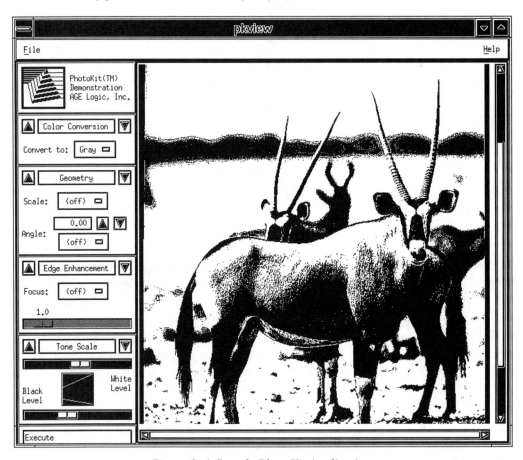

Figure 1: A Sample PhotoKit Application

The PhotoKit, in conjunction with a user interface toolkit, could be used to build either a simple viewing widget with surprising flexibility, or it might be used to build a medical application with multiple concurrent image views. The PhotoKit is intended to help create XIE pipelines, it does not involve itself directly in the creation of a GUI interface. Figure 1 shows an application built with the PhotoKit which will be discussed throughout the article. The GUI along the left hand side represents a logical pipeline allowing various types of image enhancements. The ordering of the pipeline can be modified by clicking the up and down arrows on each element. The application adapts to a variety of image types and visual classes.

Brief Review of XIE and XIElib

XIE allows "image programs" to be written using primitive building blocks. A processing pipeline, or more generally, a directed acyclic graph (DAG) is constructed by a client program from a variety of Import, Process, and Export elements. When such a photoflo is transmitted to the server and then executed, image data from the client program or from internal X server resources is piped through the photoflo, typically ending up in a viewable window.

The design of the XIE V5 protocol was based upon previous experience with an earlier version of XIE, the V3 protocol developed and promoted by Digital Equipment Corporation starting approximately 5 years ago. The V5 design included a heavy emphasis on symmetry, mechanism, flexibility and integer data types; full support for DAGs emerged, and policy-laden export elements were broken down into simpler parts.

XIE V5 adds several new resource types to the X server (Photomap, LUT, ROI, colorList), supports single band and triple band data, and supports image data of constrained (varying number of quantization levels) or unconstrained (floating) types. The V5 sample implementation performs well on a wide variety of platforms and should become ubiquitous as vendors start shipping X11R6 based servers.

Typical Problems in Using XIElib

XIElib is a direct encapsulation of the XIE wire protocol; the XIE V5 protocol reference manual and the XIElib reference manual each comprise approximately 200 pages of very terse documentation. The documentation provides excellent details on the individual flo elements and techniques, but provides little overall guidance in putting together realistic photoflos. XIElib itself contributes little to the ease of use of XIE; but instead externalizes a variety of bookkeeping problems with allocation and freeing of supporting data structures.

Although XIE can import several formats of raw image data, it is left to the programmer to decode image file headers, prepare appropriate technique parameters, and push raw data towards the server at the appropriate time.

Similarly, the programmer is left with a morass of details to ponder when trying to export an image to any of the six visual classes and various screen depths supported by X. To make matters worse, the most prevalent visual class, PseudoColor, has its own set of problems with colormap allocation policies.

A straightforward coding job may result in a large procedural program, with many testing permutations; the nature of XIElib seems to discourage modular programming. The programmer must also account for expose and resize events, and perhaps application based panning or zooming. The entire program needs to be recast in terms of the typical X event loop model.

The typical situation is that a program that works with one image or on one display will often produce `FloMatch` or `FloValue` errors when run in a different environment. In short, XIElib presents a formidable learning curve due to the large size of XIE, the focus on pure mechanism, the unfamiliar programming model, and the lack of protocol level imaging expertise.

PhotoKit - an Xt Compliant Extension

The PhotoKit is closely based on the X Toolkit Intrinsics. It uses the familiar Xt programming model with resources, the create/set/get paradigm, callbacks, and the Xt event loop. To illustrate this, the following code fragments from Figure 1's implementation are presented.

First we create an overall PhotoKit shell and the PhotoKit equivalent of a Photomap resource:

```
ps = XpkVaCreateObject("photo_shell",xpkPhotoShellPhidgetClass,top,NULL);
imgres = XpkCreateImageResource("final-form-image", ps);
```

The logical photoflo, including two user defined elements, is instantiated once as the program starts. Note the use of Xt name/value pairings to set resource values, and the lack of conditionals.

```
flo1    = XpkCreateObject("Flo1", xpkExecutePhidgetClass, ps, NULL, 0);
import = XpkVaCreateObject("Import", xpkLoadImagePhidgetClass, flo1,
                            XpkNprocessData, TRUE,
                            XpkNstoreData, TRUE, NULL);
chrome = create_chrome("ColorSpaceConverter", flo1);
geom   = XpkCreateObject("Geom",xpkSimpleGeometryPhidgetClass,flo1,NULL,0);
sharp  = XpkCreateObject("Sharpen", xpkSharpenPhidgetClass, flo1, NULL, 0);
tnscl  = create_tn_scl("ToneScaleAdjust", flo1);
render = XpkVaCreateObject("RenderWin",xpkRenderPhidgetClass,flo1,NULL,0);
edraw1 = XpkVaCreateObject("EDraw", xpkExportDrawablePhidgetClass, flo1,
                            XpkNdrawable, XtWindow(draw),
                            XpkNgc, gc, XpkNgcBitonal, gc2, NULL);
ephoto = XpkVaCreateObject("EPhoto", xpkExportPhotomapPhidgetClass, flo1,
                            XpkNconnections, "RenderWin><",
                            XpkNimageResource, imgres, NULL);
```

A second flo is created for handling expose events, and some callbacks are hooked:

```
flo2    = XpkVaCreateObject("Flo2", xpkExecutePhidgetClass, ps,
                            XpkNstoreFloGraph, TRUE, NULL);
iphoto = XpkVaCreateObject("IPhoto", xpkImportPhotomapPhidgetClass, flo2,
                            XpkNimageResource, imgres, NULL);
edraw2 = XpkVaCreateObject("EDraw2", xpkExportDrawablePhidgetClass, flo2,
                            XpkNdrawable, XtWindow(draw),
                            XpkNgc, gc, XpkNgcBitonal, gc2, NULL);

XtAddCallback(flo1,    XpkNdoneCallback, flo_cb,    NULL);
XtAddCallback(geom,    XpkNprepCallback, prep_geom, NULL);
XtAddCallback(sharp,   XpkNprepCallback, prep_sharp, NULL);
XtAddCallback(edraw1,  XpkNprepCallback, prep_edraw, NULL);
```

At this point, the application will enter the Xt event loop. As the GUI interface widgets are tickled by the user and their callbacks are invoked, individual calls to XtVaSetValues are made to change the respective options in the abstract elements in the logical photoflo. When the user hits the **Execute** button, a chain of callbacks are triggered. If a new file name has been chosen it is passed down to the import element. A new physical photoflo is realized and executed:

```
void execute_cb(Widget w, String new_file, XtPointer call_data)
{
  if(new_file || image_ready) {
     XtSetSensitive(do_it, FALSE);
     if(new_file) {
       XtVaSetValues(import, XpkNfileName, new_file, NULL);
       if(image_ready) XpkPurgeImageResource(imgres);
     }
     image_ready = FALSE;
     if(!XpkRealizePhotoflo(flo1) || !XpkStartPhotoflo(flo1,FALSE))
       XClearWindow(XtDisplay(draw), XtWindow(draw));
  }
}
```

As the physical flo is being realized, various element "prep" callbacks are invoked to allow final setup of the actual flo. Other callbacks or phidget methods may examine image characteristics such as size, or number of bands, and dynamically configure photoflo elements as discussed later.

```
void prep_sharp(Widget sh, XtPointer client_data, XtPointer call_data)
{
  int    slider;  float factor;
  XmScaleGetValue(sharp_scale, &slider);
  factor = (float)slider * sharpen_multiplier;
  XtVaSetValues(sh, XpkNsharpenFactor, XpkFloatArg(factor), NULL);
}
```

When the primary flo completes, the secondary flo responsible for expose callbacks is realized:

```
void flo_cb(Widget w, XtPointer client_data, XtPointer call_data)
{
  if(image_ready = ((XpkFloOutcome)call_data == XpkFloSuccess &&
                    XpkRealizePhotoflo(flo2)))
    XtSetSensitive(do_it, TRUE);
  else
    XClearWindow(XtDisplay(draw), XtWindow(draw));
}
void expose_cb(Widget w, XtPointer client_data, XtPointer call_data)
{
  if(image_ready && !XpkStartPhotoflo(flo2,TRUE))
    XtWarning("Can't execute a photoflo to handle an expose event");
}
```

The up and down triangles in the GUI allow the logical pipeline order to change. Several lines of code like the following adjust both Xt container geometry constraints, and PhotoKit connections resulting in a very simple visual programmer.

```
XtVaSetValues(controls[below_1].widget, XmNtopWidget,
              controls[above_1].widget, NULL);
XpkMakeConnection(controls[below_1].phidget, NULL,
                  controls[above_1].phidget, NULL);
```

Parallels Between the X Toolkit and the XIE PhotoKit

The PhotoKit uses Xt to solve a unique non-GUI problem. The PhotoKit introduces a new direct subclass of *Object* called the *Phidget*; all PhotoKit objects descend from the phidget class. Whereas widgets are combined together to create a GUI, phidgets are combined to create an image processing engine or photoflo. One can draw many parallels between the two paradigms.

1. Complex widgets are often formed from combinations of simpler widgets. Similarly, phidgets are combined into more complex abstract phidgets or into a complete photoflo.

2. The exact widgets which are visible can change dynamically, or certain widgets may be grayed-out or otherwise inaccessible. The phidgets used to instantiate a photoflo can dynamically respond to current conditions and configure varying sets of photo-elements, or bypass themselves completely.

3. Widgets within containers have geometric positions specified by constraints which can change dynamically. The connections between phidgets within a photoflo can be readily altered.

4. Widgets have a look and feel which can be tailored by resource settings. Similarly, phidgets support resource setting hints which might affect storage or colormap policies.

5. Widgets and phidgets have a functionality which can be completely replaced by substitution of a new component respecting the given class rules.

First View of PhotoKit Object Class Hierarchy

The basic PhotoKit contains the classes illustrated in Figure 2. All PhotoKit classes are subclassed from the base Xt Object class, as well as the new Phidget class; since all PhotoKit objects have Phidget as a superclass, they are often referred to generically as *phidgets.*

Each non-data-transport XIE pipeline element has a directly analogous subclass of the PhotoKit *Element* class. Although a complete list of *Technique* and Element subclasses is not illustrated, the PhotoKit provides support for each photo-element and technique defined by XIE. These simple elements form the basis of most pipelines. The basic (intrinsic) objects can be further subclassed to provide a more abstract interface to the XIE photo-elements, or more typically, higher level operators can be constructed by encapsulating objects within an element class container. The demo program shown in Figure 1 uses both of these variations.

The *Connect* subclass of Phidget allows data-flow connections to be made between Element phidgets; most interconnections will be of subclass *Image*. The *ImageData* subclass corresponds closely to the ImportClientPhoto and ExportClientPhoto XIE elements, and includes client side support to interact with an extensible set of file readers/writers and data transport code. The *ImageResource* subclass represents the XIE Photomap resource. Special Connect subclasses are also provided to represent LUT, ROI, or Histogram transport or resources.

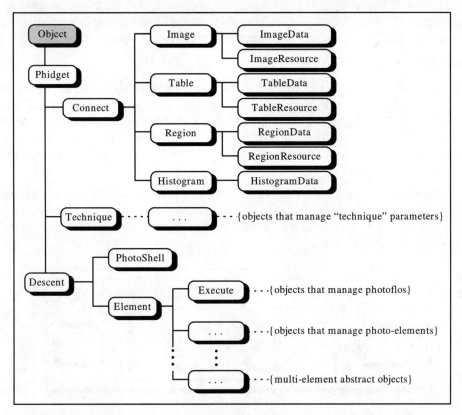

Figure 2: PhotoKit class hierarchy of the base object set (the intrinsics)

Subclasses of Element can act as containers for other elements and their respective connections. A combination of simpler elements can then appear as a single logical element - an abstract element. The *Execute* subclass takes this a step further and adds the necessary bookkeeping to manage an actual XIE photoflo, including data transport.

Simple Elements ↔ Mechanism

The programmer retains full access to all the primitive XIE elements, and to their respective techniques. All parameters, including technique parameters, are specified via the familiar Xt name/value pairing to set the PhotoKit element resources, the programmer is insulated from the actual *Technique* subclasses and the bookkeeping problems of XIElib technique access.

Element classes may be subclassed. An example provided in the PhotoKit is the *SimpleGeometry* subclass, which supplants Geometry's cryptic transformation coefficients with abstract operatives such as *scale-to-fit* or *mirror-x*.

Soft or Abstract techniques can be readily added to elements. One example is the *AutoSample* technique which chooses an actual geometry technique based on input image attributes, geometry scale factors, and a speed versus quality trade-off. This also allows for portable handling of new XIE techniques; if the underlying technique is not supported, the soft technique can utilize a standard technique. It may also insert ancillary phidgets, for instance, AutoSample might insert a Point or Constrain ClipScale element to prepare for a scale-to-gray operation for fax viewing.

Connections ↔ Topology

An XIE photoflo may be arbitrarily complex, as long as the interconnection of its photo-elements forms a DAG - a graph that does not contain any feedback loops. Any legal photoflo can be expressed using PhotoKit objects. Each Element class phidget can encapsulate any number of elements as children, and these children can do likewise to any depth. The PhotoKit only permits connections within an element's immediate family. The immediate family includes the element itself, its siblings, and its parent. Valid PhotoKit connections are illustrated in Figure 3.

Unless connections are explicitly specified, the PhotoKit will automatically connect the input of each newly created element to the output of its most recently created sibling. The scheme works well for building simple linear photoflos; in fact the use of abstract elements tends to make the high level logical flo a simple pipeline.

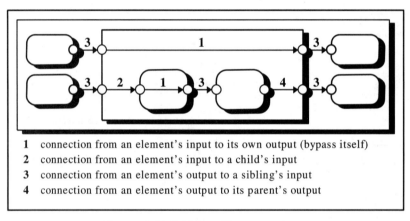

1   connection from an element's input to its own output (bypass itself)
2   connection from an element's input to a child's input
3   connection from an element's output to a sibling's input
4   connection from an element's output to its parent's output

Figure 3: Valid PhotoKit connections

The flow of data between elements is expressed using subclasses of Connect. Connections contain a dynamic representation of the data characteristics in the photoflo; for instance an image connection maintains the width, height, the data type and number of levels, and the number of bands. The PhotoKit augments this with new types representing the color space of the image and its luminance polarity. These attribute values are represented as object resources of a Connect subclass which may be interrogated via `XtGetValues`. They are usually considered read-only and cannot be set by the application unless the Connect object represents a data-transport photo-element. These characteristics are propagated through connected elements when the photoflo is realized.

Simple elements embody the knowledge of how the data characteristics will be transformed by the physical XIE implementation. Most elements will pass this information through unchanged.

Altered characteristics will be correctly passed to downstream elements, for instance the Geometry element will modify the image width and height. This knowledge is built into the PhotoKit, and also includes processing for ROIs, LUTs, and Histograms.

While simple elements act obediently to this characteristic data (or produce a warning message), abstract elements can react intelligently to this information, make dynamic decisions about how to configure their contained elements, and pass the transformed characteristics downstream. This is the magic that makes the PhotoKit.

An element can contribute photo-elements to a physical photoflo only if it is connected in the logical path between an import phidget and an export phidget. The PhotoKit intrinsic routines, XpkMakeConnection and XpkBreakConnection, allow the application and abstract elements to dynamically include or exclude elements by changing their connections. The decision to make and break connections is usually determined after examining element parameters, input connector data attributes, or other external factors. Since a connector can have only one source of data, using XpkMakeConnection to establish a new connection will implicitly break any previous connection to the connector.

An Abstract Element Example

An abstract element is an instance of a container class element which encapsulates other element instances. From the outside, the abstract element is subject to the same rules as individual elements. It can connect to its parent or siblings. It produces transformed characteristics when requested.

A static connection of objects would make a rather naive abstraction, for instance to specify a convenience function. A potential example might be to sharpen or blur an image by combining an edge detecting convolution operator with arithmetic elements operating on unconstrained data. To use this element the application would either statically include it in a higher level flo, or would be forced to connect it into the flo upon request.

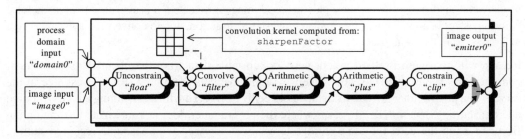

Figure 4: Schematic of the abstract Sharpen phidget

The actual Sharpen class included in the PhotoKit is shown in Figure 4. It supports a process domain or ROI input, forwarding the process domain (if any) to the Convolve element is sufficient to give the abstract element the desired functionality. Another major feature, often used in abstract elements, is the addition of a bypass path. When the sharpenFactor is set or defaulted to zero, the result should be an identity operation. At prep-time, the emitter0 tap is connected back to either the final Constrain output, or to the original image input, image0. When the PhotoKit detects that the five internal elements are a dead end, no actual XIE photo-elements will be generated. These improvements to the naive Sharpen element only require a few lines of code in the Sharpen class implementation. The description from the manual reads:

> The image is input via `image0`, optional process-domain data can be input via `domain0`, and the final image is output from `emitter0`. The names of the internal phidgets are shown in quotes below each phidget class name: *"float"* unconstrains the image (if necessary), *"filter"* convolves the image with the kernel, *"minus"* forms the difference (`SubRev`), *"plus"* recombines the difference with the original (`Add`), and *"clip"* constrains the image back to its original number of quantization levels (`HardClip`).

> The convolution kernel is computed internally using `sharpenFactor`. A value of 0 causes `emitter0` to be connected to `image0`; the phidget is bypassed and no photo-elements are placed in the target photoflo. For any other `sharpenFactor` value, `emitter0` is connected to *"clip"*, and a 3x3 convolution kernel is calculated (*kernel_size* is 3).

From the programmer's perspective, the Sharpen class is equivalent to the Math class in terms of topology and ease of use. The programmer has avoided the plumbing complexity of five strangely interconnected elements, and benefited from image processing knowledge required to envision the filter. In the future, alternative abstract filters, or perhaps even a direct connection to a new XIE server technique could be readily substituted.

Abstract Elements ↔ Policy (and More)

The PhotoKit comes with an ever growing number of built-in abstractions. Many of the newer PhotoKit abstractions are built upon other abstractions. A widely used class in this respect is *ReMap* shown in Figure 5. ReMap encapsulates a point element with the import and export elements that are necessary for managing a server LUT resource. In our example program, it is used by the LoadImage class when a palette based image is detected, it is also used to create a false coloring effect in application *ColorSpaceConverter* abstraction, and to convert a gray scale image to TrueColor in the *Render* class.

ReMap will configure itself to accept new lookup table data from the client if its table input connector has been initialized, otherwise it will retrieve data from an XIE LUT resource in the server. The programmer is freed from the bookkeeping involved with maintaining an XIE resource and transporting data to XIE. In cases where the programmer does not anticipate re-running the flo or re-using the data, the table storage is easily suppressed with a simple resource setting. ReMap can be easily subclassed to synthesize common lookup tables automatically.

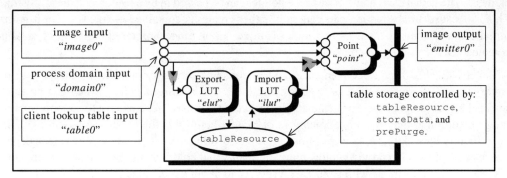

Figure 5: Schematic of the abstract ReMap phidget

The *LoadImage* class is shown in Figure 6. It utilizes the ReMap class to help load palette based images. The instance hierarchy is at least 4 levels deep. As in ReMap, LoadImage maintains a Photomap resource in the XIE server representing the current image. Setting the XpkNfileName resource triggers loading of an image file using an extensible set of file reading routines and callbacks; the image characteristics (size, levels, bands, ...) are used to prime the propagation of characteristics through the DAG. Later execution of the same logical flo will use the stored Photomap until XpkNfileName is set again.

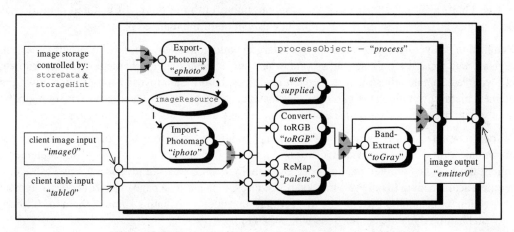

Figure 6: Schematic of the abstract LoadImage phidget

The XpkNstoreData resource enables or suppresses server storage of the Photomap and is also passed down to the ReMap element to enable or suppress storage of any palette. The XpkNstoreHint allows the image to be captured as it comes off the wire, or to wait and capture the potentially decompressed or palette expanded image; thus allowing for a space versus time tradeoff when images are re-used. When optimizing for space, the ReMap element is instructed to preserve the palette in the LUT table resource.

Another interesting feature shown in Figure 6 is the ability to include an unknown user specified element. The actual class name or instance pointer can be passed in by a resource value at any time. This is because an abstraction can generally either create its contained elements when it is first initialized and connect them as required, or utilize an alternate programming style of creating contained elements only when needed.

Abstract elements provide convenience, and intelligence through dynamically adapting to the environment. Resources such as `XpkNstoreHint` are a form of policy which can be easily selected by the programmer, or made available to the final user. The extensive support for final image rendition to the screen in *ShowImage* or *Render* help solve the major shortcoming of XIE: the difficulty in mapping a variety of image formats to various X visual classes and screen depths. These abstractions also provide policy hints for quality and colormap usage and take advantage of several non-obvious tricks with ColorList resources to avoid the dreaded "flashing" effects.

In addition to PhotoKit-provided abstract classes, the programmer can create their own classes, or register callbacks with existing abstractions to gain additional dynamic control at realization time.

Photoflo Realization

In our example program, we create the logical flo only one time. Every time we modify GUI parameters and click on the **Execute** button, we call `XpkRealizePhotoflo`. An Execute phidget is said to be *realized* when the logical photoflo that is expressed by the current state of its descendants has been transformed into a physical photoflo. Realization involves such tasks as examining element interconnections, parsing image files to seed the data attributes, generating an XIElib PhotofloGraph, and sending the resultant photoflo to the server (if a stored photoflo has been requested). Realization does not include execution of the realized photoflo.

Realization is a very complex process, but is largely hidden in class methods. A programmer can register and receive a callback at a point where an element's input characteristics are known, allowing last minute adjustment to element resources, before the process is propagated down the element hierarchy or along the photoflo. For instance, adjustment to a Geometry element might be appropriate based on the current size of the input image and the display window size.

A programmer actually writing new abstract phidgets has roughly the same view, but communication would occur via invocation of its method instead of a callback. Abstract elements inherit most of the complex method code from their superclasses. In practice, a new abstraction requires actual coding in only two method procedures, each taking a page or less of code. A typical abstraction will examine current resource settings, consider propagating some of them to children, and establishing dynamic connections within its family.

A completely different XIE pipeline may be generated each realization. Figure 1's demo example can generate as few as 3 or as many as 20 actual photoflo elements.

Photoflo Execution

Once Execute's logical photoflo has been realized, it may be executed or re-executed by calling the intrinsic routine `XpkStartPhotoflo`. If XIE import-client elements exist in the current flo, then connect methods are used to obtain data; these typically result in callbacks to the image file reading library or to the application. Exported data, if any, is detected by monitoring XIE events and then executing the appropriate connect methods. Errors from the XIE server are also collected and filtered in this stage.

In the example program, a second photoflo is used to handle window expose events and scroll bar panning. The primary flo always exports a copy of the final image to a photomap. The second flo is instantiated at program startup since it can always refer to the same ImageResource object. It is realized when the `flo_cb` callback has been notified that the primary photoflo completed successfully. It may never be executed, or could be executed many times before another primary photoflo is realized.

File Input and Output

The PhotoKit includes an extensible file input/output mechanism bound to the ImageData class. The current implementation includes support for most TIFF 6.0 files including the various fax compression formats supported by XIE. Hooks are provided so that processing routines for additional file formats can be specified at runtime, or so that raw application data can be transported.

Early stages of the photoflo realization process detect when import data-transport photo-elements are required and make callbacks to determine the initial resource characteristics. In the default case, this would result in the opening of a file, determining the file type from an extensible set of pattern matching routines, parsing enough of the file to determine the image characteristics, and setting the image characteristics and a data callback into the input connector. During photoflo execution, the PhotoKit will invoke the data callback routines of all active import connectors. This process is also able to accommodate palette images where both the image and the associated palette need to be transported to LoadImage or ReMap.

Export data-transport photo-elements are managed by using data available notification events provided by XIE. When these events are detected, the available data is retrieved from the server by the associated output connector and passed to the application or file writer via a callback.

Errors, Events, and other Interesting Xt Issues

Naive XIE programming often leads to `FloMatch` or `FloValue` errors during early development or later when the execution environment changes. XIE generated events may be useful but are difficult to integrate into an application. The PhotoKit provides some interesting solutions here. The following warnings are examples we received when adding a ROI capability to the sharp demo which utilizes the *Sharpen* class:

```
Warning: badMatch (_XpkInheritAttributes) cannot inherit
    from sharp.photo_shell.Flo.ROI
      to sharp.photo_shell.Flo.Sharpen.domain0

Warning: badSyntax (AugmentConnections) cannot parse "<ROI #domain0",
         for sharp.photo_shell.Flo.Sharpen
```

By utilizing intelligent abstract elements, a PhotoKit program will tend to be much more robust by its very nature. The pipeline will simply adjust to the conditions at hand; we have been surprised ourselves at what some pipelines have handled.

The next line of defense arises somewhat by default as well; since individual elements must determine how image characteristics will be affected as they flow through the DAG; they can simulate the error checks that the XIE server would apply for free. When an error situation is predicted, a clear warning message or callback is provided which includes the ASCII name of the offending element.

Of course, it is still possible to generate true XIE errors; a common case might be during decode of a badly formatted compressed image. This is an especially bad case since the client may already have queued up more image data to the connection, which will now generate more errors since the target photoflo has already terminated. An XIElib application could request event returns for many cases such as this and XIE is defined to return the events before the corresponding errors; however the error will tend to get to the application first anyway. The PhotoKit has been enhanced to solve both of these problems by collecting and filtering error messages and photoflo events; and hopefully producing a more meaningful and concise error response. An exception callback is available to pass Error or Warning (event) information back to the application.

XIE export-client data elements are designed to send notification events to the client so that the correct element data can be drained. The PhotoKit intercepts these events and activates the corresponding PhotoKit connector to retrieve the data, which it then passes to the application or file writer via callbacks.

Because the PhotoKit objects are based on the Object class of Xt, rather than the Widget class, event handling is quite complex, and is unfortunately sensitive to interface conflicts between the R5 and R6 versions of Xt. A similar issue currently under investigation is the ability to support the *editres* protocol to help display the currently instantiated object hierarchy.

SimpleGeometry - A Sample Man Page

Synopsis

Public headers:	`<xpk/abstract/sgeom.h>`
Private headers:	`<xpk/abstract/sgeomp.h>`
Class pointer:	`xpkSimpleGeometryClass`
Ancestry:	Object→Phidget→Descent→Element→Geometry→SimpleGeometry
Inputs:	Image - image0
Outputs:	Image - emitter0

Description

SimpleGeometry is an abstraction of Geometry that simplifies the specification of scale and rotate operations.

New Resources

Name	Class	Type	Default	Access
fit	Fit	Enum	SGeom_NoFit	CSG
box	Box	Enum	SGeom_FitPostRotation	CSG
angle	Angle	Float	0.0	CSG

`fit (CSG)`   Specifies how to scale an image so as to match the width and height resources that are defined in the Geometry superclass part. The choices are:

fit options	Description
`XpkSGeom_NoFit`	no scaling
`XpkSGeom_Width`	scale to match `width` -- maintain aspect ratio
`XpkSGeom_Height`	scale to match `height` -- maintain aspect ratio
`XpkSGeom_Within`	scale to match `width` and `height` -- maintain aspect ratio
`XpkSGeom_Stretch`	scale to fill `width` and `height` -- ignore aspect ratio

`box (CSG)`   When an image is both scaled and rotated, box specifies whether the scale factors are computed before or after rotation. The choices are::

box options	Description
`XpkSGeom_FitPreRotate`	use pre-rotate dimensions as input to fit computation
`XpkSGeom_FitPostRotate`	use post-rotate dimensions as input to fit computation

`angle (CSG)`   Specifies the angle of rotation in degrees. Positive angles cause clockwise rotation.

See Also

Geometry - XieFloGeometry()

Future Work

The current focus on PhotoKit development remains on rounding out the basic product. The obvious areas include:

1. Extensive support for reading file formats, and finishing the infrastructure for file output.

2. Rounding out a set of abstract phidgets for a variety of convenience and policy domains.

3. Creating several *SuperPhidget* classes - subclasses of Execute, which would generate a complete viewing pipeline in a given policy domain.

4. Exploring changes required for tighter integration with GUI builder tools.

Visual Programmer

While not an explicit goal of the PhotoKit, it continues to evolve as a good match for a visual programming environment for XIE or other pipelined metaphors supporting directed acyclic graphs. The demo shown in Figure 1 is a good start on a linear visual programmer. Phidgets can be freely instantiated, removed, or reconnected to other phidgets. Abstract phidgets will attempt to adapt to changing circumstances, and will try to produce graceful warning messages when they are not reasonably connected. A related issue here might be the generation of libraries of icons and GUI widgets tuned for the various Element classes.

Other Uses

While the PhotoKit was spawned by the need for a high-level interface to XIE functionality, it can also be layered above other imaging libraries, or as a means of conjoining these libraries with XIE. Thus transparent distributed image processing would be possible under the cloak of the PhotoKit. The underlying design makes some provision for this; note that the client host is already involved in image transport functions.

At a more basic level, the underlying PhotoKit technology is a natural fit for describing any pipelined based processing, for instance NAS sound pipelines. The SUN XIL library is an excellent example of a system which would benefit from the abstraction level provided by the PhotoKit.

Summary

The PhotoKit provides a consistent, extensible, object-oriented programming model that capitalizes on XIE's powerful photoflo model, while easily integrating into the typical widget based programming environment.

A significant amount of XIE expertise is already bundled into the abstract elements provided with the PhotoKit, substantially reducing the amount of imaging code and potential defects in many applications. An advanced programmer can readily extend or tailor the PhotoKit to their own unique requirements.

The PhotoKit is an evolving commercial product of AGE Logic. Release 1 has been available to early adopters for several months. Versions exist for most major workstations and include various example programs and example abstract phidgets in source form.

About the Authors

Larry Hare is the Chief Software Architect at AGE Logic, where he has been responsible for various RISC and Embedded X Server projects. Larry has been heavily involved in the XIE SI and the XIE PhotoKit for the last two years. Prior to joining AGE, Larry has worked with multiprocessor UNIX kernels, multiprocessor window systems, object oriented micro-kernels, 2D and 3D CAD systems. Larry can be reached at *hare@age.com*.

Bob Shelley is the Imaging Architect at AGE Logic. He was the Lead Architect of the XIE V5 Sample Implementation delivered to the X Consortium one year ago, and has since been focused on creating the XIE PhotoKit. Previously, Bob was involved with the original XIE V3 implementation at Digital, working on the SI, several proprietary server implementations, and an image viewing widget. While still at DEC, Bob was the Architect and Document Editor for the V5 version of the XIE protocol. Bob can be reached at *shelley@age.com*.

Intelligent Reusable User Interface Components

Veikko Punkka[†]

Abstract

This paper is about implementing and using intelligent reusable user interface components. Motivation for such components is provided. A standardized approach for constructing and using them using X11, OSF/Motif and C++ is introduced.

A sample implementation of the paradigm is introduced. The sample implementation has recently been adopted as the standard method for creating and using reusable user interface components within Nokia Telecommunications Corporation. A future development concept is introduced as "User Interface Factory".

Introduction & Motivation - The Why

Writing interactive software is difficult. Writing reusable software is difficult. Writing intelligent software is difficult. Why would one then try to combine these three difficulties?

The first argument for the project came from the sheer size of the software project I am involved in, the Nokia Operating and Maintenance Center for Cellular Networks (OMC). The system consists of over 2 million lines of C++ code. In order to keep the project manageable, we needed to separate the layout and the functionality of the system. For this we developed an architecture we call MVC++ [1]. This architectural solution is an essential part of the OMT++ methodology [2] widely used in Nokia Telecommunications Corporation and beyond. OMT++ is a modification and enhancement of the OMT approach [3]. OMT notation is also used in the meta models throughout of this paper.

MVC++ Paradigm

The MVC++ paradigm is a modified version of the MVC paradigm [6] earlier introduced in conjunction with Smalltalk [4]. MVC++ separates the applications into three functionally different parts: the Model, the View and the Controller. The Model (M) of an application represents the "real

---

[†]*Veikko Punkka is the Principal Architect of Reusable User Interface Components at Nokia Cellular Systems Oy. He may be reached by e-mail at veikko.punkka@ntc.nokia.com.*

world" the application simulates, uses or serves. It is a collection of objects representing the concepts of the problem domain. It knows how the "real world" works. The Model has no user interface elements. The View (V) is the outer layer of the user interface that is visible to the end user. It represents the manipulation methods (MM) the application provides the user with and the feedback methods (FM) the application uses for conveying information to the user as well as the query methods (QM) the application uses for inquiring information from the user. The View knows how to represent these methods and the data involved to the user and how to receive the user input. The Controller (C) controls the interaction between the Model and the View. It knows how this particular application works and what it is supposed to do.

A View object generally represents a single dialog within the user interface. One of the View objects of the program, the one representing the main window of the program, is denoted the Main View. There is a single Controller object for every View object and at most one View object for each Controller object. A Controller object may, however, have relations with several Model objects and the same Model object may be related to several Controller objects. The Controller of the Main View is denoted the Main Controller. Other Controllers are known as Subcontrollers.

The manipulation, feedback and query methods of a View are grouped into entities that are known as View Components. The main differences between a View and a View Component are: a View Component does not necessarily form a complete dialog and a View Component does not have a Controller of its own. A View component may consist of View components itself. Figure 1 attempts to clarify the relationships between the Views, Controllers and View Components of an MVC++ application.

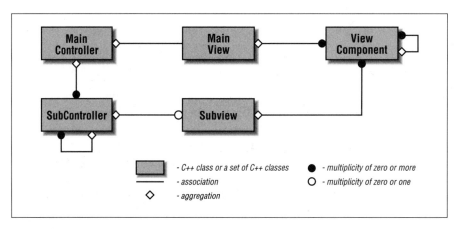

Figure 1: Meta model of the relationship of the Views, Controllers and View Components of an MVC++ application.

The View Components of various Views and even various applications often resemble each other, they perform similar tasks to the user as well as the application. Therefore, the View Components are a natural choice for reuse.

Reusability

The second argument for the project arose from the need of reusability. We often use similar combinations of widgets over and over again, for this we need to be able to create reusable components from them with ease. This can only be achieved if there is a standardized way for creating such components, such that the same wheel does not need to be invented many times.

The consistent way of creating reusable user interface components is an important aspect, but the consistent way of using them is maybe even more so. This can only be achieved by a standardized interface to the user interface components. This, in turn, requires a standardized methodology for creating the components.

If we could find out what kind of problems user interfaces are used to solve, we could make rules and guidelines for creating and using user interface components to solve these problems. Now, the rules and guidelines would not only make the components more reusable by making them look similar from the outside, but also increase their reuse by making them more easily approachable. The software designer could find the component she needs by following links in the rules and guidelines.

Division of Layout and Functionality of View

Since the View also often has some functionality that is associated with the way things are shown to the end user, MVC++ has separated the layout and the functionality of the View into two classes. The class that implements the functionality inherits the class that implements the layout. The class that implements the functionality is called the Functional Class, while the class that implements the visuality is known as the Visual Class. This way we can quickly change the functionality of the View by changing the Functional Class. The Visual Class aggregates any of the View Components the View uses.

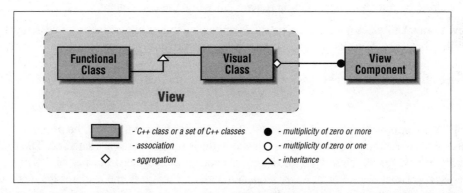

Figure 2: The Visual Class of the View aggregates all the View Components used

Since the View Components can aggregate other View Components, it looks natural that also View Components are divided into a Visual and a Functional part. This would make the View

Components easier to use, since their structure would be similar to that of the View. It would also enable us to make complete Views as if they were View Components.

Extensibility

In order to increase the value of reusable components to software designers we need to attach functionality to layout. This requirement seems to contradict the general requirement to separate the functionality and the layout, but they do so only superficially. We can achieve both by encapsulating the layout to a C++ class and then inheriting this class to another class that defines the functionality.

Convertibility

We don't always know what components should be made reusable before we have made them. For this reason we need to be able to turn parts of the layout we are already using into reusable components with ease. This, once again, requires a standardized structure to the View Components and rules and guidelines for creating them. For the purpose of View Components, a ready made widget hierarchy should be easily convertible to a Visual Class. The functionality can then be attached to it by the standard methods.

Expandability

A ready made component layout does not always satisfy the needs of a software designer. Therefore, we need a standard method for extending the layout of the components with ease. This can be achieved by letting the components aggregate each other and raw widgets in a controlled way. It would be most convenient if this could be made in some kind of GUI builder, to reduce the amount of work associated in setting attachments and other layout relates resources.

The functionality of a ready made component may not satisfy all needs either. Therefore, we need a standard method for changing and enhancing the functionality of the components with ease. For this purpose, the functionality of the component must be enclosed in it in a standardized way. There must be a rule or guideline for including functionality into the component.

A View Component does not have a Controller of its own, but it may sometimes wish to perform Controller functions. For this purpose, it would be beneficial, if a Controller Component object could be attached to it. This would enable us to connect the View Component with Model objects, just as a complete View can associate with Model objects through its Controller object.

Compatibility

Complicated components often require certain functionality from the part of the program using it, for this we need a standard method for making sure these requirements are satisfied. The MVC++ approach solves this problem by introducing a concept called "abstract partner". An abstract partner is an abstract class. It is closely associated with another class and declares the methods the other class requires from its partner. It declares these methods pure virtual. A third class, wishing to use the class the abstract partner is associated with, inherits the abstract partner and implements the methods declared in it. When we create abstract partners to View Components, we ensure that the components are compatible with the Views that aggregate them.

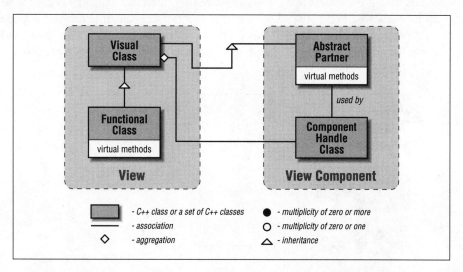

Figure 3: The abstract partner of the View Component is inherited to the Visual Class, but the pure virtual methods are implemented only in the Functional Class of the View

Another compatibility issue is compatibility amongst various user interface components. We may have various components with the same layout but different functionality, or different layout but same functionality or even different layout and functionality. If we wish to be able to swap these components easily, we need a standardized interface for the components.

Consistency

A complicated user interface can be intimidating to the user. Especially so, if the user interface does not function consistently. User interface consistency can be easily achieved by using the same components for similar tasks. It can be made even better by using the same layout for creating components doing similar tasks.

Expertise, Productivity, Quality, Customer Satisfaction

Experts of user interface design are few and far between. Therefore, these critical resources should be used in the most beneficial way. If they could generate reusable user interface components and rules and guidelines for using them, other designers possibly more experienced in the other areas of software engineering or the problem domain could combine the components with their own expertise. This would not require them to learn the intricacies of user interface design, but this would enable them to create quality applications with quality user interfaces. This means not only better productivity, but also greater customer satisfaction, the most important aspect in commercial software development.

Intelligent Reusable User Interface Components - The How

From the motivation it is obvious that a single kind of user interface components cannot possibly achieve all the goals we have stated. What we need is a hierarchical structure of components of scalable complexity and functionality. We call the collection of these rules and guidelines combined with the actual components "Intelligent Reusable User Interface Components".

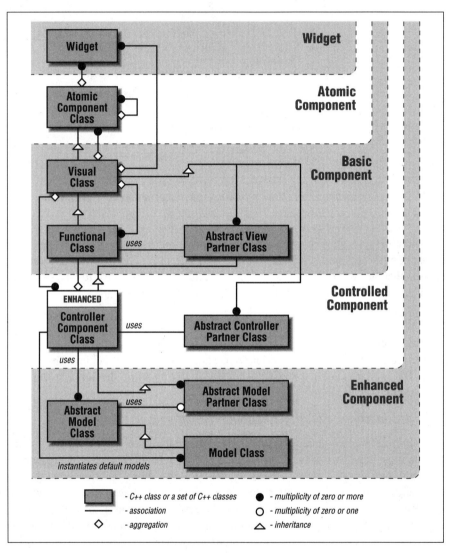

Figure 4: The general structure of various View Components

Various Kinds of Components

Reusable User Interface Components are hierarchical structures of View Component, Controller Component and Model objects. The simplest components only have the View part. The View part is associated with an abstract partner that declares the requirements the View part makes to its Controller part. The second most simple components have both the View and Controller parts. The Controller part inherits the abstract partner of the View part and the View part uses the Controller part through this abstract partner. This way we can change the functionality of components easily by simply replacing the Controller part. The most complex components contain View, Controller and Model parts. Each Model object is associated with an Abstract Model it inherits. This way we can easily swap new Model objects in place and be sure the new Model object satisfies all the requirements stated by the Controller. Model objects may also be associated with an Abstract Model Partner that defines the requirements the Model imposes to its Controller. This way we can be sure the Controller Component really can handle the Model.

Within our taxonomy, there are five different kinds of View Components: Widgets, Atomic, Basic, Controlled and Enhanced View Components. Figure 4 attempts to describe the structure of each kind. Classes denoted with a pound sign (£) are usually generated by a GUI builder such as X-Designer.

Widgets

Widgets are the simplest kind of View Components. They are used as they have always been used, for building up the layout and attaching the functionality of the View to. Widget wrappers may be used, but it is not a necessity. In our vocabulary widgets are sometimes referred to as Motif Based Objects.

Atomic View Components

Atomic View Components are C++ classes that contain the layout (a hierarchy of widgets and associated attachments &c) and possibly some functionality of the View. The class is called the Atomic Component Class. Most often Atomic Components are generated with some GUI builder. An Atomic View Component does not have an abstract partner.

Examples of typical Atomic Components: message area, radio button box, version dialog, working dialog.

Basic View Components

Basic View Components are collections of C++ classes that contain the layout and functionality of the View. The class that contains the layout is called the Visual Class and the class that contains the functionality is called the Functional Class. They are used by instantiating the Functional Class and inheriting the Abstract View Partner. The Functional Class inherits the layout from the Visual Class and includes the functionality. The Abstract View Partner defines the requirements the Basic View Component requires from the class using it. Most often Visual Classes are generated with some GUI builder. The difference between the Atomic Component Class and the Visual Class is subtle but significant. A Visual Class of a Basic View Component includes pure virtual methods as callback methods, it is an abstract class, and therefore it cannot be instantiated as itself. An

Atomic Component Class does not include any pure virtual methods. Therefore, it can be instantiated as it is.

Examples of typical Basic Components: button bar, text entry field, confirmation dialog.

Controlled View Components

Controlled View Components are collections of C++ classes that contain a layout of widgets and functionality of the View and the Controller. The class that contains the layout is called the Visual Class, the class that contains the functionality of the View is called the Functional Class and the class that contains the functionality of the Controller is called the Controller Component Class. They are used by instantiating the Controller Component Class and inheriting the Abstract Controller Partner. The Controller Component Class includes the layout and functionality by aggregating a Functional Class of a Basic View Component. The Abstract Controller Partner defines the requirements that the Controlled View Component requires from the class using it.

Examples of typical Controlled Components: time entry field, password entry field.

Enhanced View Components

Enhanced View Components are collections of C++ classes that contain the layout and functionality of the View, the Controller and the Model. The class that contains the layout is called the Visual Class, the class that contains the functionality of the View is called the Functional Class, the class that contains the functionality of the Controller is called the Enhanced Controller Component Class and the classes that contain the functionality of the Model are called the Model Classes. They are used by instantiating the Enhanced Controller Component Class, inheriting the Abstract Controller Partner and either setting or leaving as default the Model Classes. The Enhanced Controller Component Class includes the layout and functionality of the View and the Controller in a similar fashion as the Controller Component Class of a Controlled View Component does. It also includes the functionality of the Model by aggregating the Model Classes. The Abstract Controller Partner defines the requirements that the Enhanced View Component requires from the class using it. The Model Classes implement the Abstract Model Classes that include the functionality of the Model. For Enhanced View Components the Controller Component Class (as in Figure 4) is called the Enhanced Controller Component Class.

Examples of typical Enhanced Components: managed object browser, file selection dialog

Creating Various Kinds of Components

The creation of each kind of a component is highly automated within the sample implementation. The automation is based on step by step instructions, check lists and template files. They don't fit into the page limit of this publication, but they are available by contacting the author. For further details of the sample implementation, see the conclusions of this paper.

Creating Atomic View Components

The creation of all kinds of components starts by creating the Atomic View Component. This is usually done with a GUI builder. The task basically consists of designing the layout of the component and generating code for the Atomic Component Class. The actual look of the code may depend on the GUI builder used, but the following example is a typical case of a declaration file in the sample implementation.

```
/*
** Generated by X-Designer
*/
#ifndef _auiatabtdlgmx_h
#define _auiatabtdlgmx_h

#include <auidismx.h>

class auiAboutDialogViewCAtomic_c: public auiDialogShell_c {
public:
    virtual void create (Widget parent, char *widget_name = NULL);
    virtual void SetOkInsensitiveFM();
    virtual void SetOkSensitiveFM();
protected:
    Widget MainForm;
    Widget MessageLabel;
    Widget Separator;
    Widget OkButton;
};

typedef auiAboutDialogViewCAtomic_c *auiAboutDialogViewCAtomic_p;
#endif
```

The widgets are created and the callbacks attached in a virtual method called "create". Callbacks are implemented by static callback methods that are used as the callback functions to the XtAddCallback function as described in the Object Oriented Motif book [5], page 63. The pointer of the object is passed in the client_data field and the static function calls the actual instance of the object. For this purpose the object has another, identically named method. Most often, however, the manipulation methods (the callbacks) are not introduced in the Atomic View Components, but only in the Basic View Components. The above example, does not have any manipulation methods. The auiDialogShell_c is a simple wrapper class encapsulating the Dialog Shell widget. The FM suffixes denote feedback methods.

Creating Basic View Components

Basic View Components are created on top of Atomic View Components. They are created by first creating the Visual Class. The Visual Class inherits the Atomic Component Class of the Atomic View Component and may aggregate other widgets or Atomic View Components. Besides these, the Visual Class may aggregate other Basic View Components by aggregating their Functional Classes and inheriting their Abstract View Partners. The Visual Class may even aggregate Controlled and Enhanced View Components by aggregating their (Enhanced) Controller Component Classes and inheriting their abstract Controller Component Partners. The Visual Class is the last chance to modify the layout of the component and the only component class that can aggregate Basic, Controlled and Enhanced View Components. The actual look of the code may depend on the GUI builder used, but the following example is a typical case of a declaration file in the sample implementation.

```
/*
** Generated by X-Designer
*/
#ifndef _buivsabtdlgmx_h
#define _buivsabtdlgmx_h

#include <auiatabtdlgmx.h>

class auiAboutDialogViewCVisual_c: public auiAboutDialogViewCVisual_c {
public:
    virtual void create (Widget parent, char *widget_name = NULL);
protected:
    static void OkPressedMM( Widget, XtPointer, XtPointer );
    virtual void OkPressedMM( Widget, XtPointer ) = 0;
};

#endif
```

The Functional Class and the Abstract View Partner are created by a simple text editor, using template files. The process can be highly automated searching and replacing keywords in the template files. This is also the method adopted in the sample implementation. The Functional Class declares and implements the pure virtual methods it inherits from the Visual Class and the Abstract View Partner classes it inherits via the Visual Class. The MM suffixes denote manipulation methods.

A typical definition of the Functional Class of a Basic View Component might look like the following. The Abstract View Partner is declared in the same header file as the Functional Class.

```
#ifndef _buiviabtdlgmx_h
#define _buiviabtdlgmx_h

// DEFINITION OF USED CLASSES **********************************
#include <buivsabtdlgmx.h>

// DEFINITION OF ABSTRACT VIEW PARTNER ************************

class buiAboutDialogViewAbsVP_c
{
protected:
    virtual void buiOkPressed() = 0;
};

// DEFINITION OF FUNCTIONAL CLASS ****************************

class buiAboutDialogViewC_c
:public buiAboutDialogViewCVisual_c
{
public:
    buiAboutDialogViewC_c();
    virtual ~buiAboutDialogViewC_c();
    virtual void create(Widget parent, char *widget_name = NULL);
    void SetPartner(buiAboutDialogViewAbsVP_c *partner);
protected:
```

```
    virtual void OkPressedMM();
private:
    buiAboutDialogViewAbsVP_c *myPartner;
};


typedef buiAboutDialogViewC_c *buiAboutDialogViewC_p;
#endif
```

The SetPartner method is used by the partner class to set its this pointer to the myPartner pointer. The Manipulation methods check if the myPartner pointer has been set and then call the appropriate method through the Abstract View Partner.

Creating Controlled View Components

Controlled View Components are created on the basis of a Basic View Component. The controlled View Component has exactly the same layout as the Basic View Component, but adds new functionality to it. For example, as the View part cannot make any decisions about what to do with the user input, the Controller part can.

The Controller Component class and the Abstract Controller Partner are created by a simple text editor, using template files. The Controller Component class declares and implements the pure virtual methods it inherits from the Abstract View Partner class it inherits. The Abstract Controller Partner declares the methods the Controller View Component requires from the class using it. It declares these methods pure virtual. Whoever then uses the component, inherits the Abstract Controller Partner and implements the methods in it.

A typical definition of the Controller Component Class of a Controlled View Component might look like the following. The Abstract Controller Partner is defined in the same header file as the Controller Component class.

```
#ifndef _kuiccabtdlgmx_h
#define _kuiccabtdlgmx_h

// DEFINITION OF USED CLASSES *********************************
#include <buiviabtdlgmx.h>
#include <kuiczabtdlgmx.h>

// DEFINITION OF ABSTRACT CONTROLLER PARTNER *****************

class kuiAboutDialogControllerAbsCP_c
{
protected:
    virtual void kuiAboutDialogExited() = 0;
};
// DEFINITION OF CONTROLLER COMPONENT CLASS *****************

class kuiAboutDialogControllerC_c
: public buiAboutDialogViewAbsVP_c
{
public:
    kuiAboutDialogControllerC_c();
    virtual ~kuiAboutDialogControllerC_c();
```

```
      virtual void create(Widget parent, char *widget_name = NULL);
      void SetPartner(kuiAboutDialogControllerAbsCP_c *partner);
      void PostAboutDialog(kuiApplicationData_s *app_data);
protected:
      virtual void buiOkPressed();
      buiAboutDialogView_p  basicComp;
private:
      kuiAboutDialogControllerAbsCP_c *myPartner;
};

typedef kuiAboutDialogControllerC_c *kuiAboutDialogControllerC_p;
#endif
```

The kuiApplicationData_s is a data structure containing the application data shown in the About Dialog. It is declared in kuiczabtdlgmx.h. For simplicity, this header file is omitted here.

Creating Enhanced View Components

Enhanced View Components can be created either on the basis of existing Controlled View Components or directly on the basis of existing Basic View Components. The difference between a Controlled View Component and an Enhanced View Component is that an Enhanced View Component aggregates Model objects that contain Functionality of the problem domain while a Controlled View Component does not.

The enhanced Controller Component class and the Abstract Controller Partner are created by a simple text editor, using template files. Once again, this process can be highly automated and this approach has been chosen in the sample implementation. The enhanced Controller Component class declares and implements the pure virtual methods it inherits from the Abstract View Partner or Abstract Controller Partner class it inherits. The Abstract Controller Partner of the Enhanced View Component declares the methods the Enhanced View Component requires from the class using it. It declares these methods pure virtual.

A typical definition of the Enhanced Controller Component Class of an Enhanced View Component might look like the following. The Abstract Controller Partner is defined in the same header file as the Enhanced Controller Component class.

```
#ifndef _xuicxabtdlgmx_h
#define _xuicxabtdlgmx_h

// DEFINITION OF USED CLASSES **********************************
#include <kuiccabtdlgmx.h>
#include <kuiczabtdlgmx.h>

// DEFINITION OF ABSTRACT CONTROLLER PARTNER ******************

// uses kuiAboutDialogControllerAbsCP_c as Abstract Partner

// DEFINITION OF ENHANCED CONTROLLER COMPONENT CLASS **********

class xuiAboutDialogControllerCX_c
: public kuiAboutDialogControllerC_c
{
```

```
public:
    xuiAboutDialogControllerCX_c();
    virtual ~xuiAboutDialogControllerCX_c();
    virtual void create(Widget parent, char *widget_name = NULL);
    void SetPartner(kuiAboutDialogControllerAbsCP_c *partner);
    void PostAboutDialog();
    void SetApplicationDataModel(kuiApplicationDataModel_c *Model);
protected:
    virtual void kuiAboutDialogExited();
private:   kuiAboutDialogControllerAbsCP_c *myPartner;
    kuiApplicationDataModel_c *app_data_Model;
};

typedef xuiAboutDialogControllerCX_c *xuiAboutDialogControllerCX_p;
#endif
```

The kuiApplicationDataModel_c is a class handling the application data shown in the About Dialog. It is declared in kuiczabtdlgmx.h. For simplicity, this header file is omitted here. The PostAboutDialog() method uses this Model to acquire the kuiApplicationData_s data structure and then passes it to the PostAboutDialog(kuiApplicationData_s *app_data) method of the kuiAboutDialogControllerC_c. The example above shows how the abstract partners can be reused in the next level component, if no modification to the abstract partner is needed. The SetApplicationDataModel(kuiApplicationDataModel_c *Model) method is used for setting the model object. Each model object the Enhanced Controller Component aggregates, must have a similar method for setting it from outside the component. If the model object is not set by the time the create method of the component is called, the create method sets default model objects instead. For simplicity, Abstract Models and Abstract Model Partners are omitted from the example above.

Developing Components

View Components can be developed to suit the actual needs of a software designer. Since the components are real C++ classes, the development can be done most simply by declaring a new class, inheriting the ready made component to it and adding the new functionality or layout to the new class. This way, new functionality can be added to components without disturbing the applications aready using these components. This also makes incremental development of components possible. Only those features that are actually needed at the time a component is created need to be implemented in it.

Conclusion - The What

This paper was written based on experiences gained in a project designing and implementing methodology for creating and implementing reusable user interface components for the Nokia OMC. At the time of writing, the first component production project is under way. It has advanced to the implementation phase and almost one hundred components have been successfully completed.

Sample Implementation

A sample implementation has been produced within Nokia Cellular Systems Oy to be used in the platform of Nokia OMC for Cellular and Fixed Networks. The sample implementation was made using OSF/Motif, though there is no fundamental reason why other widget sets would be unusable. The sample implementation was built using X11R5, HP-UX 9.0 and Motif 1.2. The sample implementation uses X-Designer Release 3.2 [7,8] for building the layout and combining the components into applications. Other GUI builders have not been tested for this purpose. As with layout tools always, they are not absolutely necessary, but they make the life easier. X-Designer was found out to be particularly useful for the purpose, since it has a modifiable palette that accepts components made in this technique. The sample implementation was recently adopted as the standard method for creating and using reusable user interface components within Nokia Telecommunications Corporation.

User Interface Factory

User interface engineering, as it stands today, is still often seen as manual labor. Certainly, sophisticated equipments are used for producing user interfaces, but the way these tools are used does not differ much from the way a shovel is used to dig a drain. User interfaces are tailored individually for each application. There is practically no reuse of components. We are only about to enter the age of industrialization in user interface engineering. If successful, the Intelligent User Interface Components and the methodology for creating and using them may provide us the missing "Model T".

Acknowledgments

I wish to thank Nokia Cellular Systems Oy and particularly the Platform section for the possibility to develop this methodology. I owe deep gratitude to Ari Jaaksi from Nokia Cellular Systems Oy for providing me with great insights of the MVC++ paradigm and loads of support in the development phase. This project was partly supported by Finnish Technological Development Center (TEKES). Numerous people provided helpful comments in the development phase, but I would like to extend my special thanks to Jyrki Kaski, Juhani Puska, Ossi Ahola, Timo Rasi, Pia Närvänen and Ansa Lilja from Nokia Cellular System Oy. I would also like to thank Toni Sormunen also from Nokia Cellular Systems Oy for several ideas I have stolen from him.

References

[1] *Implementing Interactive Applications in C++*, Ari Jaaksi, to be published in Software Practice & Experience

[2] *Object-Oriented Development of Interactive Systems with OMT++*, Juha-Markus Aalto and Ari Jaaksi, published in TOOLS 14, Technology of Object-Oriented Languages & Systems, 205-218, R.Ege, M.Singh, B.Meyer (eds), Prentice Hall, 1994

[3] *Object-oriented Modeling and Design*, J.Rumbaugh,, M.Blaha, W.Permerlani, F.Eddy, W.Lorensen, Prentice-Hall, 1991

[4] *Applications Programming in Smalltalk-80. How to use Model-View-Controller*, S.Burbeck, 1986, 1987

[5] *Object-Oriented Programming with C++ and OSF/Motif*, Douglas A. Young, Prentice-Hall, Inc., 1992

[6] *A Cookbook for Using the Model-View-Controller User Interface Paradigm in Smalltalk-80*, G.E.Krasner, S.T.Pope, Joop, August/September, 1988

[7] *X-Designer User's Guide Release 3*, Imperial Software Technology Ltd., 1993

[8] *X-Designer Release 3.2 Supplement,* Imperial Software Technology Ltd., Issue 1, April 1994

Common Desktop Environment Architectural Overview

Steve Evans[†]

Abstract

This paper presents a high-level architectural view of the Common Desktop Environment. Concepts that are likely to be familiar to most X Window System™ graphical user interface (GUI) programmers are glossed over, while concepts not universally familiar to this group are highlighted, particularly, ToolTalk™ message sets, actions, workspace management, the GUI shell, network transparency, and the desktop object paradigm.

Introduction

In March 1993, a group of UNIX™ platform vendors agreed to develop a joint implementation of a collection of technologies targeted at defining a common application look, consistent interaction feel, and uniform desktop paradigm. The system is called the Common Desktop Environment (CDE). This paper is an architectural overview of CDE. Most of the application programming interfaces (APIs), formats, and conventions alluded to in this document are being standardized through X/Open. Likewise, the future development of CDE is likely to be managed under the guidance of the X Consortium, the Open Software Foundation (OSF™), and X/Open.

Goals

The goal of this project was to provide the open specification for, and sample implementation of, an integrated, standard, and consistent graphical user interface (GUI) desktop environment. In order to accomplish this in a timely manner, the major focus has been on the smooth integration of existing technologies. This involved looking at some duplicative technologies and picking only one. Most of the engineering during the development of CDE was directed at integrating the chosen technologies.

Another goal was to have CDE standardized by X/Open. A great deal of energy has gone into developing specifications and deciding what to put into the standard. Competing interests have

---

[†]*Steve Evans is a Distinguished Engineer at SunSoft, Inc.*

struck a balance that encourages innovation and competition, while ensuring a consistent programming environment and end user experience between CDE platforms.

In order to accomplish the above mentioned goals, CDE defines policy, in addition to supporting mechanisms. This is a significant break with X-based and many other standardized technologies. This approach has ensured that end user consistency is valued at least as high as the ability to customize the environment.

Also, effort has been expended to hide configuration files from nontechnical end users by offering GUI or direct manipulation alternatives to modifying the environment. These users also represent the target audience for CDE. For system administrators and advanced end users, there are plenty of additional configuration options available.

On a final note, users of other UNIX and PC desktops should be comfortable using CDE. CDE has not gone out of its way to differ from other desktop environments. Also, some of the features in CDE are appearing in other desktop environments. As one example, the Microsoft™ Windows 95 [AK94] desktop looks much more like CDE than Microsoft Windows 3.1 does.

Conceptual Overview

The architecture of CDE has many cross-process relationships. The usual three-process relationship of an X client, a window manager, and the X Window System [SG92] server seems simple by comparison. The area covered by CDE is broad, and the layering in the system is not as rigorous as that of Motif™, Xt, and Xlib. There are relationships between high-level system components that are diverse and extensible. This paper groups the technologies to illustrate that each component fits into an overall whole. The information is oriented toward the developer, although others should find it valuable; coding details are not explored. CDE [CDE95] [XO194] [XO294] can be divided into:

- Data interaction GUIs—Application-level components that are available for user interaction, invocable by other applications. Developers can think of these as programming components at a larger granularity than widgets.

- Multiuser collaboration—Defines and uses APIs that enable collaboration between users on the network, particularly in the areas of calendar management, network resource naming, and network file sharing.

- Desktop management—Provides components that negotiate the visual relationships between entities on the desktop. These include the following: Window Manager, Workspace Manager, Session Manager, Application Manager, File Manager, Style Manager, and the Front Panel.

- Motif GUI engine—Includes those components that implement the controls available to the user and includes the Motif toolkit, additional widgets, a GUI shell (Desktop KornShell), and a GUI construction tool (Application Builder).

- Integration technologies—Represent technologies that do not generate GUIs, but are used as infrastructure by the rest of CDE. These technologies include process execution control, application messaging (mechanism and protocols), data typing, and operation invocation.

The overall structure of CDE is depicted in Figure 1.

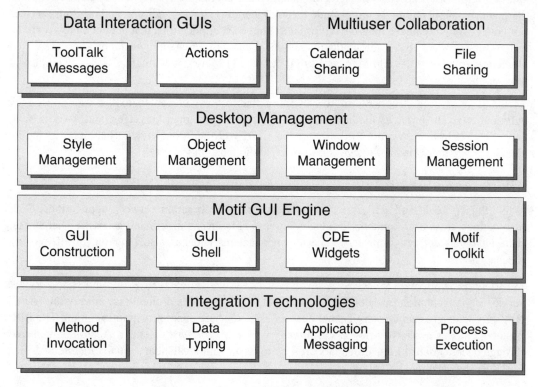

Figure 1: Conceptual overview of CDE.

Data Interaction GUIs

Within CDE, there is a philosophy of why implement something if someone else has already done so. CDE supplies a registration service that allows an application to find an available service provider. This registration service is actually the ToolTalk messaging system. ToolTalk provides the low-level messaging infrastructure. A companion mechanism, called the *actions* system, provides a consistent abstraction layer on top of both the traditional UNIX command-line interface to applications and the CDE recommended ToolTalk interface to applications. Actions, as semantic entities, are exposed to the end user through higher levels of software. Both actions and ToolTalk are discussed in more detail in *Integration Technologies* near the end of the paper. The reader should be able to make it through the intervening sections by holding on to the above short explanation of the purposes of these components.

CDE contains components that are available to the application developer through action and ToolTalk APIs. Examples include GUIs to show a view of a directory, submit a print job, view the contents of the Trash Can, edit some text, show help information, compose a calendar appointment, and compose a mail message.

In turn, application developers are encouraged to supply actions and ToolTalk message support so that the application specific services they supply are available to CDE and other applications. Particularly, applications should provide the composition, viewing, editing, and printing services for both proprietary and standard data formats. This way, applications that are coded to accept an extensible set of data types automatically gain more capabilities as more *media* handlers are added to the system. The CDE File Manager, Front Panel, and Mailer attachment GUI are examples of such applications.

Media is used as a generic term for anything that can be presented to the user to convey information. CDE provides media handlers for appointments, mail messages, mail folders, text, icons, and help data. Vendors have extended CDE with additional media handlers, including PostScript™, many kinds of image file formats, audio data, and so on.

Multiuser Collaboration

While the ToolTalk and action mechanisms encourage cooperation between applications, CDE also defines cross-user collaboration technologies. This means distributed access to shared user data. CDE has defined some basic sharing mechanisms and has also built on top of existing mechanisms.

An example of building on an existing mechanism is the remote procedure call (RPC) client/service implementation of calendar management. CDE provides a client-side library and API[†], RPC protocol, and daemon/service that enables users to share appointment information. The RPC protocol enables a user to browse and directly edit another user's calendar. Access is managed through access control lists. Calendars are tied to hosts, and a calendar's data is maintained by a host-specific daemon.

One of the problems faced by any network collaboration effort is that of naming the target resource. CDE names calendars through a `user@host` format. As a possible future direction, the X/Open Federated Naming API, XFN, promises much more interesting network resource naming. XFN comprises a generic API and base set of policies that are useful for naming services on the network relative to hosts, users, organizations, and locations. Once a network resource can be named, calendar services can be associated with them and scheduling information can be shared. For example, once organizations can be named, calendars of events relevant to the entire organization can be maintained. As another example, once locations can be named, calendars of scheduled meetings in particular conference rooms can be maintained.

CDE uses conventional distributed file systems to name files that are sharable on the network. To provide a distributed file system neutral interface, CDE provides an API to translate host relative file names into locally expressible file names. Although the CDE sample implementation is NFS™ based, CDE can be ported to run on top of other distributed file systems. Using the CDE file-name mapping API, an opaque file name object can be constructed and passed between desktop clients across the network and resolved in a host-specific way. Also, to simplify the programming task and end user metaphor, CDE applications should present remote file references as local file paths.

[†]*The API is being standardized through the X.400 Application Programming Interface Association (XAPIA) due to a strong industry interest in enabling a cross UNIX, PC, and palmtop calendaring standard.*

One of the fundamentals of building multiuser collaboration applications is the ability to share files. The conventions for naming network files, in conjunction with a ToolTalk file-sharing mechanism called *file scoping*, enable multiuser collaboration through file sharing. File scoping is more than a mechanism for simple, exclusive access control. Cooperating clients can use file scope access to negotiate for access to files. For example, an application that has exclusive access to a file could ask whether the user was done with the file when another application wanted to gain exclusive access to the file.

Desktop Management

The physical metaphor associated with CDE is loosely one of a user sitting in a chair surrounded by a bank of desks (workspaces). As the user swivels the chair (by pushing a button on the Front Panel), another desk becomes accessible. On each desk, the following is available:

- A collection of drawers (File Manager views) in which folders (directories) and reports (files) are organized.

- A collection of papers in use on the desktop (windows). Some papers are pushed out of the way (as icons), but are within easy reach.

- Continuous display (through Front Panel icons) of a clock, the date, an indication of new mail, and an indication of something in the trash can.

- Direct access (through Front Panel buttons) to an appointment book (Calendar), a pad of paper (Text Editor), a terminal (emulator), a mail box (Mailer), a printer (Print Manager), office environmental controls (Style Manager), a list of electronic agents at ones beck and call (Application Manager and Front Panel personal tool box), and a guide book (Help).

The user drags and drops objects to change their location and make copies of them. By dropping objects on services, the user gains assistance with appointment scheduling, editing, mail composition, printing, and so on.

Session Management

The state of the desktop can be remembered. At a later time, and perhaps at a different X display station, the state of the desktop can be re-created. A session is the state of a user's desktop. CDE supports two session snapshots from which the user can choose:

- Home session—A snapshot of desktop state that reassembles in the same way each time it is started.

- Current session—A snapshot of the state of a desktop at logout time.

The CDE Session Manager coordinates these activities, but applications are responsible for saving their own state.

CDE uses the X11R5 Interclient Communication Conventions style of session management. This consists mostly of conventions for setting properties on top-level windows. CDE extends this mechanism by providing a facility that allocates specific files into which applications can store their state. A command-line flag then points to this file when the application is restarted. Applications that maintain multiple top-level windows must save the state of each of them. The next version of CDE is slated to expand to take advantage of X11R6 session management, which is more full featured than the X11R5 conventions.

A session is associated with a particular user. In CDE, the Login Manager is responsible for initial user login. The Login Manager is an alternative GUI for the UNIX login program. Normally, it checks the entered password with the user's registered password. However, individual vendors may provide authentication schemes tuned to their platform.

The Login Manager is network-aware. When faced with an X display that is normally served by host A, a user can log into the their desktop by running a session from host B that has full access to the user's normal set of files and services. This is possible by Login Manager acting as CDE's X Display Manager (XDM). The XDM Control Protocol (XDMCP) is used between X window servers and XDMs on the network. The Login Manager displays its login window or host chooser window on any X server requesting either of these XDM services. This makes CDE a good match for use with XDMCP-aware X terminals.

For connections to the X server, CDE uses the X magic cookie scheme to control access. If a user on some host machine can read a certain file within a session owner's home directory, then access to the X server is granted. An alternative to this per-user authorization is per-host authorization. This is useful for installations supporting pre-X11R4 clients, which will be unable to connect to X servers using the X magic cookie scheme.

X resources files are handled in the context of CDE sessions in the following manner: a CDE set of default resources is merged with a host-specific version of this file, followed by the user's `$HOME/.Xdefaults` file, followed by a session-specific file of resources that have changed through user interaction with the Style Manager. The result is stored in the `RESOURCE_MANAGER` property of the root window. To enable fine-grain customization, the C preprocessor is run on resource files.

Being limited to two sessions could be a hardship for users who commonly run on display systems with differing characteristics (display size, display depth, connection bandwidth, and so on). With the CDE Session Manager, it is possible to have sessions that differ depending upon the value of `$DISPLAY`. This capability essentially extends the number of possible sessions beyond the home session and current session.

Application Management

One of the obstacles preventing end users from taking full advantage of the network environment is the difficulty of accessing remote applications. CDE provides conventions for:

- Installation of applications so that they can be run remotely
- User navigation of available applications
- Execution of remote applications

The user can browse the collection of available applications with a GUI tool called Application Manager. Applications can be dragged onto the desktop for easier access. Even remote applications are started by a simple double-click, hiding the network location of a running application. The user is not aware of any distinction between local and remote applications.

This network transparency is accomplished by installing applications on network hosts designated as *application servers*. The parts of the installation relevant to CDE requires placing of certain files in conventional places in the application's installation hierarchy. The application server maintains a list of applications that it is serving. Each host on the network maintains a list of the application servers on the network that it queries when a user logs into CDE. This process is referred to as *application gathering*. It results in a dynamically generated file hierarchy of actions arranged in folders. Remember, actions represent operations end users can invoke, including starting applications.

The Application Manager provides a specialized view of the file system for the end user. Applications are arranged into groups and groups can be nested. An application's installation script associates the application to a group. This association can be overridden by the system administrator as part of application server configuration. The set and arrangement of the actions shown through the Application Manager is considered a system resource that is typically shared between multiple users. Users cannot modify this view.

The user can drag an icon from the Application Manager onto the desktop, File Manager, Front Panel, and so on. The associated action remains valid as long as the gathered application that it refers to remains valid. Because actions represent a form of abstraction and indirection, the actual location of the application can change over time. This change remains transparent to the end user (more on this in *Method Invocation*, below). The user typically double-clicks on an action icon to invoke it.

Object Management

A critical part of the CDE user model is that of convincing the user that there is a physical metaphor that corresponds to the abstract electronic representation that the computer knows about. To this end, abstractions have graphic onscreen images that the user can pick up and move about, dropping them anywhere it makes semantic sense. These are viewed as "objects" by the user. The File Manager promotes the object abstraction by providing a graphical way to browse and modify file and directory objects within the file system. Also, the File Manager provides a GUI to invoke actions. When the user selects a file, the actions that are defined for the selected type of file are presented to the user.

Objects managed by CDE based applications do not have to be file-based; in-memory buffers may represent desktop objects, too. The CDE Mailer handles Multipurpose Internet Mail Extensions (MIME) messages by displaying attachments to a message as icons in a scrollable panel. These are objects that behave just like file-based objects during activities such as drag and drop. The user can drag between the File Manager and the Mailer. Applications that use drag and drop should maintain this important user model by supporting both file-based and buffer-based objects.The CDE drag-and-drop API and protocol make this straightforward.

CDE captures some object oriented system attributes without being dependent upon a completely object oriented infrastructure. Within CDE, the goal is to create the illusion of physical objects for the end user. This is in contrast to the Object Management Group (OMG) in which the fundamental building block of the system is the software "object".

Window Management

The Window Manager is essentially the Motif 1.2 window manager with extensions to provide the Front Panel GUI and workspace abstraction.

The Front Panel can be thought of as a graphic version of the root window menu supported by many window managers. It can also be thought of as a tuned object manager in which common objects are readily available to the user. The Front Panel can show dynamic system information, and it allows the user to invoke actions and system functions. The user dynamically customizes the Front Panel by dragging and dropping action icons from the Application Manager and File Manager onto subpanels. Applications can come equipped with special configuration files that extend the Front Panel, possibly defining drop behavior, drop zone animation feedback, and so on. The user can optionally install these configuration files depending on customization preferences. Figure 2 shows a typical Front Panel.

Figure 2: A typical Front Panel

Workspaces are abstractions supported by the Window Manager that can be thought of as virtual desktops. Figure 2 shows four available workspaces that the user has named Filing, Communication, Office, and Engineering. Application windows exist within one, some, or all available workspaces. The user usually determines which workspaces an application window exists in as part of the user's customization. Applications should rarely use the workspace API other than to explicitly designate in which workspace to appear on session restart. In general, an application should not place itself within multiple workspaces, because this overrides the user's prerogative. There are exceptions, such as displaying a critical asynchronous warning message, e.g., "Reactor Core Overheating".

A problem with putting Window Manager, Front Panel, and Workspace Manager functionality within the same process is that it is expensive, memory wise, for vendors to simply embed this code into X terminals. For X terminals to retain traditional window management facilities within the terminal, some type of private protocol back to a host to display and handle Front Panel interactions would be required. It is possible that a future version of the CDE Window Manager could be factored more favorably for X terminals that want to embed part of CDE. For CDE 1.0, XDMCP aware X terminals that allow login and window management functions to be controlled by the host station are the best match.

Style Management

The Style Manager enables users to customize their desktop using a GUI. Users are shielded from advanced concepts, such as X resources, for most common customization options. The Style Manager provides controls for desktop-wide properties that adjust backdrops, keyboard settings, mouse settings, screen saver options, window management, and session management. These properties either do not affect applications directly or indirectly affect them through the X server or window manager.

Application writers are more directly influenced by font choices, color choices, and input device mappings. The Motif toolkit and CDE handle many of these settings transparently for widgets. However, applications will appear more integrated with the rest of the desktop if they respond to user font and color preferences. Applications that directly interact with the mouse will feel more integrated with the rest of CDE if they are consistent with other applications, for example, utilizing the same mouse button double-click minimum interval value (`multiClickTime` resource).

To accommodate differences between platform vendor's display technology and available font sets, CDE defines font aliases that are indirect names to actual font names. Application writers are encouraged to use these aliases in ways that match how the rest of CDE uses them. For example:

- There is a font alias whose XLFD name begins with "`-dt-interface system-...`" that is used by CDE to display user interface control labels.

- There is another alias known as "`-dt-interface user-...`" that is used to render text that has been entered directly or indirectly by a user. CDE text widgets default to using this font.

- There is another set of aliases that start with "`-dt-application-...`" that don't have CDE dictated semantics, but instead offer mappings based on generic typographic properties such as serif versus sans serif, proportionally spaced versus mono spaced, and so on.

The Style Manager provides the user with color selection options to adjust the CDE color scheme. In CDE 1.0, this color information is private to CDE. Applications doing widget subclassing can indirectly access some of the color scheme by looking at inherited background pixel values. A call to `XmGetColors()` generates 3–D shadow colors.

While on the topic of color, it is worth mentioning that the X/Open Common Desktop Environment standard submission does not dictate color usage, such as colors used within icons. However, it is strongly advised that simple usages of color in the user interface be constrained to the colors offered by the CDE Icon Editor in order to enhance color sharing. These colors include:

- X color names: `red`, `green`, `blue`, `cyan`, `magenta`, `yellow`, `black`, and `white`.

- Eight gray values: `#e1`, `#c8`, `#af`, `#96`, `#7d`, `#64`, `#4b`, and `#32`.

The Motif GUI Engine

Think of the Motif toolkit as the GUI engine of the desktop. This section discusses Motif, CDE widgets, and alternative modes of Motif programming.

Toolkit

CDE Motif toolkit designers have been extremely cautious to avoid producing incompatibilities with Motif 1.2 from OSF. As a result, additional functionality has been added such that it takes explicit resource settings to enable the new features. Functional additions include file selection box GUI modifications, different default settings of existing resources (primarily to lighten up the default border widths), color management enhancements, internationalization of error messages, and minor usability fixes (some of which have the affect of easing migration of OPEN LOOK™ users to CDE).

CDE Motif and OSF Motif 2.0 are also highly compatible. Most functions put into CDE Motif have made their way into Motif 2.0. As a result, application developers have compiled their applications with CDE Motif, relinked to Motif 2.0, and the applications ran successfully. Of course, widget subclassing that has not followed Motif 1.2 subclassing guidelines designed to shield programs from widget size changes are likely to fail. All this being said, the exact binary compatibility story for CDE 1.0 Motif based applications to Motif 2.x is being worked at the time of this writing.

As mentioned in the section on *Object Management*, a drag-and-drop convenience layer has been added on top of Motif 1.2's drag-and-drop API. In addition, CDE has standardized upon the use of the Motif 1.2 *prefer preregister* drag feedback protocol. A drop site drag manager process keeps track of visible drop zones on the desktop. This data is used by a drag source client process to manage drag feedback interaction. Limited drag time validation of drop zones is followed by full validation at drop time with "snap back to source" animation upon drop failure.

Another addition to CDE Motif has been a substantially expanded GUI style guide and certification checklist. This is based on the Motif 1.2 style guide. Additions affected the input models, window management, and GUI design principles.

Widgets

There are two types of widgets that have been added to those available with Motif 1.2. The first type are low-level control widgets, with names like:

- SpinBox—increment and decrement a text field.
- ComboBox—list of valid choices for a text field.
- MenuButton—a menu that doesn't need to be in a row column widget.

These all have equivalents in Motif 2.0 (except for the MenuButton) and were added primarily to ease porting of applications from a Microsoft Windows or OPEN LOOK environment.

The second type of new widget available with CDE are rich and full-featured. The CDE Terminal Emulator widget is useful for applications designed to mix the best of a command-line user interface with a GUI. The CDE Editor widget is available for embedding a more full-featured plain text editor than that available from the Motif Text widget.

Most widely applicable are the CDE Help widgets that handle navigation and interaction with application help *volumes*. Help is delivered with an application in the form of Semantic Description Language (SDL) files that have been compiled from a form of Standard Generalized Markup Language (SGML) files known as *HelpTag*. Both SDL and HelpTag are SGML Document Type-Descriptions (DTDs) tuned for different tasks. CDE Help features mixed text and graphics, hyper links, dynamic reformatting of text, and structured navigation capabilities. The question may be raised about why not just use raw Hyper Text Markup Language (HTML) files popularized by Mosaic. Part of the answer is that, while HTML is very good for hyper link style navigation, it is inefficient at table of contents style navigation because the entire HTML file has to be parsed in order to determine the table of contents. For the very large help volumes anticipated for CDE applications, this is not a viable runtime option. However, a future direction would be to consolidate SDL and HTML formats.

GUI Shell

A marriage between the KornShell and CDE has produced the Desktop KornShell, which is an interpreted scripting language alternative to straight C programming of the Motif toolkit. Selected frequently-used CDE, Xt, and Xlib APIs are cast in the Korn script style. To access the full power of the environment one has to use a compiled language. Nonetheless, one can write Desktop KornShell scripts that participate in desktop integration activities such as drag and drop, session management, and ToolTalk messaging.

People comfortable with shell programming may prefer use of the Desktop KornShell for modest programming tasks for some of the following reasons:

- It is particularly well suited to system-administration-type applications due to the ease by which shell commands intermix with GUI controls.

- It is also good for putting a GUI control program on top of character based applications due to the natural way that character based interaction is handled by the shell environment.

- Desktop KornShell scripts are also a great way to deliver instruction set independent programs to a heterogeneous collection of hosts. The CDE Mailer makes it trivial to attach a program to a message that the recipient simply double-clicks to invoke.[†]

GUI Construction

The easiest way to produce a CDE application, and perhaps the fastest, is to do almost no Motif toolkit programming at all. By taking advantage of the CDE Application Builder, also known as App Builder, one can utilize direct manipulation and forms fill-in to completely construct the GUI control portion of an application. A focus of App Builder, unlike some other user interface construction tools, is that of making the normal default usage of widgets easy to access. It does this by hiding many of the more esoteric resources that are available on most widgets. Another focus is on making it as easy as possible to plug into the desktop integration infrastructure, including drag and drop, session management, and ToolTalk messaging.

App Builder maintains the state of the user interface in an intermediate form called the Builder Interface Language (BIL). BIL files are consumed by a Motif code generator. Differing back ends are possible; one that generates Desktop KornShell scripts would be a valuable addition to CDE. App Builder will also generate and consume the User Interface Language (UIL), supported by Motif and consumed by other GUI builders.

As changes are made to a user interface using App Builder, code entered directly by a programmer is automatically merged with generated code. Generated code is designed to be exemplary in its use of CDE APIs and is a good source of example code, even if not using App Builder to maintain

---

[†] *Of course, users need to be trained to understand that this feature can be used as a vehicle for virus delivery. Prompting the user for confirmation, after warning about possible danger, can help in this regard. Also, it should be possible for a system administrator to configure an installation to disable easy invocation of mailed scripts.*

the GUI state of a project. For programming shops in which GUI design is not done by the programmer, App Builder is great for use by nonprogrammers for producing a prototype. In addition, the prototype can roll forward to programmers for the production phase of development.

Integration Technologies

Up to this point, CDE technologies discussed have been directly involved with putting up a GUI onto the screen. The integration technologies described in this section are underlying infrastructure, not GUI providers.

Process Execution

To provide a network-leveraging environment, CDE had to venture into the realm of remote execution management. This means providing a mechanism to start, manage, and collect results from applications running on a remote host. This is accomplished through the Sub Process Control (SPC) mechanism delivered with the sample implementation of CDE. A remote host installs an SPC daemon that serves as the remote end of a socket-based control mechanism. This control mechanism tries to maintain the illusion that the remote process is a local "child" to the "parent" process. Authentication of the user that owns the parent process is based upon the ability of the parent process to write a `setuid` file to the user's home directory and the ability of the child process to read the result.

The SPC API and associated control programs are considered interim and private to CDE; this is not a general mechanism for nonCDE usage. Actions represent the public API for running applications remotely. CDE looks forward to the adoption of a remote execution standard that provides functionality that could replace SPC.

Application Messaging

The application messaging mechanism of CDE is called the ToolTalk Messaging Service. Application messaging addresses inter-application control and cooperation for applications working on behalf of a single user. There is a local message-routing process, known as the ToolTalk session daemon, whose control scope typically corresponds to that of the X server. This means that clients within a session issue requests, the ToolTalk session manager finds or starts some client within a session that is able to handle the request, and the ToolTalk session daemon tracks the request until completion. A description of the entire ToolTalk messaging system is covered elsewhere [JH94] [SS93]. Instead, a description of the CDE centric usage of ToolTalk is the focus for the rest of this section.

CDE provides two standard ToolTalk protocols known as *messages sets*. A message set contains a number of messages that may be exchanged between a sender and a handler process. These messages are grouped together because they describe related requests and notices. The sender and handler may be within the same process or on different hosts. Message sets have associated utility functions that allow the programmer to concentrate on the semantics of the protocol without getting involved in the low-level messaging details. Some of the message set functions allow the application writer to defer to default behavior with almost no work on their part. These functions represent what CDE has contributed to the original definition of ToolTalk.

Desktop Message Set

The Desktop Message Set has three areas that it encompasses. The first is windowing behavior (see *Handle Desktop* and *Send Desktop*, below). The second involves file access and short term file life cycle control (see *Desktop File*, below). The third is specific to applications that have extension languages and is therefore not generic enough to warrant library support.[†]

- Handle Desktop—Handling Desktop requests is the most basic level of messaging integration. Any application that sends ToolTalk messages, either through the ToolTalk or actions API, should handle the Desktop requests. Handling Desktop requests allows other applications to set or query a request sending application's current working directory, iconic state, $DISPLAY, and so on. As an example, the CDE Mailer handles Desktop Message Set requests so that attachments may position themselves away from the Mailer window when an attachment is opened.

- Send Desktop—When an application is started by ToolTalk to handle some ToolTalk request, it is a child of the ToolTalk session daemon rather than of the request sender. The application will usually be started on the same X display as the sender, but not necessarily on the same X screen or in the same current directory context. Or, if the application is implemented as a server process, it may already be displaying on another screen or in another directory context. Using Desktop requests allows a handling application to inherit from the sender these attributes that might otherwise be inherited through command-line invocation. Using the messaging toolkit in this way can reset the locale, current working directory, and even $DISPLAY, allowing a carefully-coded request handling application to come up on the same X screen as the sender. A request handler can also find out the window geometry of the request sender. Knowing the window geometry allows the request handler to position itself on the screen so as to be less likely to obscure the window associated with the request sender. Media handlers (described below) should send Desktop Message Set requests so as to not position themselves on top of their request senders.

- Desktop File—The toolkit makes it easy to send and receive the Desktop messages about files. These messages allow applications to coordinate their access to files.

Media Message Set

The Media Message Set allows an application to be a container for arbitrary media, or to be a media player/editor that can be driven from such a container. The Media message interface allows a container application (such as Mailer or File Manager) to compose, display, edit, or print a file or buffer of an arbitrary media type, without understanding anything about the format of that media type. ToolTalk routes a container's requests to the user's preferred tool for the given media type and operation. This includes routing the request to an already-running instance of the tool if that instance is best-positioned to handle the request.

[†]*Author's note—Numerous reviewers encouraged elimination of the details represented by the bulleted items in this subsection and the next. However, the author believes that it is important for application developers to be exposed to the basic semantic flow of these two protocols.*

- Handle Media—The toolkit makes it easy for an editor to handle the standard Media requests for the media type(s) for which the editor is responsible.

- Send Media—The toolkit makes it easy for a container to send Media requests and manage any subsequent results produced by the handler. In those cases in which the container doesn't engage in any on going ToolTalk dialog with a media handler, the actions API should be used instead of directly using these ToolTalk APIs. This is due to the fact that equivalent actions (`Open` and `Print`) represent a higher level of abstraction that supports the equivalent of ToolTalk and non-ToolTalk aware media handlers.

Data Typing

CDE provides a uniform user interface to the objects contained on the desktop. To do this, there must be agreement between players on the desktop as to the type of each object. Since there is no ubiquitous object system underlaying CDE similar to that being specified by OMG, CDE has a mechanism by which the types of objects are determined using a set of externally observable criteria. The criteria includes properties potentially shared by file-based and buffer-based objects such as name pattern and content pattern. Other criteria are the exclusive domain of files and include path-name pattern and file permissions. Associated with every CDE type is an extensible set of attributes, including icon name, name template pattern, list of actions suitable for presentation to a user, equivalent type names for other type spaces (for example, MIME type), and a textual description of this type.

CDE defines, and platform vendors supply, a set of desktop type definitions. Application vendors are expected to augment the database with both proprietary and public data types at application installation time.

Information is extracted from the database through a CDE library API. A prime function of this API is that of matching an object's properties with the database type criteria to determine the object's CDE type. The matching algorithm uses a set of precedence rules to resolve conflicts.

The CDE type space is defined by the X/Open CDE standard and exists primarily to support desktop oriented activities such as icon display and action association. The MIME type space is defined by the Internet Engineering Task Force and exists to deal with exchange of mail message parts. A ToolTalk media type space exists in order to match data with handlers, and is defined to be a subset of X selection target types as defined by the X Consortium. Thus, to do a complete job of type definition, one has to define a CDE type, X selection target, and MIME type. Types should be registered with the appropriate authority. X/Open is not currently set up to register CDE types beyond those defined in the standard. For CDE types, one should append the type name to an organization's name. Doing so partitions the name space without need for centralized allocation of types. The prefix of *Dt*, for DeskTop, is claimed by CDE. This plethora of type spaces may seem excessive, but given the differing scopes and existing legacy mechanisms, this is the minimum necessary to support CDE.

Method Invocation

A CDE type can be thought of as the class of a CDE object. Using this analogy, actions can be thought of as the methods available on instances of a class. Thus, the actions attribute in a type attribute list describes operations that are available for the type. Action and data typing information is actually stored in a single database. A single action in the database has multiple parts, many of which are optional. These parts include:

- A description of how to invoke the operation, including through ToolTalk, through an execution string passed to the SPC mechanism, from within a terminal emulator, and so on.

- A description of the type of arguments associated with the action. The type of the desktop objects (files and buffers) that it accepts are defined by the type portion of the database. A key benefit of this integration with the typing mechanism is that actions are polymorphic with respect to data types. For example, the Open action will invoke a text editor for arguments that are text files and a graphics editor for arguments that are graphics files.

- A description of the number of arguments associated with the action. Actions need not take any arguments. In this case, the method analogy breaks down in as much as actions need not be associated with a particular data type. Such actions are identified only by name.

- An optional indication as to where to carry out the operation, including the local machine, a particular remote machine, the machine on which the executable resides, and so on. In addition, these execution locations can be included in a list so that if a host is not available then the next host on the list is tried. This provides a measure of redundancy that can be used to increase the likelihood of application launch, even in the face of remote host unavailability.

- An optional label, help string, and icon that the user sees when interacting with the action's GUI. These are hints to an application about how to represent the action to the user. These hints may be ignored, as is done by the Front Panel where it will ignore the icon if an alternative icon(s) has been supplied by Front Panel configuration files.

The collection of actions available to the user is assembled at the same time as the system is collecting data typing information. In fact, related action and type information usually resides together in the same file. CDE-defined, system-administrator-defined (host-specific), and user-defined files are assembled into a single database, with later definitions taking precedence. This ordering of search path precedence and traversal is utilized elsewhere in CDE for such things as help volume and icon file searches.

Action files are the mechanism chosen by the actions and data typing database mechanism and the File Manager to instantiate actions as file system objects that can be viewed, invoked, moved, copied, and so on. The actions and data typing database contains references to the actual implementation of an action (e.g., "run /usr/bin/app on machine net_app_svr"). However, a representation is needed of an action as an object that the user can directly manipulate. An object's name identifies it as an action to any object manager that is looking for actions. Thus, if there is an executable file named Dtstyle and an action named Dtstyle, the File Manager will interpret that file, regardless of its content, as the Dtstyle action reference. In addition, the File Manager utilizes the action's label as the name that the user sees for this file. Action labels are localizable, whereas action names are programmatic entities that should not be localized.

The good feature about using files simply as pointers into the actions database is that the underlying implementation can evolve without the user having to do anything. On the other hand, one user's actions and data typing database may not match another user's actions and data typing database.

Thus, a user can not exchange an action reference, for example as a mail message attachment, and reasonably expect another user to have a comparable definition for that action. Exchanging a Desktop KornShell script is the best device for solving this problem, because it involves explicit programmatic behavior encapsulation.

Actions are useful because they integrate both legacy command-line applications and ToolTalk applications into the desktop as polymorphic, distributed operations on desktop objects.

Futures

The first version of CDE is a complete desktop environment. Future versions of CDE should continue to evolve by bringing increased power and ease-of-use to the end user. The most obvious areas include:

- Information access—use CDE Help as the starting point for carrying information access across document formats, the enterprise, and around the network.

- PC integration—enhance the desktop infrastructure so that PC compatibility solutions, like Wabi™, have all the hooks necessary to provide smooth inter-environment interoperability.

- Printing model—provide a "printing through X" architecture.

- Compound document architecture—migrate toward a document oriented metaphor. Users want to access information in the most natural format, which continues to be page oriented with mixed media on the page.

- "Real" object leverage—incorporation of OMG based technology. Indeed, the ToolTalk messaging team is already studying interoperability approaches. It should be possible to migrate to include OMG based technology in such a way as to be smooth for the end user.

There are smaller scale areas that deserve attention in future versions of CDE. These areas include:

- Error handling—more guidelines and library support.

- Name registry—clearer guidelines. Promotion of uniformity and avoidance of conflicts in the name spaces used by CDE is important.

- Color usage—firmer guidelines and library support. Limited color resources should be more aggressively shared.

- Action definition—enhanced inheritance and more flexibility in argument specification. The inheritance issue applies to data typing as well.

- Drag and drop—move toward dynamic drag behavior. This includes the ability to navigate between workspaces and locate hidden drop zones during drags.

- Session management—use of X11R6 session management.

- Style management—more extensible, as opposed to its current fixed set of options.

Some of the areas on the above two lists have plans on the drawing board already.

Conclusion

CDE represents the next evolutionary step beyond existing GUI standards. By defining a common desktop environment:

- End users benefit from cross-application interoperability and cross-platform usability.

- Application developers benefit from having a uniform runtime environment.

- System administrators benefit from capabilities that are designed to allow control over end user options across heterogeneous platforms.

Acknowledgments

CDE is a direct result of contributions from many people at Hewlett-Packard, IBM, Novell, and SunSoft. The cooperative efforts of people from OSF, X/Open, and the X Consortium have contributed greatly to the result. Other companies have made contributions through their involvement and adoption of CDE as well as their interest in contributing to future versions of CDE.

As to this paper, particularly thanks go to those that have taken the time to do a thorough review of it and generate substantial comments: Brian Cripe, Daniel Dardailler, Kathy McGovern, Doug Rand, Bill Shannon, Ralph Swick, and Steve Uhlir. Numerous other CDE engineers reviewed sections with which they are expert.

Trademarks

X Window System is a trademark of the X Consortium, Inc.

UNIX and OPEN LOOK are registered trademarks of UNIX Systems Laboratories.

ToolTalk and NFS are registered trademarks and Wabi is a trademark of Sun Microsystems, Inc.

PostScript is a registered trademark of Adobe Systems, Inc.

OSF and Motif are trademarks of the Open Software Foundation, Inc.

Miscrosoft is a registered trademark of Microsoft Corp.

References

[AK94] Adrian King, *Inside Windows 95*, Microsoft Press, 1994, ISBN 1-55615-626-X.

[CDE95] Hewlett-Packard, IBM, Novell, and SunSoft CDE Joint Development Teams, *CDE: Programmer's Overview, CDE: Programming Guide, CDE: Help System Author's and Programmer's Guide, CDE: Internationalization Programmer's Guide, CDE: Application Builder User's Guide, CDE: Style Guide and Certification Checklist, CDE: ToolTalk Messaging Overview, CDE: Dialog and Scripting Services, CDE: User's Guide, CDE: Advanced User's and System Administrator's Guide*, CDE 1.0 sample implementation, 1995.

[JH94] Astrid Julienne and Brian Holtz, *ToolTalk and Open Protocols: Inter-Application Communication*, SunSoft Press and PTR Prentice Hall, 1994, ISBN 013-031055-7.

[SG92] R. Scheifler and J. Gettys, *X Window System: The Complete Reference to Xlib, X Protocol, ICCCM, XLFD*, Digital Press, 3$^{\underline{rd}}$ Edition, 1992.

[SS93] SunSoft Press, *The ToolTalk Service: An Inter-Operability Solution*, SunSoft Press and PRT Prentice Hall, 1993, ISBN 0-13-088717-X.

[XO194] X/Open, *CAE Specification: Common Desktop Environment—Definitions and Infrastructure (Company Review Draft)*, X/Open Company Ltd., 1994.

[XO294] X/Open, *CAE Specification: Common Desktop Environment—Services and Applications (Company Review Draft)*, X/Open Company Ltd., 1994.

Author Information

Steve Evans is a Distinguished Engineer at SunSoft, Inc. He has recently been working on desktop architectural issues. In the past, he has worked on 2–D graphics, window system components, user interface toolkits, structured graphics editing software, and has done a fair bit of management. He is currently the Sun Microsystems, Inc. advisor to the X Consortium. He can be reached at steve.evans@eng.sun.com.

The X Public Access Mechanism

Software Cooperation For Space Science And Beyond

Eric Mandel
Ralph Swick
Doug Tody[†]

Abstract

We describe a simple and effective use of the *X Toolkit* (*Xt*) selection mechanism that allows an *Xt* program to define named public access points through which data and commands can be exchanged with other programs. We will discuss our design goals, the technical challenges we faced -- including extensions to the *Xt* selection implementation -- and the user interface and application programming interface that we developed to meet these challenges.

We also describe our application of the X Public Access (*XPA*) mechanism to a new version of the popular *SAOimage* astronomical image display program. *XPA* makes possible the external control of the program's main functions, including image display, image zoom and pan, colormap manipulation, cursor/region definition, and frame selection. It also supports "externalization" of internal algorithms such as image file access and scaling. Finally, we describe how *XPA* is used to support user-configurable "quick-look" analysis of image data and bi-directional communication with other processes.

Introduction

In the past decade the astronomical world has witnessed the development of several highly successful scientific analysis systems that offer great functional improvement over previous software. Taking advantage of the explosion in hardware computing power over the past ten years, astronomers now enjoy software functionality only dreamed of in the days when programs fit into

---

[†]*Eric Mandel is the software R&D group leader in the High Energy Astrophysics Division of the Smithsonian Astrophysical Observatory. Ralph Swick is Technical Director of Integration Technology at the X Consortium. Doug Tody leads the IRAF Development Group at the National Optical Astronomy Observatories.*

64 kilobyte address spaces and when 5 megabytes of disk space was all the data storage one could reasonably expect.

All of these different analysis systems have special strengths. There are excellent packages available for plotting, for image processing, for spectral and timing analysis, for statistical analysis, and for image display. General systems also are available that provide a broad range of functionality. But it is clear that no one system can satisfy all of a user's analysis needs. It is inevitably necessary to combine the functions of two or more of these systems in order to carry out a research program (see Figure 1).

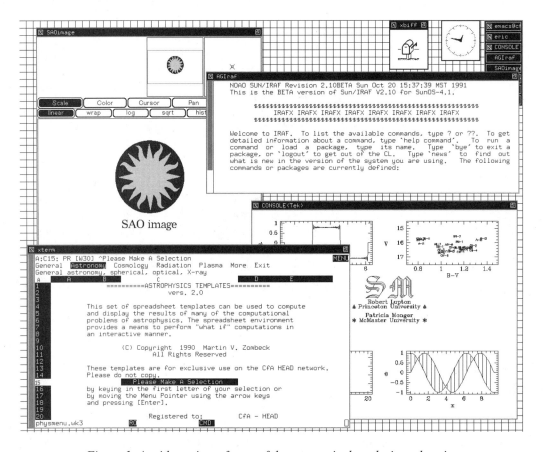

Figure 1: A wide variety of powerful astronomical analysis tools exist, but they do not work together effectively.

Until recently, little effort has gone into developing the means by which these different systems could interface easily with one another. Each system supports its own input and output data formats, its own graphical view or command syntax, and its own help system. The systems are effectively closed to one another. As a result, it is difficult for researchers to become proficient at more than one or two systems and it is even more difficult to make these systems work together as part of a unified research program.

The absence of cooperation between heterogeneous analysis systems is leading to a crisis in the world of astronomical software development. Users increasingly want to extend existing software and combine tasks from different systems in order to create their own individualized research environments. At the same time, the resources available for astronomical software development are shrinking. Our software designs must balance the increasing need for open-ended flexibility and extensibility without sacrificing functionality and without violating budget constraints.

A case in point is the *SAOimage* display program, one of the most successful astronomical image display programs ever written. Developed ten years ago at Smithsonian Astrophysical Observatory (SAO), *SAOimage* is an X Window System program that has been used by thousands of astronomers throughout the world. It requires updating to satisfy the increasing user demand for features such as:

- an easy means by which users can support their own data file formats, data scaling algorithms, and colormaps.

- an easy way to integrate user-defined analysis routines with the image display.

- an easy means by which the program can be controlled by external processes, such as data archive and retrieval systems.

These needs represent a whole new class of "open software" requirements that has come into existence as a result of increasing user expectations combined with frustrations concerning the limitations of our powerful but closed analysis systems.

Meeting these new needs will require new collaborative techniques, both for the way in which our software systems interact and for the way in which software development groups interact. To explore these collaborative issues, software developers at SAO and the National Optical Astronomy Observatories (NOAO) are combining forces in the development of a new high-quality image display program to replace *SAOimage*. This effort will be based on the *ximtool* image display program developed by D. Tody for the worldwide astronomical Image Reduction and Analysis Facility (IRAF). *Ximtool* provides a high-level image display programming interface as well as low-level access to graphical widget functions[1]. SAO will layer software collaboration functionality on top of the NOAO *ximtool* program in order to develop *SAOtng* (SAOimage: The Next Generation).

The X Public Access Mechanism

To add "open software" functionality to programs such as *SAOtng*, we developed a general mechanism by which *Xt* programs can exchange data and information with external programs. From the outset, our design goals included the following:

- The mechanism should be driven by the external process, which exchanges "named" data and commands with an *Xt* program.

- The mechanism should allow for the simultaneous sending and receiving of data associated with the same "name".

- *Xt* programs should send or receive data using the standard event-driven callback paradigm already familiar to *Xt* application programmers.

- External processes should be able to access data in *Xt* programs using a simple application programming interface (*API*) that does not require knowledge of *Xt* or linking against the *Xt* libraries.

- In addition to a low-level *API*, there should be a set of high-level programs that send or receive data at the command line.

- The mechanism should not add substantial overhead to the application, so that it can be applied liberally and remain dormant until invoked.

The result of our initial efforts is the "*X* Public Access" mechanism (*XPA*), a layered interface built on top of the existing *Xt* selection interface [2], which allows an *Xt* program to define points of public access through which data and commands can be exchanged with external programs (see Figure 2).

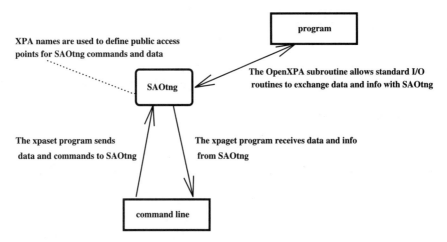

Figure 2: XPA allows Xt programs to cooperate with other processes and programs.

We chose to implement *XPA* using the *Xt* selection mechanism because of the universal availability of the *Xt Toolkit* and also because the selection mechanism provides platform-dependent implementation of interprocess communication. Layering *XPA* on *Xt* selections also allows an analysis program to be executed on a remote network host with no additional effort on the part of either the programmer or the user.

The Layered Implementation of XPA

The *XPA* mechanism is designed to be useful both to software developers and to users. It contains function libraries as well as high-level user programs built on top of these libraries. The major components of this layered interface include:

- a function library centered on the *NewXPA* routine, which is used by *Xt* programs to tag public access points with string identifiers and to register send and receive callbacks for these access points.

- a function library centered on the *OpenXPA* routine, which is used by external applications to exchange data and commands with an *Xt* application.

- two high-level programs, *xpaset* and *xpaget*, which allow data and information to be sent or received from the command line. These programs have the command line syntax:

```
<data> | xpaset  [qualifiers ...]
          xpaget  [qualifiers ...]
```

Conceptually, the *XPA* mechanism is straight-forward. An *Xt* application such as *SAOtng* calls the *NewXPA* routine to create a named public access point. One can specify "send" and "receive" callback procedures which will be executed by the program when an external process either sends data or commands to this access point or requests data or information from this access point. Either of the callbacks can be omitted, so that a particular access point can be specified as read-only, read-write, or write-only. Client data can be associated with these callbacks in the same manner as is done for *Xt* widgets. Having defined one or more public access points in this way, the *Xt* program creates its graphical interface of widgets and enters its usual event loop.

External communication with these *XPA* public access points is accomplished using either *xpaget* or *xpaset* (at the command line) or *OpenXPA* for reading or writing (inside a program). Both methods require specification of the name of the access point. The *xpaget* program returns data or other information from the *Xt* application through its standard output. The *OpenXPA* routine (called for reading) returns a Unix file handle which can be used to retrieve the data using standard Unix I/O calls. The *xpaset* program will send data or commands from its standard input to an *Xt* application, while *OpenXPA* (called for writing) will return a Unix file handle through which data or commands can be written to the *Xt* application using standard I/O calls. *OpenXPA* simply opens a pipe to *xpaset* or *xpaget*. The *XPA* code is not added directly to the application and thus the *Xt* libraries need not be linked into the external program.

Arbitrarily large amounts of data can be transferred to and from *Xt* programs using *XPA* (subject, of course, to system limitations on available memory). The interface is designed so that the data associated with a given access point can be read and written simultaneously. This is accomplished by having the application manage its own "current" copy of the data, which is sent to external requesting processes. Newly received data are maintained internally by *XPA* until the user-specified receive callback can be executed safely to replace the old data with the new. Because of this double buffering, a program can retrieve data from *SAOtng*, transform it in some way, and then send the transformed data back to *SAOtng* for display with one filter command:

```
xpaget data ... | transform ... | xpaset data ...
```

Originally, *XPA* was designed specifically to facilitate the transfer of large amounts of data to and from *Xt* programs such as an image display program that exchanges image data with external processes. It quickly became apparent that, in addition to data, external processes need to send commands to *Xt* programs. We therefore added a function layer on top of the basic *XPA* library to deal specifically with such commands. These routines are centered on the *NewXPACommand* function, and they allow an *Xt* program to define a list of known commands through which the program can be controlled by external processes. These *XPA* commands perform essentially the same function as pushbutton or menu widgets which execute callbacks when activated. In addition, *XPA* commands can return state information to a requesting external process. They have been used extensively to support cooperation between processes, as discussed below.

Other features of the *XPA* interface include:

- the ability to retrieve the names of all public access points in an application.

- the ability to include a descriptive string in communications with the *Xt* application to qualify the data being transferred or requested.

- the ability for real-time applications (e.g., real-time data acquisition) to trigger the receive callback each time data is sent to the *Xt* program, rather than only once at the end of the data transfer.

Extensions to the Xt Selection Mechanism

The *Xt* selection mechanism, which allows *Xt* applications to exchange data, required extensions in order to implement *XPA*. The selection mechanism, as supplied by the X Consortium, Inc., relies on timeouts to determine whether a transfer has been interrupted. For *XPA*, we had to disable the *Xt* timeouts in order to allow the computation and sending of data over an arbitrarily long period of time. This would be the case, for example, if a convolution program was sending image data to an *Xt* application one line at a time.

Instead of timeouts, therefore, *XPA* uses two mechanisms to ensure that both sides of a transfer are active. The receiver code (for *xpaget* or *OpenXPA*) sets a special X property on an X window. The sending process monitors this property. If the receiver terminates, the property will disappear and the sender can take appropriate action to abort the transfer and clean up. On the other hand, to monitor a sending process, the receiver code checks to make sure that the owner of the selection is the same window as the original owner when the receive request was issued. In *XPA*'s use of selection names, if the selection owner changes, this means that the original sender no longer is sending data. The receiver then can take appropriate action.

Applying Public Access Programming Techniques To SAOtng

We have utilized *XPA* to extend the *ximtool* image server into an open-ended *SAOtng* display service that can cooperate with other processes and programs. Indeed, we have added *XPA* functionality at many different levels of the program. Thus, the standard *SAOtng* graphical user interface is a simple menu-based GUI that parallels the original *SAOimage* menu/command paradigm, providing menus for image and frame selection, scaling, colormaps, zoom/pan, regions, etc. All of these menu functions also are defined to be *XPA* public access points using the *NewXPACommand* function. As a result, *SAOtng* can be controlled directly through its menu-based GUI or externally through the *XPA* mechanism. For example, Figure 3 shows how the scaling algorithm is changed and the current scale value is queried using the external access interfaces.

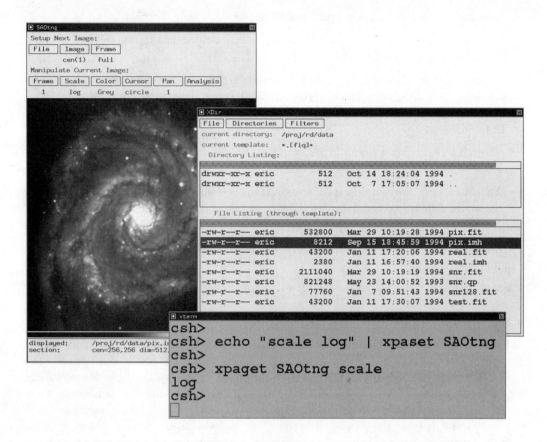

*Figure 3: SAOtng has a simple menu-based GUI. It can be commanded externally
(lower right) and can communicate with programs such as XDir (upper right).*

In fact, the *SAOtng* GUI uses *XPA* to send commands to itself. This implementation ensures that support for external control of *SAOtng* does not lag behind the internally-supported user interface: the GUI initiates commands as if it were just another external process!

External Support For File Access

The astronomical community long ago defined a data exchange and archiving standard based on the Flexible Image Transport System (*FITS*). *SAOtng* supports *FITS* files internally, so that a standard *FITS* image file can be sent directly to *SAOtng* for display using *XPA*:

```
cat foo.fits | xpaset SAOtng
```

However, *FITS* image format generally is considered an inefficient format for data analysis and it is common for astronomical analysis systems to make use of more efficient run-time image formats. Support for these "proprietary" image file formats (or any other image format) is added to *SAOtng* by writing two external file access programs:

- a header access program to generate a *FITS* header describing the full image.

- a data access program to generate a *FITS* image of a specified data section (given the center, dimensions, and block factor).

These program pairs are made known to *SAOtng* at start-up time in a user-configurable ASCII file. To load an image, the access programs are run externally (using the *system( )* function) to create a *FITS*-format data stream of a specified data section, which is passed back to *SAOtng* for display using *XPA*:

- When a new file name is sent to *SAOtng*, the appropriate header access program is run to gather the overall image dimensions.

- The data access program then is run to extract the desired image section, which is scaled to the image display depth and displayed on the screen.

- Finally, the data access program again extracts the data section and stores it as raw *FITS* data for later use (e.g., in order to re-scale the image without having to run the data extraction program again).

Note that adding new formats does not require re-compilation of *SAOtng*.

Integration Of Analysis Routines

Each file type known to *SAOtng* can have user-defined analysis commands associated with it. These analysis commands are defined at start-up time by means of ASCII descriptions. The analysis commands associated with the currently displayed image are available for execution, either via an analysis menu in the *SAOtng* GUI or using *SAOtng*'s *XPA* "analysis" command. When activated, an analysis command first is macro-expanded to fill in user-defined arguments and then is executed externally using the *system( )* function. Results can be displayed in a separate window or even can be sent back to *SAOtng*, i.e., an analysis command can create an image and send it to *SAOtng* for display:

```
xpaget SAOtng data | smooth ... | xpaset SAOtng "frame new"
```

In the example above, the *FITS* representation of the currently displayed image in *SAOtng* is piped into the standard input of an image smoothing program. The *FITS* image generated by this program then is piped back into a new frame buffer of *SAOtng* for display.

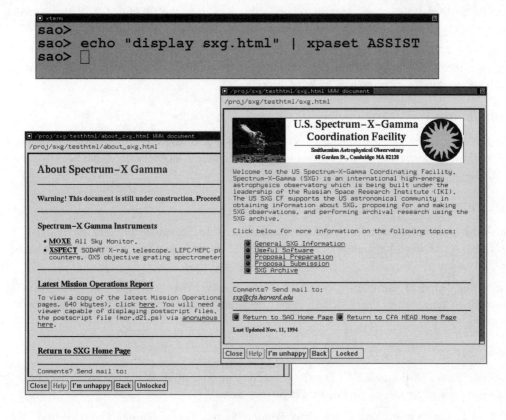

Figure 4: XPA can be used to display WWW documents at the command line, by sending a "display node" command to the ASSIST.

Cooperation With Other Processes

XPA encourages the re-use of GUI programs so that new systems can be built from existing high-level components. For example, the *SAOtng* "Load Image" menu option pops up the *XPA*-based *XDir* directory and file browser (see Figure 3). *XDir* can be used to browse through directory trees using template filters. Double clicking on an image file causes *XDir* to send an *XPA* command to *SAOtng* to load the new image. Thus, *SAOtng* can make use of *XDir*'s sophisticated capabilities without linking them explicitly.

As a final example, consider the use of *XPA* in the *ASSIST* application. The *ASSIST* is an X Window System program developed by E. Mandel and M. Ackerman (University of California, Irvine) that implements a uniform graphical interface to analysis systems, documentation (including WWW HTML documents), and other organizational memory [3]. One of the *XPA* commands that has been added to *ASSIST* is a "node display" command that directs the *ASSIST* to display an information node in a window. This command can be used, for example, to display WWW documents from the command line, as shown in Figure 4. It also allows external programs to utilize *ASSIST* as a help system: these programs can send a "node display" command to *ASSIST* in order to display their documentation, and in this way, reap the benefit of the latter's special capabilities for collecting and accessing organizational memory.

Using *XPA*, GUI programs can make collective use of their individual strengths without having to link all of the different types of functionality into each program separately: in effect, GUI programs can be re-used in the same manner as subroutines!

Conclusion

The X Public Access mechanism makes possible a new type of analysis program that is extensible and that can cooperate with other processes. It takes us closer to an era in which our heterogeneous analysis systems can work as an integrated whole.

Acknowledgments

This work was supported under NASA contracts to the *IRAF* Technical Working Group (NAGW-1921), the *AXAF* High Resolution Camera (NAS8-38248), and the *AXAF* Science Center (NAS8-39073).

The National Optical Astronomy Observatories are operated by the Association of Universities for Research in Astronomy, Inc. (AURA) under cooperative agreement with the National Science Foundation.

References

[1] Doug Tody. "A Portable GUI Development System: The IRAF Widget Server", to appear in the *Astronomical Society of the Pacific Conference Series*.

[2] Paul J. Asente and Ralph R. Swick. *X Window System Toolkit*, Digital Press, Bedford MA, 1990.

[3] Eric Mandel, Mark S. Ackerman, John Roll, and Stephen S. Murray. "AXAF User Interfaces for Heterogeneous Analysis Environments'", *ESO Conference and Workshop Proceedings*, 43, 361.

A Remote Access Protocol for the X Window System

W. Keith Edwards
Susan H. Liebeskind
Elizabeth D. Mynatt
William D. Walker

Abstract

This paper presents a protocol which communicates information about graphical interfaces between X applications. This protocol, called Remote Access Protocol (RAP), can be used to script or test graphical applications, or, as in our case, translate a graphical application to a non-visual presentation. We present details on how applications begin communicating via RAP and describe the messages in the protocol itself.

Introduction

This paper describes an inter-application communication protocol called Remote Access Protocol, or RAP. RAP is designed to allow a process (called an *agent*) to be notified of changes in the state of another application's interface, and to even cause changes in the state of other applications.

The basic framework needed to support RAP transparently has been included in Release 6 of the X Window System, in the form of a new HooksObject within the Xt toolkit. The RAP protocol itself, along with its rendezvous mechanisms, are being proposed as a new standard to be supported in Release 7.

RAP can facilitate the construction of new classes of applications. One category of systems that RAP supports (and, in fact, the reason that design work on RAP was undertaken in the first place) is interface translators. Via RAP, an agent can receive notifications of changes in an application's interface and can present that interface in a new (and possibly even non-visual) modality. For example, a RAP agent could allow access to existing X Window System applications via a car phone, or could allow blind users to operate graphical applications by translating those applications to an auditory presentation.

Other applications include batch scripting of graphical applications, automated testing, and interactive resource editing, a la Editres. While our focus has been on providing a software infrastructure for interface transformation, we have tried to ensure that RAP is usable for other applications as well.

In this paper, we first discuss a motivational example for RAP, namely Mercator, Georgia Tech's screen reader for X Window applications. We follow with a discussion of the infrastructure that will support the RAP protocol, both existing infrastructure and a proposal for additional infrastructure. Next, we discuss our goals for the RAP protocol, followed by a section covering the messages that form the protocol. Lastly, we discuss the status and future directions for the RAP protocol implementation.

Motivation

As a motivating example of RAP, we shall consider the case of translating an existing graphical interface into a non-visual presentation. This transformation has been the goal of the Mercator Project, a research effort at the Georgia Institute of Technology. The Mercator effort has been concerned with the construction of a system which can permit blind or severely visually-impaired computer users to access graphical applications. The system translates graphical output into nonvisual (primarily speech and non-speech audio), and provides new input modalities for controlling applications (for example, the system translates keyboard input into the mouse input "expected" by most applications). Such a system is also useful for providing access to graphical applications in situations where only a limited visual display, or even no visual display at all is present (car phones and PDAs come to mind).

When we began the Mercator Project, we based our system on a completely external approach for capturing information about changes in the state of an X application. We used a pseudoserver process to both trap and synthesize X protocol to and from applications. The pseudoserver, in conjunction with Editres, allowed us some degree of access to the interface of X applications. However it became clear that programming the system to deal flexibly with highly dynamic graphical interfaces was problematic with the pseudoserver approach [1].

For our second version of the system, we began to investigate a set of modifications to Xt itself which would provide more complete and high-level information about application interfaces. The rationale for this approach was that by instrumenting Xt to notify us about changes in an application's widget hierarchy and widget resource values, our agent process would be able to construct a more robust model of the application's graphical interface. Further, this approach would be independent of the various widget sets layered atop Xt (that is, we would not need to provide additional code changes every time a new widget class was written) [2].

RAP Design Goals

Before we begin our discussion of the Remote Access Protocol itself, we must present some of the design goals we felt were important.

Transparency

Transparency means that an application with the requisite set of modifications can participate in the protocol without programmer intervention. That is, no special action is required on the part of the application developer to take part in the services provided by RAP.

To implement transparency, the infrastructure provided by Xt and Xlib must be extended so that the entire process of initiating communication, responding to requests, and generating notifications occurs within Xt and Xlib themselves. However this feature does not mean that "RAP-aware" clients cannot exert control over their participation in the protocol, if they are specifically written to do so. Further, clients can specifically choose to not participate in the protocol, for security or other reasons.

Arbitrary Rendezvous Order

It is important that applications and agents be able to connect to each other in arbitrary order. For example, a blind user may begin an X session by starting the interface translation agent, and then running any desired applications. In the case of an interactive resource editor, the agent may be started after the application is already running.

For maximum flexibility, and to support a range of different agents, arbitrary start-up ordering is a requirement.

Support for Multiple Agents

The protocol and initiation procedures should not prevent multiple agents running at the same time. It is easy to envision a situation in which a given user may be running a testing application, a resource editor, and an interface translator at the same time. The protocol infrastructure must support connection of an arbitrary number of agents to a set of applications, whether those agents are speaking RAP or some other protocol.

Support for Multiple Protocols

While our work has focused primarily on the RAP protocol for communication of interface changes, it is possible that the infrastructure required for RAP may be used for other protocols in the future. Thus, we should provide support for arbitrary multiple protocols to share the connection set-up and hook infrastructure used by RAP.

Non-Xt Specific

Although our current implementation is for the Xt toolkit, and our work has resulted in a number of changes to Xt itself, there is no reason that a RAP implementation could not be provided for other Xt (or even non-Xt) toolkits. For this reason, it is important to not include any constructs in the protocol which are specific to Xt and might not be implementable in other toolkit paradigms.

Information Filtering

Even though RAP is a general tool for communicating changes in application interfaces to an agent process, different agents may require different information even though they all participate in RAP. For example, an interface translation system requires access to all interface change information, while an interactive resource editor only needs to be informed of changes in resource values. Thus we must provide a mechanism to limit the types of information which are sent from an application to an agent via RAP.

Light-weight

The protocol should be lightweight, and not impact the performance of the clients by its presence. It is possible that some clients will choose not to participate in the protocol; such clients should not have to pay the price for unused functionality.

RAP Infrastructure

In order to translate graphical interfaces to non-visual equivalents, a certain amount of infrastructure must be supplied within the X Window System. Some of the necessary translation support was added as of Release 6. This support, discussed in the *Existing Infrastructure* section, will permit translation to take place, assuming that the protocol connection has been established and initialized. But support to establish and initialize the protocol is still lacking in the current release. In the *Additional Required Infrastructure* section, we outline our proposal to resolve this deficiency. With this extra functionality, we will have all the necessary components to support the RAP protocol.

Existing Infrastructure

Over the course of this second phase of the project, a set of code changes were proposed to the X Consortium and accepted as a Consortium standard with Release 6. These code changes provide a new, private, implementation-dependent widget to Xt called the HooksObject. The Hooks object is associated with an application's display connection, and maintains a set of callback lists (see Table 1, "HooksObject Callback Lists,"). These callback lists hold callback routines which are fired whenever certain changes occur in the state of the application's interface. Xt has been instrumented to call into the appropriate HooksObject callback list. For example, whenever a new widget is created, Xt will invoke any callbacks present in the WidgetCreation callback list in the HooksObject. Some additional APIs were added to Xt to allow applications to retrieve the HooksObject associated with a display connection [3] and the shells associated with the display.

Callback List	Description
CreateHook	Called whenever a new widget instance is created.
ChangeHook	Called whenever a widget resource value is updated.
ConfigHook	Called whenever a widget's configuration (size or position) change.
GeometryHook	Called whenever a widget's geometry is updated.
DestroyHook	Called whenever a widget is destroyed (when a widget's phase 1 destruction is complete).

Table 1: HooksObject Callback Lists

The changes to the R6 Xt library do not specify *what* code will be installed in the various callback lists; they merely provide the infrastructure to have Xt call out to some installed set of procedures whenever interface changes occur.

Along with the R6 HooksObject in Xt, a new client-side extension hook was added to Xlib. An extension procedure may be installed via XESetBeforeFlush() which is called whenever the Xlib request buffer is flushed [4]. The motivation for this change was that an interface transformation system (or other applications interested in low-level protocol information) could install a procedure via XESetBeforeFlush to pass the low-level X protocol information which was previously available only through pseudoserver-based approaches.

Like the changes to Xt, the R6 Xlib does not specify any code to be installed in the BeforeFlush hook; it merely provides infrastructure which applications can use to install code.

These changes to the Release 6 Xlib and Xt libraries were based on our experiences with two versions of the Mercator system. The types of information which can be provided by these modifications are necessary to enable translation of graphical interfaces to non-visual modalities at runtime.

With the framework in hand to enable translations, we turn our attention to designing a protocol that can actually pass the information required for translation. The Inter-Client Exchange Protocol (ICE), new to X11R6, facilitates the process of developing inter-client communication protocols, such as RAP. ICE provides functionality common to many protocols (opening connections, validation of requests, closing connections to name but a few). This set of services allows protocol developers to concentrate on designing the protocol-specific messages and message handlers, while leveraging the generic protocol framework in ICE. Additional details on ICE may be found in [5] and [6].

Additional Required Infrastructure

Unfortunately, although we have the necessary framework in Release 6 to support the translation of graphical interfaces, we do not have the sufficient framework to support this translation. We lack a way to jump-start the process, initiating the RAP protocol as soon as the prospective partners can participate in the protocol.

This problem is not specific to the RAP protocol -- all ICE-based protocols face the issue of initiating the communication process. For many custom protocols, this is not a large problem. The clients on either end of the wire are explicitly aware of the protocol, and at the proper point in their execution, can take steps to setup the communication channel, via the appropriate ICE calls. But for the RAP protocol to work with off-the-shelf X clients, written without foreknowledge of the RAP protocol, transparent initiation is a significant problem.

The solution that we will propose for inclusion in Release 7 is the ICE Rendezvous Mechanism [7]. The rendezvous mechanism is designed to establish an ICE connection between an agent and a client in a manner which will not require explicit awareness of the RAP protocol. Briefly, clients wishing to speak ICE-based protocols follow this set of steps to fire up the ICE connection to support the protocol:

1. The client registers interest in the common protocol with the ICE library.

2. The client either actively tries to make an ICE connection to its partner(s) if this client is the Protocol Originator, or passively waits for its partner(s) to make the connection, if this client is the Protocol Acceptor. Authentication at this step is optional.

3. Once the ICE connection is made, the Protocol Setup request and Protocol Reply response messages are exchanged between originator and acceptor. Following the successful, possi-

bly authenticated, exchange of these messages, the custom protocol's messages may be passed back and forth.

The information that must be made known to both sides of the channel is

- the common protocol (in our case, RAP)
- the network connection point (network id), dynamically assigned by the ICE library

To transfer this information, we are proposing the use of the Client Message mechanism to pass the protocol and network ID information, used in conjunction with a new data object, a table of protocol initialization routines. Calls will be provided to install, remove, and retrieve the protocol routines in the table.

The ClientMessage event handler, specific to each protocol, will be responsible for installing the appropriate protocol initialization routine. The protocol initializer routine, supplied by the protocol developer, will handle any required bookkeeping to fire up the protocol. This protocol initializer routine is not necessarily tied to setting up an ICE connection (although the RAP protocol will use its routine for this purpose.) Any client capable of being monitored by an agent must have its routine installed in its address space.

But one question remains: how does the RAP ClientMessage event handler get installed in the first place, to make all this happen without requiring clients to be RAP aware. The answer lies in the VendorShell source file, specific to each toolkit. Just as the Editres [8] Client Message handler is installed in Athena widget set's VendorShell implementation, so that all clients can be queried transparently by the editres program, so would the RAP client message handler be installed in the VendorShell implementation for all toolkits (Motif and Athena). In this way, any Motif or Athena-based client will be RAP aware, simply by being linked against the toolkit libraries.

The Remote Access Protocol

This section of the paper describes the format of the Remote Access Protocol itself. We describe the semantics of each message in the protocol (that is, what each message *means*), the circumstances under which each message is sent, and the format of the messages. This list is not meant to be definitive or final; it represents the current state of the protocol as used by Mercator [9][10].

Whereever the term "widget ID" is used in the description of a particular message, we are referring to a 32-bit unique identifier for a toolkit object in the application. While in the Xt implementation of RAP these 32-bit values will map directly onto widget IDs, other toolkits may use them to identify their particular constructs.

Further, some messages may not be implemented for certain toolkits. See the DoActionRequest for example.

There are three basic types of messages in RAP: requests, replies, and notifications.

Requests are RAP messages which travel from an external agent process to an application. They are used to ask the application for information about its interface, or to control some aspect of the application.

Replies are responses to specific requests for information sent from the agent. Replies travel from the application to the agent.

Notifications are asynchronous messages which are used to notify an interested agent in a change in the status of the application's interface. Via a set of notification-control requests, the generation of notifications within the application can be selectively filtered.

GetResourcesRequest

The GetResourcesRequest message passes a list of widget IDs to the application; the application responds with a list of the names and types of the resources in the specified widgets (see GetResourcesReply).

QueryTreeRequest

The QueryTreeRequest asks the application to transmit its entire widget hierarchy back to the calling agent via a QueryTreeReply.

GetValuesRequest

GetValuesRequest is used to ask for the values of a set of resources on a set of widgets. The message passes a list of structures; each structure includes a widget ID and a list of resources to retrieve the values of for the specified widget. The application generates a GetValuesReply with the requested information.

SetValuesRequest

The SetValuesRequest message is used by an external agent to change the value of a particular set of resources in a particular set of widgets. The message encodes a list of structures; each structure contains a widget ID, and a list of resource-value-type tuples specifying all of the resources to change in the particular widget, the new values, and the type the value is expressed in.

AddNotifyRequest

The AddNotifyRequest is used to control filtering of notifications sent from the application. The message passes a list of names of callback lists in the HooksObject. Any callback lists specified in the request will be "turned on," meaning that they will generate notifications to the external agent.

RemoveNotifyRequest

RemoveNotifyRequest is used to disable particular notifications by "turning off" callbacks in the HooksObject. Like AddNotifyRequest, it takes a list of names of callback lists to disable.

ObjectToWindowRequest

The ObjectToWindowRequest is used to resolve a widget ID into the primary window used by that widget. The message takes a list of widget IDs to resolve, and generates an ObjectToWindowReply message from the application.

WindowToObjectRequest

WindowToObjectRequest it used to resolve a window ID into the primary Xt widget associated with that window. The message sends a list of window IDs to resolve, and generates a WindowToObjectReply from the application.

LocateObjectRequest

The LocateObjectRequest message is used to find the on-screen locations of a specified list of objects. The message generates a LocateObjectReply return from the application.

GetActionsRequest

The GetActions Request is used to retrieve a list of actions associated with a group of widgets. The message contains a list of widgets.

DoActionRequest

This request is used to invoke an action. It contains a widget and an action name which together specify the action to run.

This message will most probably not be provided in the Xt implementation of RAP, because there are situations in which Xt-based applications may become unstable if actions were invoked directly.

SelectEventRequest

The SelectEventRequest message is used to control which event types are sent from the application to the agent. Whenever connection between an agent and a client application is initiated, a procedure is installed in the WireToEvent client-side extension slot which can transmit X Events to an agent. This message can be used to filter what events are actually sent.

SelectRequestRequest

This message is used to filter the transmission of X Protocol requests from the application to the agent. Requests are "caught" by a routine installed in the BeforeFlush client-side extension and are sent to the agent if their types have been selected by SelectRequestRequest.

CloseConnectionRequest

This message is generated by an agent whenever it wishes to terminate its communication with a client application. The client should take any appropriate clean-up action and then disconnect.

GetResourcesReply

This message is generated in response to a GetResourcesRequest; it contains a list of structures. Each structure contains the ID of a requested widget, and a list of the resource names, classes, and types for that widget.

QueryTreeReply

QueryTreeReply is generated in response to a QueryTreeRequest and returns the widget tree of the application. The information is formatted as a list of tuples, with each tuple containing the widget ID, name class, window ID, and parent widget ID.

GetValuesReply

This message returns a list of resource values for specified widgets to the caller. The format of the message is a list of structures, with each structure containing the ID of a requested widget, and a list of the requested resource names and values for that widget.

ObjectToWindowReply

The ObjectToWindowReply message returns a list of the windows corresponding to the objects requested via ObjectToWindowRequest.

WindowToObjectReply

WindowToObjectReply returns a list of the objects associated with the windows passed via WindowToObjectRequest.

LocateObjectReply

The LocateObjectReply message returns an X, Y coordinate pair for each of the objects requested via LocateObjectRequest.

GetActionsReply

The GetActionsReply is generated in response to a GetActionsRequest and contains a list of action names for each widget specified in the GetActionsRequest message.

CreateNotify

The CreateNotify message is generated by code installed in the CreateHook callback list in the HooksObject. CreateNotify is used to inform an agent whenever a new widget has been created. The messages passes the widget ID, name, class, window ID, and parent widget ID to the agent.

ChangeNotify

The ChangeNotify message is generated via the ChangeHook whenever a resource value is updated. The message sends the widget ID, resource name, and new resource value to the agent.

ConfigNotify

A ConfigNotify message is sent to any interested agents whenever the ConfigHook callback is executed. This message contains information on widget configuration changes: the widget ID, a geometry mask specifying the actual changes which have taken place, and an XWindowChanges structure describing the changes. The message is sent after the changes have taken place.

GeometryNotify

GeometryNotify is generated whenever the GeometryHook callback is executed. This occurs when Xt application makes a geometry request. The message contains the resulting widget geometry, expressed as an XtWidgetGeometry structure. The message is sent after the geometry negotiation has completed.

DestroyNotify

DestroyNotify is used to inform an agent that a widget has been destroyed. The message contains the ID of the newly-destroyed widget, and is generated via the DestroyHook callback list.

RequestNotify

RequestNotify passes X protocol requests to the agent. The actual requests which are sent may be selected by the SelectRequestRequest message. The message contains one or more wire-format X protocol requests; it is generated by code installed in the BeforeFlush client-side extension.

EventNotify

EventNotify passes X events to the agent. The event types which are sent may be selected via the SelectEventRequest message. The message contains one or more wire-format X events, and is generated by code installed in the WireToEvent client-side extension.

Status and future directions

Our current implementation of the Mercator system is built using a protocol which predates (but is essentially similar) to RAP. This protocol runs over standard TCP/IP sockets. Implementation of RAP itself, as well as implementation of the changes to Mercator to use RAP, are ongoing.

Will Walker is serving as the RAP architect, and has begun implementation work on the ICE rendezvous mechanism, and the RAP protocol messages. The public forum on which RAP-related issues are discussed is the x-agent public mailing list, x-agent@x.org. This mailing list is sponsored by the X Consortium for the purposes of developing protocols like RAP for external agent software. Anyone who is interested in contributing to the effort may join the list by sending a message to

```
x-agent-request@x.org
```

The body of this message should contain the single word "subscribe". The subject line of the message will be ignored.

At last year's X Technical conference, Philippe Kaplan and Anselm Baird-Smith of Bull France announced their efforts in a next generation Editres protocol, called K-Edit. K-Edit is "an attempt to provide a simple multipurpose protocol, suitable (in particular) to export an application user interface state" [11]. There is enough overlap between the goals of the K-Edit protocol and the RAP protocol that there has been continuing discussion over the last year, with the possibility of combining the two efforts into a common protocol.

The ICE rendezvous mechanism and ClientMessage handler outlined in the Additional Infrastructure section will be proposed for inclusion in Release 7. However, those proposed changes can be added to R6 clients today. For dynamically-linked applications, all that must be done is to rebuild the Intrinsics library from source modified to support the rendezvous and ClientMessage. The next invocation of the dynamically linked clients will be RAP aware, as the library they utilize dynamically will have been made RAP aware. Statically linked clients will need to be relinked against a newly compiled static Intrinsics library, but in keeping with the goals for the RAP protocol, the clients themselves will not need to be modified at the source code level in any way.

Since the format of the RAP protocol is still evolving, we expect changes in the protocol between now and the Release 7 cut-off date. One area where we need to focus is resource type negotiation. Certain types used by resources within an application may not be known to a particular external agent; yet the application may have the ability to convert these types to a format which the agent can understand. Conversely, the agent itself may have the ability to convert certain types internally, even if the agent does not have the required converters linked into it. Thus a process where resource types are negotiated between agents and applications may be useful.

Summary

We have presented a protocol for communicating changes in interface state between X applications and agent processes. This protocol is powerful in that it can support a variety of useful agents including interactive resource editing, scripting, testing, and interface translation.

The protocol builds on a set of hooks, some of which are already present in Release 6 of the X Window System, and some of which are still pending.

We acknowledge the contributions of many people to this project: Tom Rodriguez (formerly of Georgia Tech, now at Sun Microsystems, who designed the protocol on which RAP is based; Bob Scheifler, Donna Converse, Ralph Swick, Daniel Dardailler, and Kaleb Keithley (of the X Consortium) who provided much-needed design guidance; and the members of the Disability Action Committee on X (DACX). Thanks also to Sun Microsystems and the NASA Marshall Space Flight Center for their sponsorship of Mercator.

Author Information

Keith Edwards, Susan Liebeskind, and Beth Mynatt work at the Graphics, Visualization, & Usability Center at Georgia Tech. Their email addresses are keith@cc.gatech.edu, shl@cc.gatech.edu, and beth@cc.gatech.edu; they can be reached via telephone at (404) 894-3658. Will Walker is a Software Engineer at Digital Equipment Corporation. His email address is wwalker@zk3.dec.com.

References

[1]   Elizabeth Mynatt and W. Keith Edwards. *Mapping GUIs to Auditory Interfaces*. In Proceedings of the Fifth ACM Symposium on User Interface Software and Technology (UIST), Monterey, CA, November, 1992.

[2]   Elizabeth Mynatt and W. Keith Edwards. A*n Architecture for Transforming Graphical Interfaces.* In Proceedings of the Seventh ACM Symposium on User Interface Software and Technology (UIST), Marina Del Rey, CA, November, 1994.

[3]   Joel McCormack, Paul Asente, Ralph Swick. *X Toolkit Intrinsics C Language Interface.* X Consortium Standard. Version 11, Release 6.

[4]   James Gettys and Robert Scheifler. *Xlib C Language Interface.* X Consortium Standard. Version 11, Release 6.

[5]   Robert Scheifler and Jordan Brown. *Inter-Client Exchange (ICE) Protocol, Version 1.0.* X Consortium Standard. Version 11, Release 6. 1994.

[6]   Ralph Mor. *Inter-Client Exchange (ICE) Library, Version 1.0.* X Consortium Standard. Version 11, Release 6. 1994.

[7]   William D. Walker. *An ICE Rendezvous Mechanism for X Window System Clients.* Unpublished report, Disability Action Committee for X, 1994.

[8]   Chris D. Peterson. *Editres: A Graphical Resource Editor for X Toolkit Applications.* In Proceedings of the Fifth Annual X Technical Conference, Boston, MA, January, 1991.

[9]   W. Keith Edwards and Tom Rodriguez. *Runtime Translation of X Interfaces to Support Visually-Impaired Users.* In Proceedings of the 7th Annual X Technical Conference, Boston, MA, January 18-20, 1993.

[10]   William D. Walker. *Remote Access Protocol (RAP), Version 0.2.* DACX Work In Progress. November 11, 1993.

[11]   Philippe Kaplan and Anselm Baird-Smith. *The K-edit System.* Unpublished report available via http://zenon.inria.fr:8003/koala/k-edit.html.

The Double Buffer Extension

Ian Elliott[†]

Abstract

The Double Buffer Extension (DBE) provides a standard way to utilize double-buffering within the framework of the X Window System. DBE supersedes the Multi-Buffer Extension (MBX) which never became an X Consortium standard. At the time of the X Conference, DBE should be in the final stages of public review.

This presentation will give an overview of the design of DBE, its intended usage, status of the DBE sample implementation, and the relationship of DBE to MBX, PEX, and OpenGL. Various implementation strategies will be discussed, and a demonstration will be given of one or more DBE implementations.

[†]*Ian Elliott (ian@elliott.fc.hp.com) is a Technical Contributor for Hewlett-Packard Company.*

Loadable Server Architectures

Rob Lembree
Ian Elliott

Abstract

The X Window System has grown by leaps and bounds over the last decade. As new demands have been placed on X, these demands have been met by a proliferation of new graphic adapters, extensions, and other components. In addition to growth, the X industry has found itself head to head with the personal computer industry, as the gap between workstations and PCs has shrunk to virtually a difference in philosophy and software. These changes have placed challenges on X server developers to keep the server small while adding a great deal of new functionality. At the same time, X is being called upon to meet the personal computer's variety and flexibility. This paper outlines how dynamically loadable modules help X server vendors maintain a balance between size and function, while at the same time, making flexible configuration and third party contribution possible.

Part 1: Introduction

The traditional X Server is built from heavily X Consortium-based sources, and provides support for one specific graphic adapter and a pre-selected set of extensions. If someone were to build such a server, they would have to know in advance what sort of features that the server would need to support. They'd have to decide which graphic adapter they're targetting, what extensions might be needed on the server, and even what font renderers they'd like. Having selected all the right pieces from the distribution, they'd build a single server image, and name it something unique for this particular application. Clearly, this process can become unreasonable when the number of graphic adapters and extensions grows beyond a handful, or when the users of a system can have widely diverse needs. Soon, the number of desired permutations can become too numerous to even consider. This is particularly true for system vendors who are trying to target a broad set of markets with one product set.

To solve this problem, many vendors have modified the X server to be able to dynamically adapt to different hardware configurations and user needs. By doing this, they can produce a very flexible product without having to predict each and every configuration possibility. They do this by using dynamically loadable X server component modules.

What Loadable Technology Can do For an X Server

Using the concept of a dynamically loadable module, vendors have found that they no longer need to have *a-priori* knowledge of any particular configuration. Rather, the configuration decisions can be deferred to each server startup time and be at least partially dependent on the present circumstances. The trick, it seems, is to defer as much decision making as possible to as late as possible. To be able to adapt to a multitude of potential configurations requires a great deal of forethought and careful design, but the benefits in the end product are often worth the effort.

Configurability

One of the biggest wins with loadable modules is that no longer do vendors have to restrict configurations to a few popular ones. For the most part, vendors can write their servers so that regardless of how graphic adapters or extensions are installed, they will work as well: almost as if the configuration had a special server built for it.

In an example of a student workstation farm at a university, it is conceivable for one student to use a workstation for MCAD, using OpenGL or PEX, followed by the next student who needs to do desktop publishing using Display PostScript, followed by another who needs to work with multimedia. To have a monolithic server perform all of these functions would require a fair amount of skill and forethought on the part of the system administrator, as well as a significant amount of system memory for all of the X server's extension code. An X server that supports loadable modules would be able to do all of these things equally well, and without the activities of an earlier user interfering with the subsequent users.

Scalability

Scalability is important to X server vendors. The X desktop now ranges from personal computers to X terminals to high end workstations, and scalability even within these wide ranges is important. Memory and disk availability, as well as workstation graphic hardware, ranges widely. To provide the maximum amount of ready functionality with as little resource consumption as possible is key in producing a competitive product. This breaks the scalability problem into two large classes: upward and downward scalability.

For upward scalability, large multi-head configurations serve as a good example. Consider a customer who buys a shiny new workstation with one low-end graphic adapter. Six months later, the customer finds that he or she needs to start doing high-end 3D on the system, and needs a specialized graphic head in addition to the low-end graphic hardware. With a truly loadable X server architecture, the customer only has to buy the adapter, plug in a floppy with a driver and a DDX shareable, install, and restart the system.

In the case of downward scalability, the X server should occupy only the amount of physical memory absolutely necessary to perform the job asked of it.[†] For example, if a workstation is capable of supporting *G*, *H* and *I* graphic adapters simultaneously, a 'static' X server built for this machine would include all three DDX modules. On a system with just a *G*, the memory occupied by the other support modules would be wasted memory. With a loadable X server, the configuration can be dynamically supported, without the additional overhead of unnecessary DDX support.

Another example of how a loadable X server can improve downward scalability is through how it can handle extensions. As extensions have proliferated, the memory required to support a full-featured X Server has increased dramatically. Large extensions such as PEX, XIE and DPS can often occupy more memory than the core X Server itself! Without a loadable server, the choice has to be made at server build time -- should this extension be included or not? With a loadable server, the load decision can often be deferred to a much later point, such as server startup or even as late as a client's `XQueryExtension` request.

Third-Party Contributions

The transition from static X servers to dynamic X server has made possible another bold move outward for the X Window System industry: the seamless integration of third party components into established workstation products. Since components can be loadable, the only roadblock to supporting third party components seems to be a stable, documented programming interface. While a number of vendors have supported third parties, it remains a difficult task while maintaining a competitive base product. The loadable working group is tackling this at an industry wide level, and hopes to standardize methods for making this easier through better interfaces and documentation. An important side effect of this effort is that inter-vendor component porting will be far easier, creating a wider market for third party vendors.

Part 2: Technology Inventory

There are a great many ways to approach the loadable server problem, and each vendor has done so in a different way, reflecting the reasons why each has found it necessary to do so. Since there are so many reasons why it can be a good reason to implement a loadable server, and since each vendor has concentrated on a particular (and often differing) set of problems, the solutions each have their strengths and weaknesses. But, since each problem has been solved in a number of ways, the various methods of solving the problems make up a good repository of experience, which we try to outline here. The Loadable Server Architecture will draw on the best strengths of this collection of technology, and avoids the pitfalls shown by the common experience. We have chosen Digital's DEC OSF/1 and Hewlett-Packard's HP-UX as our primary example implementations, as they represent a good cross-section of the available technlogy.

---

†*While it is true that most X display systems today have virtual memory, it is not valid to assume that all do. Also, in the case of low-end systems such as notebook systems, even virtual memory space is very limited due to the limited size of mass storage. Adequate physical memory is therefore of tantamount importance to a well-performing X system.*

Digital's DEC OSF/1

DEC OSF/1 is Digital's 64-bit Unix offering running on the Alpha AXP Architecture. The Alpha AXP Architecture has been used in systems from very low-end PC-class systems to very high-end multiprocessor server systems, all of which can support graphic subsystems. Since DEC OSF/1 targets such a wide range of platforms and users, flexibility and scalability are high priorities. The loadable server that is implemented on DEC OSF/1 reflects these needs.

Loading Strategy

The DEC OSF/1 Loadable X Server Architecture is designed to provide the broadest range of ready functionality without incurring a great deal of overhead. In addition, it is important to be able to use sources as close to the X Consortium's sample implementation as possible, as a divergent source pool becomes increasingly expensive to maintain.

The core of the DEC OSF/1 loadable server source is contained within the directory `Xserver/loadable`. This directory is built at the end of the server build, as this is where the `Xdec` server executable is built. Contained in this directory is the loadable services library (`LS_`), the config file parser (`parser.y`) (`yacc`), the loadable server specific include files, and documentation.

Loadable Components

`Xdec` is actually a small (73K) bootstrap program that loads the X server components and transfers execution to them. The executable also contains the loadable service routines required by the loadable server to provide the OS-independent loading interface. The `Xdec` loadable X Server is composed of several major sections, each represented by a configuration file section.

The **System** components contain all of the system provided shareables such as the math library and network libraries. They are explicitly loaded by the X server so that these components can be specified by the X server, and run-time replacement of these libraries by the X server is possible, for whatever reason.

The **Core** components include the OS layer, DIX and WS (Digital specific driver interface layer).

The **Device** components include the MI layer, CFB and MFB libraries, and the DDX components. These are loaded as required by the hardware environment. Like all other component types, the `Device` components can have sublibrary lists specified for additional specialized hardware support.

The **Extension** components contain the protocol extension code for the X server. The components are loaded by the core components from a configurable list in `Xserver.conf`. Most extensions are not loaded at server initialization time to save memory. Instead, when the first client requests the use of an extension (via `XQueryExtension`), the extension code loads the extension and continues processing the requests. Some extensions may load additional device-specific code to provide special handling of graphics devices or input devices found on the system. An example of this is the device specific support required by the X Video Extension, which is included in separate device-specific modules loaded by the extension as required.

The **Font_Renderers** components specify the loadable font renderers available. The core X server contains native support for bitmapped fonts, but additional renderers such as `Type1` and `Speedo` are dynamically loaded as requested. One font renderer is a communication interface to a font server. These font renderers are also loaded by the font server as well, resulting in code sharing between servers where they coexist.

Finally, the `Input` components specify dynamically loadable X Input device handler modules.

Loading Process

When `Xdec` is started, it uses a set of internal default lists of components to build an X server. It also reads a system configuration file (`/usr/var/X11/Xserver.conf` or the file specified by the `-config` option), to supplement or replace components on the lists.

The `Xdec` command then searches for libraries using the `library_path` specified in the configuration file or the `LD_LIBRARY_PATH` environment variable. Each component in the colon separated path is searched. In addition, for each component in the path, the path `component/Xserver` is also searched so that X server libraries can be more neatly maintained in a subdirectory. The default search path is `/usr/shlib/X11:/usr/shlib`.

The server loads all system and core components, then resolves the symbol `dix_main` using the `LS_GetSymbol` function. Execution is then permanently transferred to `dix_main()`.

Workstation driver interface code in the core components then queries the system for graphics and input device types and loads appropriate components from the device and input lists. If the workstation driver interface cannot find a component for a device, it will ignore the device. If however the server is unable to find loadable support for any screens at all, it will exit with an error message.

The core components then load the list of "pre-load" extensions provided, and initialize the extensions. Some extensions may load further device-specific components from the sublists provided to them in the configuration file. The differentiation between extensions that are preloaded and those with deferred loading is whether or not an extension name is provided in the configuration line for that extension.

Currently, DEC OSF/1 does not use the transport handler configuration section, as these are hard-linked at build time.

When the X server resets itself (usually when the last client has exited), all extension and font renderer components are unloaded and then reinitialized when the X server begins to restart itself. In this way, extensions or font renderers which have been used can be removed from the configuration until they are required again. Since it is not currently possible to hot-swap graphic hardware, the hardware environment can be considered stable across server resets, and therefore DDX support is not unloaded.

Configuration File Syntax

The configuration file used by DEC OSF/1 is a object class oriented file that describes the possible components for the loadable server. The sections are component sections, describing one or more components of the same type. Sections are recursive, so it is possible to have components be tightly tied to or dependent on other components.

Individual components may have multiple sublibraries. In the example below, the device paragraph specifies one device, a VGA graphics device. Here, if a VGA is detected on the system, the file `lib_dec_vga.so` will be loaded, and the routine `vgaScreenInit` will be called. This initialization routine identifies the specific VGA present, obtains a list of sublibraries of its own, finds a match, requests that the matching library be loaded, resolves the initialization routine symbol, and calls it. Here, the name of the library, the library's filename, the initialization routine name, and the device supported is specified.

```
device <
        < _dec_vga lib_dec_vga.so vgaScreenInit
            < _dec_triton lib_dec_triton.so pwgaScreenInit_base QVision >
            < _dec_ati64 lib_dec_ati64.so atiScreenInit_base ATI64 >
            < _dec_ati32 lib_dec_ati32.so ati32ScreenInit_base ATI32 >
        >
    >
```

The extension type is organized identically to the device type. Here, several extensions are listed in the paragraph. Of particular interest in this example is the XVideo extension, which has hardware specific modules listed as sublibraries of the main library. XVideo has an internal policy that if it does not find a device handler that matches one of the devices available on the system (in this case PMAG-RO or PMAG-JA), it does not initialize itself. Also of interest here is how the Xie extension's MI layer is specified as a dependent shareable. Specified here again is the library name, library's file name, initialization routine name, and the extension name (if the extension is to have deferred loading).

```
extensions <

        < extSync    libextSync.so    SyncExtensionInit  SYNC >
        < extxtest   libextxtest.so   XTestExtensionInit XTEST >

        ! add the video extension along with device specific handlers
        ! for the TX device
        < xv libxv.so   XvExtensionInit  XVideo
            < _dec_xv_tx lib_dec_xv_tx.so XvropScreenInit PMAG-RO >
            < _dec_xv_tx lib_dec_xv_tx.so XvropScreenInit PMAG-JA >
        >

        ! add the X imaging extension
        < dixie  libdixie.so   XieInit   XIE
            < mixie libmixie.so >
        >
    >
```

Font renderers are specified similarly, but no examples to date take advantage of the component defined fourth argument.

```
font_renderers <
        < fr_fs      libfr_fs.so      fs_register_fpe_functions >
        < fr_Speedo  libfr_Speedo.so  SpeedoRegisterFontFileFunctions >
        < fr_Type1   libfr_Type1.so   Type1RegisterFontFileFunctions >
```

```
>
```

This is an example of an input specification. The X Input extension implicitly has both DDX and DIX layers, and DEC OSF/1 has made a clean split between the two. The following paragraph specifies that there is a dial and button box on /dev/tty01. When the XInput extension initializes, it will open the shareable library and call the initialization routine specified.

```
! enable PCM dial and button box
input <
        < _dec_xi_pcm  lib_dec_xi_pcm.so  XiPcmInit    /dev/tty01 >
>
```

The X Server has the ability to specify its own loadable library path. This is especially useful when a third party wants to keep its own shareables in its own directory. An additional library specification in this definition will permit them to do this without any source code modification.

```
library_path < /newserver/fonts/lib/font:/usr/shlib >
```

Finally, the configuration file permits the specification of default command line arguments. This allows the sometimes necessary modifications to the command line to be hidden from the casual user.

```
! you specify command line arguments here
args
       -vclass0 StaticGray
        ! first screen has a default visual of static gray
>
```

Loadable Services

The DEC OSF/1 Loadable Services (LS_) functions are part of the Xdec executable, contain a fairly complete set of functions, and provides an application programming interface that can be implemented in an operating system independent fashion. It serves as an example of the kind of API that the loadable server architecture needs to produce.

```
LS_Status LS_LoadLibraryReqs(libraries, ndx, num)
void LS_UnLoadLibraryReqs(libraries, ndx, num)
```
      Loads / Unloads specified libraries.

```
void LS_MarkForUnloadLibraryReqs(libraries, ndx, num)
void LS_FreeMarkedLibraries()
```
      Specifies libraries to be closed at a later time, and then actually closes them.

```
char *LS_GetLibName(libraries, ndx)
char *LS_GetDeviceName(libraries, ndx)
char *LS_GetLibFileName(libraries, ndx)
```
      Gets the specified name from a library record.

```
void *LS_GetInitProc(libraries, ndx)
char *LS_GetInitProcName(libraries, ndx)
```
      Gets the initialization procedure or procedure name from a library record.

```
int LS_GetLibraryReqByLibName(libraries, count, name)
int LS_GetLibraryReqByDeviceName(libraries, count, name)
int LS_GetLibraryReqByExtensionName(libraries, count, name)
```
Search the specified library list for the library with the appropriate matching name.

```
Boolean LS_GetSubLibList(libraries, ndx, liblist_return, count_return)
```
Returns a list of sublibrary records for a specified set of libraries. This facilitates the specification and use of sub library dependencies.

```
void *LS_GetSymbol(symbolName)
void *LS_GetSymbolInLibrary(symbolName, libraries, ndx)
```
Returns address of a symbol in either global name space or the name space of a specific library.

```
void LS_MarkLibraryInited(libraries, ndx)
Boolean LS_IsLibraryInited(libraries, ndx)
```
Marks / detects initialization state by the server. Keeps track of which libraries have had their initialization routine called.

```
LS_Status LS_ForceSymbolResolution()
```
Forces all currently loaded symbols to be resolved.

```
void LS_ParseArguments( options, num_options, argc, argv )
```
Parse a command line argument list for the members of the specified options list.

```
void LS_ListOpenLibraries()
```
Lists all known libraries and their states. Used in response to a command line option requesting this information -- useful for debugging.

Hewlett-Packard's HP-UX

Introduction

HP's current X server implementation that supports dynamic loading addresses problems faced by vendors, IHVs, ISVs, and end users. HP's solution covers issues such as powerful extension support (extensions that require direct DDX support), standard interfaces (to simplify IHV/ISV porting), robustness (the X server must always come up), and Plug & Play.

By Plug & Play, HP means that no administrator configuration step is required. If matching software and hardware are present the X server will start up. DDX and extension module software installation is order independent. Simply update software as it becomes available or as desired. Switch the hardware as frequently as desired. Hardware identification and software versioning issues are dynamically identified and resolved by the broker paradigm.

A *Broker Paradigm* is integral to HP's implementation. Brokers represent all potential DDX drivers and extensions during the dynamic module selection process. New, pre-screenInit() control points are introduced, which along with HP's DDX/extension co-initialization entry point, creates a very flexible and extensible server initialization process.

User/Administrator Involvement

Experience demonstrated to HP that end-user and administrator responsibilities should be as simple as possible. Therefore, HP limits involvement to the specification of non-essential (i.e. optional) feature information. For each changeable option, good default values exist, and are used if the alternate value is mis-specified. Administrators are not allowed to directly specify what modules to dynamically load; brokers provide this information, potentially taking into account user-specified options. This approach supports HP's Plug & Play and X server startup robustness goals.

HP created a file syntax, a location, and a file naming convention to store this optional information. Most users/administrators will never need to modify the file (or even know of its existence). The file utilizes key words to identify *standard* options. A special keyword signals the use of *non-standard* options, which allows DDX providers to extend the set of options that a user may set. A few examples of standard screen-specific features HP has currently defined include: the default visual (i.e. depth, layer and visual class), and monitor size.

Inside the X server, the file is parsed and the information is placed within several lists of token-value pairs (one list for server options and one list for each screen). Each of these lists is called a *token list*. These token lists are accessible throughout the server initialization timeframe. This approach proves quite flexible in conjunction with the broker paradigm where the brokers are able to make decisions based on requested features, and even modify or add feature requests (tokens) to support their requirements. Eventually these token lists are fully processed, with each screen-specific list being processed by the chosen xxxScreenInit() procedure. Tokens which aren't recognized by a xxxScreenInit() procedure are simply ignored.

Before calling the DDX brokers, HP's X server uses ioctl() calls to identify the type of hardware being used. All graphics devices supported on HP's workstations are uniquely identifiable. For graphics devices that can not be uniquely identified, HP envisions that a new token-value pair would be defined to allow a user/administrator to specify a unique ID, which the brokers will use (via the screen token list) to recognize the device.

How to Support Powerful Extensions

HP wants to support what it terms *powerful* extensions, and do so in an *open* fashion. By *powerful*, HP means extensions which require or benefit from direct DDX support. By *open*, HP means it should be relatively easy to port code from one vendor's X server to another's.

HP takes an approach of having one DDX screen driver that can support multiple extensions as opposed to having one DDX module for core X and another DDX module for each extension.

DDX/Extension Dependencies

HP defines the following four *dependency classes* for describing the level and type of interactions between extensions and DDX drivers (extensions can have a different dependency class value for screen and input DDX drivers):

None

> These extensions work without any DDX involvement. In fact, no DDX involvement is possible.

Beneficial

> These extensions will also work without any DDX involvement. However, these extensions provide an extension-specific, device-dependent (aka DDX) interface so that optional, beneficial DDX support is possible.

Tight

> These extensions ignore any screen and/or input device that doesn't plug device-specific routines into the extension-specific DDX interface.

Extreme

> These extensions can only work when `all` of the screens and/or input devices plug device-specific routines into the extension-specific DDX interface. Otherwise, the server will not operate correctly.

DDX/Extension Dependency Resolution

Because extensions of the **None** and **Beneficial** classes will always work regardless of DDX screen or input-device support, they should always be loaded. **Tight** extensions should only be loaded if at least one screen and/or input device will support the extension. Otherwise, the extension will ignore all screens/input-devices, and thus be useless. **Extreme** extensions should only be loaded if all screens and/or input devices provide DDX support for the extension. Otherwise, the server won't work.

What takes shape is that each screen and input driver that is dynamically loaded must *vote* on each extension that may be dynamically loaded. HP defined the following three voting options that a driver may choose from:

Yes

> Please load. This vote should be cast for any directly supported extension, or when the dependency is either **None** or **Beneficial**.

Abstain

> Only load if some other driver supports this extension. This vote should be cast when support is not provided and the dependency is **Tight**.

Veto

> Don't load this extension! This vote should be cast when the dependency is **Extreme** and support is not provided.

Co-Initialization Model

It can be argued that the X Consortium's sample server was biased towards extensions that have a dependency class of **None**. This is evidenced by the fact that the server's initialization sequence is missing an opportunity for extensions and screen/input drivers to *co-initialize* each other (i.e. set up extension-specific, DIX/DDX interfaces).

HP developed a model for *co-initialization*. First the core X portion of the drivers are initialized, and the drivers *register* a call-back routine with each *powerful* extension that is supported. Second, the extension initialization code is called, and powerful extensions call all of the call-back routines in order to initialize the extension-specific DIX/DDX interface.

Standard Interfaces

HP desires a more *open* X server in the context of powerful extensions, to minimize third-party porting efforts without sacrificing functionality. To accomplish this, there must be more commonality between server vendors. For example each vendor's multi-buffer extension implementation has a different DIX/DDX interface. HP is committed to helping correct this. For example, HP has contributed a sample implementation for the new Double Buffer Extension. The development of well-documented, standard porting interfaces is our highest priority for the loadable group.

Module Selection--The Broker Paradigm

HP has tied all module selection and several other dynamic loading issues together with what HP refers to as the *Broker Paradigm*. Brokers are small, dynamically loaded modules which live in pre-defined directories (e.g. `screens,` `extensions`), and contain all of the essential configuration information for the extension or driver(s) which they represent. A single DDX screen broker may represent a single driver or a collection of drivers, where a different broker is required for each extension. The X server acts as the brokerage house, facilitating all of the broker interactions, evaluating responses, and eventually loading the appropriate modules.

Extension Brokers

Extension brokers have two defined procedural interfaces, or entry points, to accomplish their role. The first entry point, `*GetExtensionInfo()` (where "*" is the prefix of the broker's filename), returns the following information: (See section with sample extension broker below)

- Extension Name
- Version
- Vendor (i.e. extension provider)
- DDX Screen Dependency Class (as described above)
- DDX Input Dependency Class (as described above)

The second entry point, `*GetExtensionModuleList()`, returns a list of modules that implements the device-independent portion of the extension, the name of the extension's initialization routine, and the name of the registration routine used for DDX/extension co-initialization, as described in a previous section.

DDX Screen Brokers

Screen brokers also have just two defined entry points. The first entry point, `*GetScreenBid()`, provides a numerical *bid* on each screen's graphics device based on the represented screen driver's ability to support each device. A low positive bid indicates limited support, such as the general, non-tuned, capability of the CFB driver. A high positive bid indicates high performance support, such as generally provided by the graphics device vendor. If a positive bid is returned (indicating support) for a particular graphics device it must also cast a vote, (i.e. **Yes**, **Abstain**, or **Veto**) on each possible dynamically loaded extension.

The second entry point, `*GetScreenModuleList()`, returns a list of modules that implements the driver, and the name of the screen driver's `xxxScreenInit()` routine. The returned module list may be influenced by which extensions were selected.

New Control Points Introduced by the Broker Paradigm

The second entry point for both types of brokers, `*GetExtensionModuleList()` and `*GetScreenModuleList()`, presents new control points during X server initialization, ones that occur before the normal screen and extension initialization control points.

Why the Broker Paradigm?

The *broker paradigm* provides robust, dynamic module selection based upon installed hardware and software. In contrast with configuration files, using dynamically loaded brokers provides more flexibility and extensibility. If more than one driver exists for the same device, brokers can be written to intelligently decide when one driver should be selected instead of another. If an additional server initialization control point is needed, it's there. Besides, configuration files can get corrupted, especially if end users are involved.

Server Initialization With The Broker Paradigm

The following pseudo-code shows the relevant portions of HP's server initialization:

- Determine user-desired options (i.e. parse `X*screens` file).
- For each graphics device, get unique ID.
- Load each screen and extension broker.
- Call `*GetExtensionInfo()` for each extension broker.
- Call each screen broker's `*GetBid()`:
  - Can read the token lists.
  - Returns a bid for each device and a vote for each extension.
- Determine *winning* graphics device bids (those drivers that will be loaded).
- Determine *winning* extensions (those extensions that will be loaded).
- Call `*GetModuleList()` for winning screens & extensions:
  - Get module lists.
  - Get initialization routine names.
  - Get DDX/extension co-initialization registration routine names.
  - Give chance to read/modify the token list.
  - Give chance for other pre-ScreenInit initialization.
- Unload broker modules.

- Dynamically load all DDX and extension modules.

- Call `AddScreen/xxxScreenInit` for each Screen. Each `xxxScreenInit` routine calls the co-initialization registration routine for each powerful extension supported, and registers its call-back.

- Call `xxxExtensionInit` for each extension. Each powerful extension's xxxExtensionInit routine calls the appropriate DDX call-back procedures in order to co-initialize the extension's DIX/DDX interface.

Sample Extension Broker

```
void mbxGetExtensionInfo(DlExtensionInfoPtr pExtensionInfoRec)
{
    pExtensionInfoRec-name = "Multi-Buffering";
    pExtensionInfoRec-vendor = "Hewlett-Packard";
    pExtensionInfoRec-version.majorNumber = 1;
    pExtensionInfoRec-version.minorNumber = 0;
    pExtensionInfoRec-version.patchNumber = 0;
    pExtensionInfoRec-inputDepend = DL_EXTN_DDX_DEPEND_NONE;
    pExtensionInfoRec-screenDepend = DL_EXTN_DDX_DEPEND_TIGHT;
}

void mbxGetExtensionModuleList(
        DlModuleListItemPtr *ppModuleList,
        char **nameExtnInit,
        char **nameExtnRegister)
{
    DlModuleListItemPtr pList;

    /* The module list must be created from a continuous block of memory,
     * allocated by this routine and later freed by the X server. */
    if (!(*ppModuleList =
            (DlModuleListItemPtr) Xalloc(sizeof(DlModuleListItemRec))))
        ErrorF("MBX broker, unable to alloc required memory.");
    else {
        pList = *ppModuleList;
        pList-moduleName = "mbx.1";
        pList-modulePath = "hp";
        pList-bindState = DL_BIND_IMMEDIATE | DL_BIND_VERBOSE;
        pList-next = NULL;
        *nameExtnInit = "MultibufferExtensionInit";
        *nameExtnRegister = "MbxRegisterFunction";
    }
}
```

Other Notable Implementations

Digital's OpenVMS

On OpenVMS, all DDXs and some extensions are dynamically loadable at server startup time. The VMS X server references a set of logical names that contain all of the server configuration information. Included in this set of logical names are the set of graphics devices which should be used (DECW$SERVER_SCREENS), and the set of extensions that should be loaded (DECW$SERVER_EXTENSIONS).

These logical names are defined within a set of DCL command procedures used to start the X server as well as other DECwindows components. A command procedure is provided for each class of graphics device, each of which is executed as part of the startup process. These command procedures will locate all of the devices that they recognize and add them to the DECW$SERVER_SCREENS list. A user modifiable command procedure is available in which the system manager can change the order or select a subset of the entries in DECW$SERVER_SCREENS.

During the standard DDX initialization in InitOutput(), DECW$SERVER_SCREENS is read. For each device name found, a loadable DDX server image is dynamically activated (assuming it has not already been activated). Its name is derived from the device name. A single entry point, a device-specific copy of the InitOutput() routine, is defined in each DDX image. After the DIX image activates the specific DDX image, it calls the specific InitOutput() routine. Each of these routines will call AddScreen() to perform the screen specific initialization.

Extensions are handled in a similar manner. The DECW$SERVER_EXTENSIONS logical is read early in the server initialization process. For each extension in the list, an extension image is activated. The image name is derived from the extension name. Later, in the InitExtensions(), the initialization routines for each extension is executed. Note that not all extensions are dynamically loadable. Those extensions that are very tightly coupled with the main server or those that are very small on VMS are built into the DIX image and are always loaded.

The user modifiable command procedure described earlier can also be used to specify the list of extensions to dynamically load.

Sun's Solaris

Sun's loadable server implementation dynamically loads graphical device support (DDXs) and some extension support. The remainder of the server is contained within discrete shareables that are linked in at build time. This permits Sun to replace discrete shareables individually, but doesn't permit the dynamic loading of those modules that are "hard linked".

The loadable services are implemented in a shareable called libowconfig, which is also a shareable resolved at link time, and is therefore essentially part of the main server.

The loadable server configuration mechanism is based on a configuration file (Xconfig). The configuration file is object-class oriented, listing various objects by type and by name. The object classes supported are XDISPLAY, XSCREENCONFIG, XSCREEN, XINPUT, and XEXTENSION. Examples of object definitions using some of these classes follow.

```
class="XSCREENCONFIG" name="my8514"
device="8514"
pmifile="/usr/openwin/etc/vesa/8514/ati.pmi"
res="1024x768";

# 8514 display adapter
```

```
class="XSCREEN" name="8514"
ddxHandler="ddxSUNW8514.so.1" ddxInitFunc="i8514Init";

# Mouseman module

class="XINPUT" name="MOUSEMAN-S"
ddxHandler="ddxSUNWx86mouse.so.1"
ddxInitFunc="ddxSUNWmouseProc"
buttons="3"
strmod="vuidm4p"
dev="/dev/tty00";
```

The Solaris implementation provides an API mechanism for retrieving the contents of the configuration file. These include functions to get all names defined for a specific class, get attributes of a specific named object of a specific class, and to get complete instances of a named object. While this is useful for loaded components to get information from the configuration file, it does not solve the problem of getting dynamic configuration information from the server, nor does it simplify the external manipulation of the config file, such as adding new components. Currently, the addition or deletion of new components is accomplished with a sed script.

At server startup time, the server examines the default graphic adapter (as specified by command line, default is /dev/fb), and determines the graphic adapter identification string. The server then examines the configuration database (Xconfig) to find the first match of this name, and retrieves the name of the shareable module and the name of the initialization function. This shareable is then opened using dlopen with lazy symbol evaluation, the initialization function symbol is explicitly resolved using dlsym, and this is then passed to AddScreen, at which point, screen startup continues unmodified.

Currently, extension loading is limited to PEX, but the framework is present to load other extensions as well. All other extensions supplied by Sun are currently hard-linked at build time, and are therefore always present.

X Inside

X Inside, Inc. provides loadable X Servers for the Intel-based PC community, on multiple operating systems.

The X Inside loadable server implementation dynamically loads DDX support, Extensions and Font Renderers.

X Inside uses a non-standard DDX layering mechanism, as it does not make use of the MFB/CFB layers. Instead, X Inside has developed a proprietary porting layer that they feel gives significantly better performance for less memory. In addition, performance is improved in that they then can write a large portion of their drawing code in assembly language for the Intel x86 CPUs. The ability to continue using such vendor-specific solutions to the DDX porting layer will be maintained by the loadable server architecture.

X Inside provides an OS-independent API for loading operations. Included are operations that initialize the loading interface, open modules, close modules, find symbols and search for symbols located near a given address (for debugging purposes). The close mechanism can unload the module if the refcount goes to zero.

X Inside implements an interesting top-down symbol resolution mechanism. Each DDX for a screen has its own namespace. This allows multihead servers to be able to have duplicate names. This may be desirable if for example, two graphic adapters have the same RAMDAC, say a Bt485, and have separate implementations for it with some common names, yet need to work together on the same system. A monolithic namespace would disallow this. Support for namespaces such as this is important to support true "blind" loadability.

SCO Unix

SCO's implementation of a loadable server loads both DDXs and extensions, based on available hardware and user specified options. When the server starts, it reads a configuration file that contains a representation of the system configuration. For each specified hardware device, the server looks for `grafinfo` file, which contains information specific to the device type, including depth, resolution support, and graphics init routines. Dynamic loading is done using a custom loader.

The dynamic extension mechanism is also based on a file, and is unique in that it permits the specification of a hardware dependency. Currently, only server startup time loading is supported. The server, like most, does not handle a multi-head configuration with adapters that require different versions of the same extension. This needs to be addressed by the loadable server architecture, and may be solvable using discrete address spaces, as is accomplished by X Inside.

```
#Ext       File Name        Load   Entry    Adaptor
#Name                       Time   Point    Driver
#-------------------------------------------------------
PEX        PEX/PEX.o        INIT   PEXInit  *
PEX        dyddx/s3c/PEX.o  INIT   PEXInit  s3c
```

Siemens Nixdorf's SINIX

Siemens Nixdorf produces an operating system descended from AT&T SVR4 w3.4, called SINIX. SINIX runs on standard Intel-based PCs.

Currently, SINIX loads only DDX components, including discrete CFB and MFB components. SNI finds discrete CFB and MFB components necessary because not all of their DDXs require CFB, and they occasionally need to switch BITMAP_BIT_ORDER between LSB and MSB for the MFB component. SNI plans to add support for loadable extensions in the very near future.

Like SCO and others, the SINIX X Server's dynamic loading mechanism has been written from scratch as opposed to being based on an OS mechanism. SNI finds better performance with their specialized loading mechanism. The loadable server architecture will allow SNI to maintain its proprietary mechanism, as the loadable services are all hidden underneath the OS-independent loading API.

The configuration mechanism that SNI provides permits the specification of many parameters, including screen size, horizontal and vertical refresh rates, and sync timing. This tuning externalizes a lot of parameters that are normally hardcoded in the DDX and/or driver. Support for such detailed tuning is important to many vendors, and should be a design feature of the loadable server architecture.

IBM's AIX

The AIX loadable server solution provides for the dynamic loading of the DIX layer, DDX support, and extensions.

The AIX operating system supplies a system configuration database, and the loadable server relies heavily on this for its configuration mechanism. The Object Data Manager (ODM) is the system database containing configuration information for all system objects, including graphic adapters. The loadable server architecture needs to allow for non-standard configuration mechanisms such as ODM.

DDXs are loaded dynamically at server startup time, and only those DDXs that support available graphic devices are actually loaded. A command line option is provided to permit a system administrator to optionally shut off support to individual graphic adapters, to specify the logical ordering of the graphic adapters, or to specify the logical placement of the graphic adapters.

Extensions on AIX are separated into two groups: those that are always loaded and those that are to be loaded at server startup time by user demand. There are two configuration files that specify these distinct sets: `static_ext` and `dynamic_ext`. The static extension configuration file contains those extensions that are always loaded at server startup time. The dynamic extension configuration file is used to specify those extensions that are valid options for the `-x` server command line options, which is how a user includes additional extensions. An example line from an extension configuration file looks like this:

```
dps /usr/lpp/DPS/bin/loadDPS
```

Part 3: The Loadable Server Architecture

The loadable server architecture outlined in this section is based on requirements submitted by participants in the loadable working group of the X Consortium. The document as you see it is a working, changing document, and is meant to serve as a plan of record for the loadable working group participants, not a final specification.

User/Administrator Involvement

Software Installation

The installation of new loadable components to a system using the loadable server architecture should be 'Plug & Play'. When a user purchases a new graphic option for their system, the installation of the card and its associated software should be trivial if the system is designed well enough. Integration with existing hardware and software should be automatic.

A mechanism needs to be designed that meets the following criteria:

- Installation order independence between components An example of this would be a user who bought a high-end graphic adapter from one vendor, and an extension from another that required the hardware support of the high-end graphic adapter. The order in which these are installed should not matter.

- Vendor file location transparency Different vendors require different installation tree locations. The standard will not specify where server files should go. Installation mechanisms should be supplied by system vendors to assist third parties.

Setting optional features

There are a number of common optional features that a user or system administrator can set that modifies how the X server starts and runs. The Loadable Server Architecture will address the following well-known optional features:

- Screen order

- Screen enabling/disabling

- Location and types of input devices

- Enabling and disabling of internal server features

- Specification of default command line options

- Overriding of default loadable paths

- Specific replacement of default libraries

In addition to these "well-known" features, the Loadable Server Architecture must address needs that can not be forseen today. Because of this, the architecture must permit "unformatted" parameters to be specified by the user or system administrator, for any component in the system, including the server itself. Hewlett-Packard's implementation comes close to addressing this issue by permitting a "component private" parameter section in its configuration file. By allowing this free-form section, and by passing it unmodified to the component, the design of the loadable architecture can be virtually extended on a per-component basis without modification.

Inter-Module Interfaces

One challenge that X Server vendors have stuggled with as long as they have used loadable X servers is that the common interfaces and data structures used by the server are in a fairly constant state of flux. When new features are added, often they add or modify critical data structures such as the screen structure. To bring this flux under control, those data structures and routines that have traditionally caused problems need to be documented as part of the X server's programming interface. Knowing that a proposed change will impact loadable server vendors, efforts can be undertaken to lessen the impact. Possibilities include:

1. Avoidance of source code and binary incompatibility by redesign. It may be the case the in light of a new incompatibility, design steps can be taken to avoid the change.

2. Early notification of vendors of future incompatibility, along with early submission of incompatible data structure changes. If it becomes obvious that a change is necessary, vendors can be notified early of the intended change, so that the functionality and the binary incompatibility may be planned into future schedules

3. `#ifdef` coverage of binary incompatibilities so that vendors can break binary compatibility in synchronization with product schedules

While a large portion of this is being done today, a more formal approach is desired by a number of vendors. The inclusion of formal function prototypes in R6 is a solid step in the right direction, but it still does not provide sufficient interface stability and documentation to support long-term interfaces between server modules. This effort is an attempt at understanding what is involved, what the functional impact may be, and how to strike the best balance between functionality and supportability.

Core X Interface and Structure Definitions

The core X server interfaces (DIX, OS, MI, CFB and MFB) contain the most frequently used interfaces in the X server, and combined with the data structure definitions in the server and common include files, account for the complete programming interface of the X server. All components that link to the X server rely on the stability of these. The interfaces and data structures contained herein need to be documented, and those that are not "public" need to be hidden such that they are not available externally.

Common Extensions Interface and Structure Definitions

Like the core X server, each extension supports at least a small set of interfaces and structure definitions. These must be maintained and documented in a formal way so as to avoid binary compatibility problems. These should all start with a common template so as to ensure consistency.

Interface Modification Process

Combined with any effort to manage the future changing of a set of interfaces, there must be an associated effort to manage the eventual changes. In the loadable server effort, we recognize the need for changing interfaces, but feel the need to perform these changes in a more controlled way than has been done in the past. The loadable server architecture will specify a process for managing change.

Module Versioning

As loadable components become more standard in how they are built, how they are used, and what formal interface they export, a need arises for a common module versioning mechanism. If, for example, a functional change is made in a module without breaking binary compatibility, it is important for other modules to be able to determine, in a standard way, what revision of a specific interface that component implements.

The module versioning mechanism needs to be implemented as part of the OS-independent loading interface so as to maintain implementation independence.

Inter-Component Dependency Handling

A mechanism needs to be designed that permits components to determine if their presence on the system is required. For example, if an extension loads, but cannot find hardware that will support it, it may choose to unload itself. The Hewlett-Packard broker model implements a mechanism similar to this.

Multi-Point Component Initialization

Many vendors have found that in order to split parts of the server off into their own shareables completely, a multi-point initialization mechanism becomes necessary. Since components often are of the nature that they need early access to server data structures (often prior to extension or screen initialization), it is difficult to remove all tendrils of such extensions, and DIX implementations are riddled with special cases for these extensions.

Examples of tasks that need to be accomplished earlier or later than normal are probing hardware, probing for the existance of a required device or extension, or static data structure allocation. The multi-point initialization mechanism can be used for advanced extensions such as OpenGL, PEX and Adobe Display Postscript. The initialization steps need not be all specified, can take place in multiple, differing shareables, and can result in the subsequent unloading of a shareable. In this way, large extensions do not need to be completely loaded to perform minor initialization -- they can have smaller 'shepherd' shareables that are loaded, perform some initialization, and are then unloaded after the work is done.

Data Structure Allocation and Access Methods

One method of hiding data structure modifications from older components is by making it possible for them to be opaque. For example, if a component requires a `Window` structure, the component should use `AllocateWindow` rather than `xalloc(sizeof(Window))`. If the component then does not make assumptions about the size of a window, additions to the end of the structure will not affect the component.

To some extent, this is being done today, but an effort needs to be undertaken to identify all of the 'public' structures, and to make allocators for them. In addition, access routines should be written to provide for opaque access to the contents of the structures, so that future code need not have direct access to them, and better information hiding can take place.

Global Symbol Usage and Resolution Rules
Global Symbol Collision

As components transition from integrated to loadable, symbol resolution moves from the developer's build procedure the user's desktop. This can result in catastrophic results, as symbols are resolved differently in this environment. Guidelines need to be established for global symbol naming, and care taken to ensure that shareables are built with private symbol spaces where possible. Since this relies heavily on operating system features, these may only be stated as guidelines rather than the strict rules of a standard.

An example guildline would be as follows. On some Unix implementations, it is possible to build a shareable such that none of its global symbol data participates in global symbol resolution. A correctly designed shareable would be built in this way, and external access to its internal global symbols would be accomplished by well-known symbol names passed to the `dlsym(3)` for explicit resolution. With this mechanism in wide use, there would be far less chance of symbol clash between loadable components.

Location Of Global Symbols

There are cases within X where the DIX layer has link dependencies on extensions because of global symbol data contained within the extension. A good example of this is the XInput extension. XInput defines global data that contains input event types, and this global data is required by the core to perform correct input processing. Since it would be considered unacceptable for DIX to have a dependency on an extension,[†] it would become necessary for DIX to have global definitions on behalf of the extension.

This problem can be solved by way of the mechanism described above, or by way of named global data, for which a sample implementation exists in vendor code.

Module Selection

As we have seen in the technology inventory section, many vendors have chosen at least as many ways to choose the modules to be loaded. There are a great many requirements placed on module selection. Some of these are:

- Module installation must have no effect on interoperability. For example, if a customer buys a graphic board from one vendor, and an extension from another, there should be no difference in how they work together based on the order in which they were installed.

- Complex extensions should be able to determine whether or not there is sufficient hardware support available to support their advanced features without *a-prior* knowledge of all hardware.

- Components must be able to determine the presence of other components

The selection of which modules to load is likely the problem with the most widely ranging set of solutions. This problem must be solved for all modules, but with special emphasis put on DDX and extension selection, since they frequently have very tight dependencies upon one another (i.e., one cannot exist without the other). While this portion of the work is technically involved, there is plenty of industry experience to draw on.

Deferred Extensions

The loadable server architecture will support deferred, dynamic extension loading. There are two general classes of extensions when viewed from a deferred loading standpoint.

In the simple case, extensions may be loaded on demand during the server's lifetime at XQueryExtension time. These extensions do not require that any prior work be done within the server when loaded.

"Complex" extensions, on the other hand, need to have work done prior to successful deferred loading. This level of support requires a initialization mechanism similar to the multi-point initialization mechanism, so that the extension may have a chance to do this advance work without being fully loaded.

[†]*Such a dependency would result in a circular dependency, making object separation difficult at best, and would require XInput to be always present*

OS-Independent Loading Interface

Since the acceptance of a standard relies heavily on the solidness and portability of its sample implementation, the Loadable Server Architecture will provide an interface specification that will permit the hiding of OS-specific loading mechanisms. These can be either implemented or stubbed by an implementor, but must be present as entry points to conform to the Loadable Architecture. The loadable services interfaces will provide at a minimum the following:

- Load module(s)
- Unload module(s)
- Find symbol
- Find symbol in module
- Find device(s)

Additional design goals of the Loading Interface are:

- Sufficiently generic design so as to encourage reuse by other parties such as client libraries, Font Server and Audio Server
- Loading Interface library to be packaged apart from the core server to facilitate code reuse.

Building/Coding Conventions

While it is a not the goal of the loadable server architecture to standardize how modules are built or written, the sample implementation that will result from the effort will suggest conventions for how to do this. So as to make the sample implementation as useful as possible, though needs to be given to the suggestion being made.

Component Packaging

The way that components are packaged carries a lot of burden in how flexible a loadable server implementation. For example, the implicit assumption that a component will exist in only one shareable will impose a policy on how complex extensions are initialized. A large, complex extension might be implemented in two shareables, one for early data structure initialization, and the other for the main function of the extension.

Imake/Header File Rules

The complete and seamless integration of the loadable server architecture will rely on correct implementation of how the loadable server sample implementation is integrated into the base SI. It is a goal to integrate cleanly and with *optional* build characteristics.

There should be provisions made to allow implementors to select loadable components one at a time, as development schedules allow. The success of the acceptance of this proposed standard relies on the ability of vendors to transition their product sets to it. The work done in the area of Imake and header files will be instrumental in the ease of porting,

Software Packaging and Installation

One of the goals that the industry has set forth for the loadable working group is to ease the support of graphic related components on the X Window System. A non-trivial part of this is the installation of a component on multiple vendors' systems.

Work must take place to agree on a methodology that will make software installation and configuration more similar on multiple vendors' platforms, while at the same time preserving the configuration autonomy that vendors require. Once completed, it should be possible for a vendor to have one installation script that will work with relatively few changes from one vendor to another. Of course, operating system differences will preclude a standardization of this, but a complete, usable example should be part of the sample implementation.

Acknowledgments

The authors would like to gratefully acknowledge the following for providing the technical details and understanding of their implementations: Doug Stefanelli (Digital) Burns Fisher (Digital), Kevin Marshall (Sun), Mike Patnode (SCO), Christian Kaiser (SNI), Thomas Roell (X Inside), Jeanne Smith (IBM). In addition, we gratefully acknowledge the direct contributions of Madeline Asmus (Digital) and Ron MacDonald (Hewlett-Packard), without whom this would have been a lot more difficult!

Author Information

Rob Lembree (*lembree@zk3.dec.com*) is a Member of the Technical Staff in the Workstation Software Group at Digital Equipment Corporation in Nashua, New Hampshire. He's the project leader for the DEC OSF/1 X Server, and is co-architect of the loadable working group. When he's not writing X Server code, he's the Assistant Brewer at Martha's Exchange Brewing Company in Nashua.

Ian Elliott (*ian@elliott.fc.hp.com*) is a Technical Contributor with Hewlett-Packard Company in Fort Collins, Colorado. He is the technical lead for HP's DDX Group, and is co-architect of the loadable working group. When he's not writing X Server code and working within the X Consortium, he spends time with his family and volunteers in his church.

What's New in PEX and PEXlib 5.2

New Features Make PEXlib Programming Easier

Karl Schultz[†]

Abstract

PEX is the X Consortium standard 3D graphics extension to the X Window System protocol. PEXlib is the X Consortium standard API (Application Programming Interface) intended for use with PEX.

The PEX specification committee of the X Consortium developed three versions of the PEX specification over several years, releasing the PEX 5.2 specification for public review in August of 1994. The PEXlib specification committee developed the PEXlib 5.1 specification as a companion to PEX 5.1 in November of 1992 and has recently completed the PEXlib 5.2 specification which it intends to release for public review in January of 1995.

This paper briefly reviews the new functionality of PEX 5.2 and concentrates on the new features of PEXlib 5.2 which are not directly related to PEX 5.2 additions. These features make PEXlib 5.2 easier to use than PEXlib 5.1 by providing an improved parameter passing mechanism reducing parameter list lengths, additional data models reducing the need to reformat and copy application data, and a smaller number of functions for generating primitives.

Introduction

The PEX 5.2 and PEXlib 5.2 specifications represent the results of an effort to improve PEX and PEXlib by adding popular and useful features that are strongly demanded by 3D graphic

[†]*Karl Schultz (kws@fc.hp.com) received a B.S. in Computer Science from the University of Illinois at Urbana/ Champaign and a M.S. in Computer Engineering from Syracuse University. He is currently a member of the Technical Staff at the Hewlett Packard Company working in the Graphics Software Laboratory. Karl is the X Consortium Chief Architect and Document Editor for the PEXlib 5.2 specification*

application programmers. These new features not only increase the capabilities of PEX-based applications, but also make them easier to develop.

Although many people describe PEXlib as a "thin-layer" or "low-level" API for PEX, PEXlib 5.2 provides somewhat more service at the API level than PEXlib 5.1 to ease the development of applications and improve performance. This paper covers these new PEXlib features in detail after a brief overview of the new function in PEX 5.2.

Specification Status

The PEX 5.2 specification entered consortium review in May of 1994, after nearly a year and a half of work to determine its content. PEXlib 5.2 entered consortium review a little over four months later, in October of 1994.

PEX 5.2 entered public review on August 15, 1994. The PEXlib committee intends to release PEXlib 5.2 for public review in January of 1995.

Because of the numerous dependencies between the two specifications, the PEX committee plans to delay the final specification for PEX 5.2 in order to facilitate any necessary changes as a result of PEXlib 5.2 specification changes and updates. Therefore, both specifications should become final in April of 1995.

PEX 5.2

The PEX 5.2 Protocol Specification documents the entire PEX 5.2 protocol, including the PEX 5.1 elements, as well as the new 5.2 elements. PEX 5.2 is compatible with PEX 5.0 and PEX 5.1, allowing PEX 5.0 or PEX 5.1 clients to work with PEX 5.2 servers. The PEX 5.2 specification is contained within a single document, in contrast to the PEX 5.1 specification which used separate documents to specify the protocol semantics and the encoding.

Why 5.2 instead of 6.0?

Jeff Stevenson presented the rationale behind developing a PEX 5.2 instead of a PEX 6.0 at the 1994 X Technical Conference. In summary:

We wanted to design PEX 6.0 for:

- fixing things that required an incompatible change in order to fix
  - remove PHIGS workstation
  - redesign structure resources
  - redesign PHIGS lookup table support
  - improve extensibility
  - remove subsets
- adding lots of functionality
- addressing conformance requirements

The PEX committee analyzed this rationale and decided to design PEX 5.2 instead:

- 6.0 incompatibility created too great a burden on applications and end users

- the installed base has continued to grow

- the exercise of defining 6.0 provided the opportunity to see alternatives and the real trade-offs

- it was the only pragmatic solution

Therefore the PEX 5.2 design effort is restricted to adding functionality and addressing conformance requirements and cannot change anything that would break backwards compatibility.

New Function in PEX 5.2

- Texture Mapping
- New Primitives
  - Drafting
  - Triangles
  - Sphere/Cone
- New Attributes
  - Drawing Functions (logical frame buffer operations)
  - Plane Masking
- Alpha and Z Buffer Access Functions
- Highlight Controls
- Conditional Traversal
- Alpha Blending
- Transparency
- Accumulation Buffer
- Improved Lookup Table Editing

Conformance Requirements

Experience with PEX 5.1 exposed some confusion over PEX subsets and the requirements for implementing optional features. The PEX 5.2 specification addresses these problems by raising the level of required functionality; requiring that implementors implement more function. A PEX 5.2 implementation must include the Immediate Rendering and Structure Rendering subsets, thus making the PHIGS Workstation subset the only optional subset. In addition, an implementation must support a clearly defined set of enumerated type values and must equal or exceed required values of implementation-dependent constants and table limits. These stricter conformance requirements ensure a higher "baseline" level of PEX implementation that application developers can rely on.

PEXlib 5.2

During the specification of PEX 5.2, when it was going to be PEX 6.0, the PEXlib committee reviewed several interface designs with the intent of creating a new PEXlib 6.0 on a "clean slate". However, the decision to design PEX 5.2 implied that PEXlib 5.2 must be backwards compatible with PEXlib 5.1 which requires the retention of all PEXlib 5.1 functions and data structures. In spite of this, the committee designed a new output command[†] interface and new data models that essentially replace the 5.1 functions, although the 5.1 functions still exist. A pure PEXlib 5.2 application can, and should, simply ignore the deprecated PEXlib 5.1 functions and focus on using the improved 5.2 versions. If the application designer puts the deprecated 5.1 functions aside, the size of the PEXlib 5.2 specification is not as great as first imagined.

Support for New PEX 5.2 Function

Providing new programming interfaces for the new PEX 5.2 functions is a requirement for PEXlib 5.2. The PEXlib programming interface is designed to provide complete access to the PEX protocol. Support for these new functions is fairly straightforward. Existing programming interfaces are extended for the new lookup tables, output commands, renderer attributes, pipeline context attributes, renderer functions, and any other new requests or features.

Output Command Context

The Output Command Context (OCC) is a mechanism designed to reduce the number of parameters in functions that generate output commands. This is accomplished by placing the most commonly-used and least-frequently changing parameters in the abstract OCC data structure. For example, most applications open a single connection to an X server running with the PEX extension. It is redundant to specify the *display* parameter in each and every function call to generate an output command. The same redundancy occurs with other parameters such as the *request_type*, *resource_id*, and *color_type* parameters. The OCC itself appears first in the parameter list, replacing several other parameters.

```
PEXOCCTriangleStrip(myocc, NULL, count, vertices);
PEXTriangleStrip(display, resource_id, req_type, PEXGANone, PEXGAColor,
                 PEXColorTypeRGB, NULL, count, vertices);
```

The example illustrates that the *display*, *resource_id*, *req_type*, *facet_attributes*, *vertex_attributes*, and *color_type* parameters are replaced by the OCC in the OCC form of the function. The assumption is that these six values are not likely to change frequently during the execution of the application. In both cases, the function call generates a Triangle Strip with no facet data and vertex data with vertex colors. Note that the OCC form of the function contains only four parameters, instead of the nine in the non-OCC form. Not only is this easier to program, but can result in significant savings in function call overhead, which is critical for DGHA (Direct Graphics Hardware Architecture) implementations[‡].

Before using one of the OCC-style functions, the programmer must create an OCC and initialize it with values appropriate to the application. PEXlib 5.2 provides a set of functions for manipulating

---

[†]*An output command is a PEX protocol element that contains a graphic primitive, attribute, or control.*

an OCC that are analogous to the functions provided in Xlib for manipulating Graphics Contexts (GC's).

Facet and Vertex Data Models

One of the more difficult aspects of programming with PEXlib 5.1 is that applications must format their graphic data to fit the prescribed PEXlib 5.1 data structures. Very few, if any, applications already have their graphic data in a format readily usable by PEXlib, forcing the applications to copy this data into temporary storage in a particular format so that PEXlib can process it.

PEXlib 5.2 addresses this issue by supplying new "data models" that are flexible enough to adapt to many applications' data structures, reducing or eliminating the need to copy and reformat the data.

Stride Data Model

The stride data model is a more general form of the existing PEXlib 5.1 "packed" data model. The data is assumed to be stored in members of a structure, where one structure contains both application and geometric data for a single facet or vertex. The structures for a number of facets or vertices are assumed to be stored in contiguous storage, as if in a "structured array"[†]. The application stores facets and vertices in separate structured arrays.

The application supplies to PEXlib the offsets into the structure for each piece of PEXlib-related data, such as coordinate data, color data, and normal data. The application also supplies the size of the entire structure or "stride", so PEXlib can locate the data for the next facet or vertex in the array. The application is able to store the PEXlib data and the application-specific data in any order it wishes in the structure. Once the application supplies the offset and stride via the OCC, PEXlib can extract the data directly from the application's data structure, eliminating the need to make a special copy of the data just for PEXlib. An illustration of the stride data model is in Figure 1.

Using the diagram in Figure 1, the application sets the values `vertex_stride`, `vertex_coord_offset`, `vertex_normal_offset`, `vertex_color_offset`, and `vertex_fp_data_offset` in the OCC. The application passes the `vertex_data_pointer` to PEXlib via a function argument. It is likely that the values the application sets in the OCC remain constant, so the application only needs to supply a new vertex data pointer for each new primitive to render.

[‡]*Several vendors have implementations of PEXlib that directly render to a window on a local X server without sending PEX protocol to the X server. These implementations benefit from not having to encode and decode protocol and have highly optimized paths from the application to the graphics accelerator hardware. Thus, the number of parameters becomes more important as they contribute to the cost of function call overhead.*

[†]*An example of a structured array in the C language is:* `struct {float x,y;} points[20];`

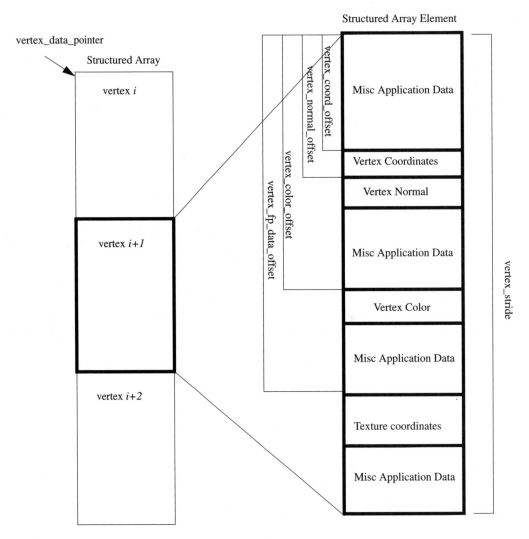

Figure 1: Diagram of the Stride Data Model

Unpacked Data Model

Some applications use a data model where they store the graphic data in lists of similar types. There is a list of coordinates, a separate list for colors, a separate list for normals and a separate list for floating-point (texture) data, as in Figure 2.

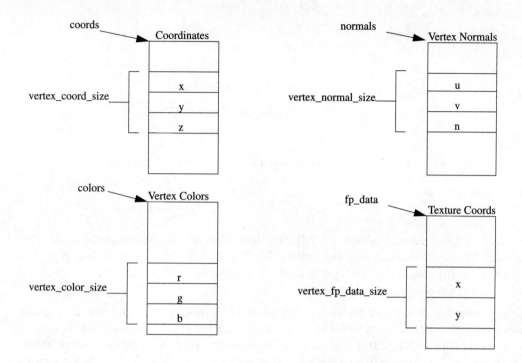

Figure 2: Diagram of the Unpacked Data Model

These lists are stored in memory independently of each other. The application indicates to PEXlib via the OCC the values for `vertex_coord_size`, `vertex_normal_size`, `vertex_color_size`, and `vertex_fp_data_size`. The application passes the pointers `coords`, `normals`, `colors`, and `fp_data` to PEXlib by placing them in a structure and passing the address of the structure in the function argument.

Primitive Function "Collapsing"

PEXlib 5.1 used a "one-to-one" philosophy when designing the functions that generate output commands. This approach resulted in a simple mapping from function to output command, but presented the programmer with a number of functions for generating primitives that were very similar. In order to reduce the total number of primitive-generating functions, PEXlib 5.2 defines fewer of these functions, many of which are capable of generating more than one type of output command.

For example, PEXlib 5.1 defines three functions for generating a Fill Area primitive:

```
PEXFillArea(Display *display, XID resource_id, PEXOCRequestType req_type,
            int shape_hint, int ignore_edges, unsigned int count,
            PEXCoord *points);

PEXFillArea2D(Display *display, XID resource_id, PEXOCRequestType req_type,
              int shape_hint, int ignore_edges, unsigned int count,
```

```
                    PEXCoord2D *points);

PEXFillAreaWithData(Display *display, XID resource_id,
                    PEXOCRequestType req_type,
                    int shape_hint, int ignore_edges,
                    unsigned int facet_attributes,
                    unsigned int vertex_attributes,
                    int color_type,
                    PEXFacetData *facet_data,
                    unsigned int count,
                    PEXArrayOfVertex vertices);
```

In contrast, the single PEXlib 5.2 function for generating all Fill Area primitives is:

```
PEXOCCFillArea(PEXOCC context, PEXPointer facet_data,
               unsigned int count,
               PEXPointer vertices);
```

PEXlib 5.2 defines fewer functions for Fill Area Sets, Markers, and Polylines using the same approach. The key to this technique lies in the OCC. The OCC contains much of the information that was explicitly specified in the argument lists. The movement of these arguments to the OCC allows for more generalized function calls.

The new functions, along with the stride and unpacked data models, allow applications to make changes to the way they invoke PEXlib more easily than before. For example, an application simply turns on the **PEXGA2D** flag in the vertex attributes to switch to a 2D form of the primitive, if using the stride or unpacked data models. Or, if an application has vertex color data but does not need to send vertex colors with the vertex data, it is a simple matter to turn off the **PEXGAColor** flag in the vertex attributes. There is no need to make a copy of the data without the vertex colors, as would have been the case with the packed data model of PEXlib 5.1.

Utilities for Visual Selection and Colormap Creation

Due to the PEX color approximation mechanism, applications that use PEX have fairly rigorous color requirements. PEX applications prefer to use deep frame buffers and use many contiguous colors in order to provide good quality shading (color interpolation). An additional constraint arises when some vendors supply PEX implementations that do not support every possible set of color approximation values defined by PEX. Although PEX supplies a request to determine support for a given color approximation, it is still no easy task to match up the correct visual, colormap contents, and color approximation to obtain the best working color set for the application. PEXlib 5.2 provides utilities that allow applications to determine all of these factors with just a few function calls.

Double Buffering

PEXlib 5.1 applications face a difficult task when setting up to perform double buffering. First, the application checks for the existence of MBX (Multi-Buffering Extension) and uses it if it exists. Otherwise, the application looks for a set of optional double-buffering escapes and finally resorts to pixmaps if the escapes are not supported and the PEX extension supports rendering to pixmaps.

Because of the lack of progress in completing the final specification of MBX, the X Consortium began work on a less ambitious effort in the latter part of 1994 called DBE (Double Buffer Extension). Since the Consortium workgroup finished the DBE specification rapidly, the PEX 5.2 specification requires that devices that support PEX double buffering must do so via the DBE. This requirement greatly simplifies the process the application uses to perform double buffering.

Although PEXlib 5.2 applications may use the DBE interface directly, the PEXlib 5.2 specification includes PEXlib functions for controlling double buffering and strongly encourages applications to use them. One advantage of this approach is to insulate the applications from any future changes to the DBE interface. Another advantage is that the PEXlib double buffering functions are simpler and use the more familiar PEXlib objects in the interface. Finally, the DBE "idiom" mechanism of grouping together requests that are potentially optimized by the server is likely to be overlooked by a PEXlib programmer and is better left to the implementation of the double buffering functions.

Future of PEXlib

Public Specification Review

We need your help!

Both the PEX 5.2 and PEXlib 5.2 specifications are available for public review. The documents can be found at `ftp.x.org` in `/pub/DOCS/PEX`. These specifications contain much more information than can be covered in this short paper. You will find details on all the new and exciting PEX and PEXlib 5.2 features. Please have a look and let us know what you think!

Window System Independent Version

Although PEX is tied quite closely to the X Window System protocol as an extension, the PEXlib application programming interface is not as dependent on the X Window System as many people first think. With a small amount of specification effort, an architect could define a "common PEXlib" that would be free of any attributes specific to any window system. The architect could also define a small specification for each of a number of window systems that describes how common PEXlib is implemented in each of those environments.

Some of the steps needed to achieve a common PEXlib include:

- Abstract X resource ID's to "handles".

- Separate any hopelessly X dependent functions (e.g., **PEXMatchRenderingTargets**) into an "X Support" library.

- Develop a set of common error definitions and map the current PEX protocol errors to that set. Will need to architect a generic PEX error handler function along the lines of the X protocol error handler, since the X handler is not present in other window environments.

- Scan specification for other things that need generalization.

The value of this exercise could be rather high, given the current work going on with low-end (PC) platforms. With the advent of more powerful processors with good floating point capability, implementing PEX on PC-class machines is no longer out of reach. There are several implementations of PEX as server extensions to X server PC software that perform reasonably well. A common PEXlib specification, as described here, would ensure the consistent implementation of "direct" PEXlib in diverse PC and workstation windowing environments.

References

Stevenson, Jeff, "PEX 6.0 - NOT!", Slide Set, 1994 X Technical Conference

PEX Protocol Specification, Version 5.2, Public Review Draft, 15 August 1994

PEXlib Specification and C Language Binding, Version 5.2, Consortium Review Draft, September 30, 1994

BACK ISSUES OF THE X RESOURCE

Back issues are available to North American customers directly from the publisher for $14.95 each plus shipping (see inside front cover). Overseas customers should contact our Overseas Distributors (listed after this section). The journal is also carried by many U.S. and foreign bookstores.

ISSUE 0: FALL 1991

Back Issues of the X Resource

Issue 1: Winter 1992

Proceedings
6th Annual X Technical Conference

BACK ISSUES OF THE X RESOURCE

ISSUE 2: SPRING 1992

BACK ISSUES OF THE X RESOURCE

ISSUE 3: SUMMER 1992

Back Issues of the X Resource

Issue 4: Fall 1992

BACK ISSUES OF THE X RESOURCE

ISSUE 5: WINTER 1993

BACK ISSUES OF THE X RESOURCE

ISSUE 6: SPRING 1993

BACK ISSUES OF THE X RESOURCE

ISSUE 7: SUMMER 1993

BACK ISSUES OF THE X RESOURCE

ISSUE 8: FALL 1993

BACK ISSUES OF THE X RESOURCE

ISSUE 9: WINTER 1994

BACK ISSUES OF THE X RESOURCE

ISSUE 10: SPRING 1994

BACK ISSUES OF THE X RESOURCE

ISSUE 11: SUMMER 1994

Back Issues of the X Resource

Issue 12: Fall 1994

Statement of Ownership, Management and Circulation

(Required by 39 U.S.C. 3685)

1A. Title of Publication	1B. PUBLICATION NO.	2. Date of Filing
THE X Resource	1 0 5 8 5 5 9 1	8/31/94
3. Frequency of Issue	**3A. No. of Issues Published Annually**	**3B. Annual Subscription Price**
Quarterly (Jan, April, July, OCT)	4	USA $65.00 or $90.00

4. Complete Mailing Address of Known Office of Publication *(Street, City, County, State and ZIP+4 Code) (Not printers)*

103 A Morris Street Sebastopol CA 95472

5. Complete Mailing Address of the Headquarters of General Business Offices of the Publisher *(Not printer)*

Same as above

6. Full Names and Complete Mailing Address of Publisher, Editor, and Managing Editor *(This item MUST NOT be blank)*

Publisher *(Name and Complete Mailing Address)*

O'Reilly + Associates 103 A Morris Street Sebastopol CA 95472

Editor *(Name and Complete Mailing Address)*

Paula M. Ferguson 1630 30TH Street Boulder CO 80301

Managing Editor *(Name and Complete Mailing Address)*

N/A

7. Owner *(If owned by a corporation, its name and address must be stated and also immediately thereunder the names and addresses of stockholders owning or holding 1 percent or more of total amount of stock. If not owned by a corporation, the names and addresses of the individual owners must be given. If owned by a partnership or other unincorporated firm, its name and address, as well as that of each individual must be given. If the publication is published by a nonprofit organization, its name and address must be stated.) (Item must be completed.)*

Full Name	Complete Mailing Address
Tim O'Reilly	O'Reilly + Associates 103 A Morris St. Sebastopol CA 95472

8. Known Bondholders, Mortgagees, and Other Security Holders Owning or Holding 1 Percent or More of Total Amount of Bonds, Mortgages or Other Securities *(If there are none, so state)*

Full Name	Complete Mailing Address
N/A	N/A

9. For Completion by Nonprofit Organizations Authorized To Mail at Special Rates *(DMM Section 424.12 only)*
The purpose, function, and nonprofit status of this organization and the exempt status for Federal income tax purposes *(Check one)*

(1) [X] Has Not Changed During Preceding 12 Months
(2) [ ] Has Changed During Preceding 12 Months
(If changed, publisher must submit explanation of change with this statement.)

10. Extent and Nature of Circulation *(See instructions on reverse side)*	Average No. Copies Each Issue During Preceding 12 Months	Actual No. Copies of Single Issue Published Nearest to Filing Date
A. Total No. Copies *(Net Press Run)*	5313	5339
B. Paid and/or Requested Circulation 1. Sales through dealers and carriers, street vendors and counter sales	426	442
2. Mail Subscription *(Paid and/or requested)*	1678	1515
C. Total Paid and/or Requested Circulation *(Sum of 10B1 and 10B2)*	2104	1957

2 only)
income tax purposes *(Check one)*
(If changed, publisher must submit explanation of change with this statement.)
9. For Completion by Nonprofit Organizations Authorized To Mail at Special Rates (DMM Section 424.1
The purpose, function, and nonprofit status of this organization and the exempt status for Federal
(1) [X] Has Not Changed During Preceding 12 Months
(2) [ ] Has Changed During Preceding 12 Months
10.

F. Copies Not Distributed 1. Office use, left over, unaccounted, spoiled after printing	2761	3001
2. Return from News Agents	72	1
G. TOTAL *(Sum of E, F1 and 2—should equal net press run shown in A)*	5313	5339

11. **I certify that the statements made by me above are correct and complete**

Signature and Title of Editor, Publisher, Business Manager, or Owner: [signature]

PS Form **3526**, January 1991 *(See instructions on reverse)*

Subscribe Now!

To the best source of timely, in-depth articles on the X Window System today!

The X Resource Journal *from O'Reilly & Associates, Inc.*

Bill to my Credit Card or call (800) 889-8969 (US and Canada, Weekdays 6 a.m.- 6 p.m. PST)

Please indicate your subscription choice. *(Prices include shipping charges)*

❏ **$65 USA Regular Subscriptions**   ❏ **$70 Canada & Mexico**

❏ **$90 Europe, Africa, Central & South America**   ❏ **$95 Asia, Australia & New Zealand**

Start my subscription with Issue # _____

Name _____ Company/Organization _____

Address _____

City _____ State _____ Zip/Postal Code _____ Country _____

Telephone _____ FAX _____ Internet or other email address (specify network)

Charge it!

❏ Visa   ❏ MasterCard   ❏ American Express

Account Number _____ Exp. Date _____

Name as it appears on card _____ Signature _____

XR15

O'REILLY WOULD LIKE TO HEAR FROM YOU

Please send me the following:

❏ *ora.com*
O'Reilly's magazine/catalog, containing behind-the-scenes articles and interviews on the technology we write about, and a complete listing of O'Reilly books and products.

❏ *Global Network Navigator*™
Information and subscription.

Please print legibly

Thank you for purchasing an *X Resource Journal* Issue!

Where did you buy this book?
  ❏ Bookstore   ❏ Direct from O'Reilly
  ❏ Bundled with hardware/software   ❏ Class/seminar

Your job description: ❏ SysAdmin   ❏ Programmer
  ❏ Other _____

What computer system do you use?   ❏ UNIX   ❏ MAC
  ❏ DOS(PC)   ❏ NT   ❏ Other _____

Name _____ Company/Organization _____

Address _____

City _____ State _____ Zip/Postal Code _____ Country _____

Telephone _____ Internet or other email address (specify network)

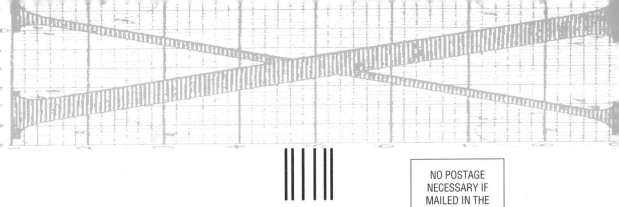

BUSINESS REPLY MAIL

FIRST CLASS MAIL   PERMIT NO. 80   SEBASTOPOL, CA

Postage will be paid by addressee

O'Reilly & Associates, Inc.
103A Morris Street
Sebastopol, CA 95472-9902

BUSINESS REPLY MAIL

FIRST CLASS MAIL   PERMIT NO. 80   SEBASTOPOL, CA

Postage will be paid by addressee

O'Reilly & Associates, Inc.
103A Morris Street
Sebastopol, CA 95472-9902